Memoirs of a Poor Relation

Also from Westphalia Press
westphaliapress.org

The Idea of the Digital University

Masonic Tombstones and Masonic Secrets

Eight Decades in Syria

Avant-Garde Politician

L'Enfant and the Freemasons

Baronial Bedrooms

Conflicts in Health Policy

Material History and Ritual Objects

Paddle Your Own Canoe

Opportunity and Horatio Alger

Careers in the Face of Challenge

Bookplates of the Kings

Collecting American Presidential Autographs

Misunderstood Children

Original Cables from the Pearl Harbor Attack

Social Satire and the Modern Novel

The Amenities of Book Collecting

The Genius of Freemasonry

A Definitive Commentary on Bookplates

James Martineau and Rebuilding Theology

No Bird Lacks Feathers

Earthworms, Horses, and Living Things

The Man Who Killed President Garfield

Anti-Masonry and the Murder of Morgan

Understanding Art

Homeopathy

Ancient Masonic Mysteries

Collecting Old Books

The Boy Chums Cruising in Florida Waters

The Thomas Starr King Dispute

Ivanhoe Masonic Quartettes

Lariats and Lassos

Mr. Garfield of Ohio

The Wisdom of Thomas Starr King

The French Foreign Legion

War in Syria

Naturism Comes to the United States

New Sources on Women and Freemasonry

Designing, Adapting, Strategizing in Online Education

Gunboat and Gun-runner

Meeting Minutes of Naval Lodge No. 4 F.A.A.M

Memoirs of a Poor Relation

Being the Story of a Post-War Southern Girl
and Her Battle with Destiny

by Marietta Minnigerode Andrews

WESTPHALIA PRESS
An imprint of Policy Studies Organization

**Memoirs of a Poor Relation: Being the Story of a Post-War
Southern Girl and Her Battle With Destiny**
All Rights Reserved © 2014 by Policy Studies Organization

Westphalia Press
An imprint of Policy Studies Organization
1527 New Hampshire Ave., NW
Washington, D.C. 20036
info@ipsonet.org

**ISBN-13: 978-1-63391-061-4
ISBN-10: 163391061X**

Cover design by Taillefer Long at Illuminated Stories:
www.illuminatedstories.com

Daniel Gutierrez-Sandoval, Executive Director
PSO and Westphalia Press

Rahima Schwenkbeck, Director of Media and Publications
PSO and Westphalia Press

Updated material and comments on this edition
can be found at the Westphalia Press website:
www.westphaliapress.org

MEMOIRS
of
A POOR RELATION

MARIETTA MINNIGERODE ANDREWS
"Why Rushed the Discords in, But That Harmony Should be Prized?"

Memoirs
of
A Poor Relation

BEING THE STORY
OF A POST-WAR SOUTHERN
GIRL AND HER
BATTLE WITH DESTINY

by
MARIETTA MINNIGERODE ANDREWS

ILLUSTRATED

NEW YORK
E. P. DUTTON & COMPANY
681 FIFTH AVENUE

To
My little granddaughters
MARY LORD ANDREWS III
HELEN TUCKER ANDREWS II
CARTER RANDOLPH ANDREWS

CONTENTS

CHAPTER		PAGE
	Introduction	xvii

PART I

I	My grandma, a "consecrated widow"—Judas Iscariot—The "common things"—My father's ancestry—The Feudal Nobility of Germany—Benjamin, Ludwig and Charles Minnigerode	3
II	Charles Frederick Ernest Minnigerode, D.D.—Revolutionary activities at the University of Giessen—Imprisonment—Expatriation—The Civil War—Association with Jefferson Davis, Robert E. Lee, Edwin M. Stanton, General Nelson A. Miles . . .	15
III	My grandfather's house in Richmond—Glimpse of Southern belles and beaux—My father, Charlie Minnigerode, Aide-de-Camp to General Fitzhugh Lee . . .	22
IV	My mother, Virginia Cuthbert Powell—Stories of the Civil War times—Her engagement to a disabled Confederate soldier	32
V	"Uncle Robert," my Aunt Ida's old negro butler, who instructs a little girl as to the significance of the word "Us"	40
VI	The fine old art of letter-writing—My parents marry for love—A homesick little bride	44
VII	My godmother's legacies	52

PART II

VIII	Childhood at Oakley—The Dulanys—Grandma . .	61
IX	My grandma's Personal God and my grandma's personal maid	70
X	Clothes—Companions—One strings grasshoppers for fishing bait and sings hymns the while	77
XI	My grandmother's memory my best library—Tales of old homes—Traditions of Kinloch, Arlington, Ravensworth, Tudor Place, Vaucluse	82

CONTENTS

CHAPTER		PAGE
XII	My little sister Lucy visits me at Oakley—We search for the two-headed lamb—Sacrilegious pastimes or Pre-Raphaelite Pageantry	94
XIII	Books—Discussions upon the theories of Darwin—How Grandma would dispose of an imaginary fortune if—	98
XIV	I accompany my handsome Uncle Hal to collect the "Post"—By way of Parenthesis, Rouge versus snuff .	104
XV	The Oakley kitchen and its presiding genius, "Aunt Kitty"	110
XVI	My solitary playmate, "Aunt Kitty's Willy" . . .	114
XVII	The ancestry, raising, curing and cooking of the old home-cured Virginia Ham	117
XVIII	My Aunt Ida's key-basket—Meat-houses—Dairies—Feed rooms—Poultry houses—Sweetmeat closet—Ice house—Vision of a beautiful death on an August day	123
XIX	Rigorous Religious training—Speculations on the Ten Commandments—Biblical precedent for evil deeds—Undue familiarity with Holy Writ	131
XX	The Law of Hospitality—When God and Grandma disagree—Old Colonel John's death-bed repentance .	137
XXI	Cousin Dick	143
XXII	Cousin Ginnie (You-Janie)—Cousin Cary	149
XXIII	Cousin Neville—Cousin Peter and Cousin Annie—Cousin Buck	154
XXIV	Cousin Arthur—Cousin Sophronia—Cousin John Henry Powell—Little Edith Bolling	161
XXV	By way of Parenthesis—A rainy October day with three baby granddaughters	167

PART III

XXVI	New Orleans—I sally forth to uplift my family—and learn that I am a person with a very unfortunate disposition—Our mother reads Tennyson to us—and we hear how she became an "abolitionist"	175
XXVII	Our first school—At the mercy of a dope fiend . . .	180
XXVIII	Sensible Lucy and Sentimental May—Spelling bottles—Increasing difficulties of applying Grandma's theological teachings to everyday affairs—The stone which the builders rejected.	183

CONTENTS

CHAPTER		PAGE
XXIX	Father's "Stag parties"—His Ex-Confederate comrades—Cousin Randolph Tucker—Cousin Mary Lee—Cousin Kinloch Fauntleroy—My father meets the Union Officer who saved his life after the Battle of Appomattox	190
XXX	Our annual trips from New Orleans to Virginia—Summers at Oatlands—Aunt Katie's heavenly character and historic heirlooms	198
XXXI	Our young Cousin Grace, embodiment of practical wisdom and domestic virtue—Our mother decides that Lucy and I are to wear corsets and to be confirmed—Willy Callahan—Mother also decides to endow us with talents	207
XXXII	I injure a schoolmate and seek to propitiate his impressive parent—A broken pen, a boycott and a broken spirit—The initial processes of life explained to Lucy and me by an enlightened young lady—Disgrace—Mammy consoles	213
XXXIII	Old Fannie and Mammy	221
XXXIV	We learn a few things—From Franklin Edwards, Democracy—From Cousin Mary Lee the proper pride of the Southerner—From Cousin Horatio Whitridge Turner the stylish way to eat shrimp and oysters—An old lady teaches us French—A young gentleman teaches us "elocution"—We "take" music and art—And tuck up our hair—I capture a "Marrying beau" and Grandma writes pleading with me to conquer my unfortunate disposition	228
XXXV	A flood on the Mississippi—My father goes with a rescue party—The Reverend Henry Harcourt Waters, Yellow Fever Hero—Father's habits and business drift into irregular ways—The last Mardi-Gras—The crash comes	235
XXXVI	One becomes a Breadwinner at the age of fifteen—The Beloved Floor-walker—Bankruptcy—The temperamental Dagoes—Back to Virginia	242

Part IV

| XXXVII | Alexandria, Virginia, an old town on the Potomac—Ancient landmarks—Relics of the Hessian prisoners—Poor Relationdom for a fact—Our Cousin Robert Carter Lee . . . . | 249 |
| XXXVIII | I become engaged to my "marrying beau"—Mother's twins are born—And one dies on my knees—Bad checks and pressing bills—No money and multifarious guests . . . . | 256 |

CONTENTS

CHAPTER		PAGE
XXXIX	Boys and girls will be boys and girls—Rough and ready hospitality—Schools—Our Cousin Rebecca	260
XL	The state of engagedness becomes intolerable—My mother explains to me the state of mind called "being in love"—My Cousin Stanley departs whence he came—Mother sepulchral—My father and I fight against depression and insomnia—My younger sisters perhaps may marry—I cast an appraising eye on certain descendants of Thomas Jefferson—And make my first visit to the Corcoran Gallery of Art in Washington	267
XLI	My mother's decision that I should have a "talent" is accepted by us all and I proceed to "cultivate" it—The Nude in Art makes me uncomfortable—Drawings submitted for admission to the Art School are refused—I go in person to look after this matter	275
XLII	My father's death—Editorial from the Charleston News and Courier—I get to work in earnest ignoring my own ignorance—Kindness of Cousin Bob and Cousin Mollie Powell—Kindness of Everybody—Renaissance of Art in Alexandria, Virginia—An elderly friend bestows upon me a pair of storm shoes, a kiss and a volume of Swinburne's Poems	279
XLIII	I become the man of the family—And rent a little house—We decide that Lucy will be a musician—Multiplicity of Mother's advisors—Emmeline—Our eleventh baby—Our Cousin Annette	290
XLIV	Foraging—Man cannot live by bread alone—Potboiling—Drawing-teacher in a country school—Cousin Lizzie and Cousin Cary Nicholas—The palmleaf fan industry is revived and special offer of portraits of Saint Peter—A bit of cast-off finery	297
XLV	Grandma's religious teaching still sticking to me—Moody and Sankey—The Prodigal Son—The things we get for nothing—The democratic spirit of an Art School	303
XLVI	My mother's conception of "business"—Alexandre Casarin—Anecdotes of painters	308
XLVII	Outdoor sketching—Strange places and strange types—"Mary the Wild Cat"—Bladensburg—Fredericktown—Georgetown	314
XLVIII	Zeal for Studio Properties—Mother's oldest son leaves home—The "Minni Barrel"	323

CONTENTS

CHAPTER		PAGE
XLIX	The psychology of clothing—Connection of the uniform with heroism—The manner in which we should hand down the "hand-me-downs".	332
L	Progress in study—Appointment as "assistant" to Mr. Andrews—Speculations as to his intentions—An observant eye on other maidens—How to educate our boys?—A "benevolent" Congressman—Powell, Fitz, Lucy, and George	334
LI	Extra ways of making money—Our Cousin Helen—Portraits of a dead Emperor—Rebecca Ramsay's errand	344
LII	Hack newspaper work—Dr. James Nevins Hyde of Chicago—Mrs. Antoinette Van Horseman Wakeman of the "Chicago Evening Post"—The love of common things—Wealth of the roadsides	348
LIII	Mr. Andrews' portrait class—Studios—Agreeable habits of some friends in the country—Rendering unto Cæsar	353
LIV	Visits to the country—Serenades—Disciples at last—Contrary to the prophecies of my family—Offers of marriage—Poverty dodges	359
LV	In mourning for a lover—Yearnings for social opportunities—The Thomas E. Waggamans	364
LVI	A first trip to Europe—The voyage—Wonderful people—Arrival at Genoa	367
LVII	Genoa—filigree silver—Naples—tortoise shell—Pompeii—Dr. Dole—Rome—Silk stockings—And an attempt to see the Pope—Florence—Mosaics—As my young cousins bought things	374
LVIII	Paris—My Uncle Meade—An atmosphere of wealth—Dresden—And familiar poverty—A bit of the old South in the heart of Dresden	379
LIX	Shinnecock Hills—How an Art School came to be there	386
LX	The Art School—William M. Chase—The words of William M. Chase	391
LXI	Clever boys and girls—Howard Chandler Christie—The Beale brothers—Gertrude Weil—Della Milhau—Alice Tinkham	401

Part V

| LXII | Catherine Carter Critcher—A first big order—the Byam Kirby Stevens of New York—Our models . . | 409 |

CHAPTER		PAGE
LXIII	Our students in Washington—The Princess Mary Cantacuzene—The connoisseur—Real temptations from within—By way of parenthesis—Grandmotherhood	414

PART VI

LXIV	At twenty-five—What is worthwhile?—My mother's religion—The doors of life swing open—Daily intercourse with highly-trained people	427
LXV	Back to my Aunt Ida and Oakley—Changes—Those precious years in which the pulses slow down—Grandma—Mr. Andrews turns the ice-cream freezer . . .	434
LXVI	Grandma's philosophy—The manner in which she awaited death—A country funeral—And mint juleps	440
LXVII	By way of parenthesis—Gates of the Soul	443
LXVIII	Epilogue	446

LIST OF ILLUSTRATIONS

Marietta Minnigerode Andrews	*Frontispiece*
	FACING PAGE
The Old Von Minnigerode Forsthof in the Rittergasse, Asfeld, Hessen	10
Facsimile of the Tombstone of Heidentrich Corrigia, 1013. Discovered by Jost von Minnigeroda, 1539, in the Churchyard at Kirchdorf	11
Ludwig Minnigerode, Wearing the *Commandeurkreutz*	16
Marianne, Wife of Ludwig Minnigerode	16
Robert Carter of Nomini Hall. Copy by Mrs. Andrews of the Original attributed to Sir Joshua Reynolds	17
Major Charles Minnigerode and General Fitzhugh Lee in Confederate Uniform	26
General Robert E. Lee	27
Virginia Cuthbert Powell (Mrs. Charles Minnigerode)	46
The Hall at Oakley	47
Tudor Place, Georgetown, D. C.	84
Ravensworth	85
Arlington House	90
Kinloch, Home of Thomas Turner	91
Rev. Charles Minnigerode of Richmond during the Civil War	132
Rev. Charles Minnigerode, D.D.	133
Robert Carter of Corotoman	164
Ann Carter of Shirley on the James River	165
Oatlands, Loudoun County, Virginia, a Carter Estate	200
Oatlands	201
Mrs. Andrews, in costume of Mrs. Jefferson, used during the campaign to preserve Monticello	270
The Mansion House, Alexandria, Va.	271
Old Carlyle House, overlooking the Potomac	271
Old Christ Church, Alexandria, Va.	292
Pulpit of Old Christ Church	293
Farmington, Albemarle County, Virginia; showing the part of the house designed by Thomas Jefferson	318
The Box-wood Labyrinth at Farmington and the Covered Corridors	319
Eliphalet Fraser Andrews, late Director of the Corcoran School of Art	336
Lieutenant-Colonel Fitzhugh Lee Minnigerode, U.S.A.	337
Lucy Minnigerode, in uniform as Chief of the Nursing Service of the Public Health Department, U.S.A.	360
Lucy Minnigerode and her Red Cross Unit, sailing for Europe	361
North Gate to the Theological Seminary of Virginia	420
Eliphalet Fraser Andrews II, Veteran of the World War	421

Build as thou wilt, unspoiled by praise or blame;
Build as thou wilt, and as thy light is given;
Then if at last the airy structure fall,
Dissolve and vanish, take thyself no shame—
They fail and they alone who have not striven.
— *Thomas Bailey Aldrich*

INTRODUCTION

THROUGH the perspective of thirty years events become impersonal and the delicacy one might feel in intimate revelations of more recent date is tempered by a larger feeling of proportion. Indeed many events, harsh and unlovely at the time, have now fallen into place, into value. No longer offensive they are yet essential spots in the whole picture, supplying the shadows necessary to the composition which without them would remain flat.

Like the hardy shrubs and flowers of old-fashioned gardens, a certain class of homely—of even sordid—human experiences hold their own in this kaleidoscopic world, and though ever-recurring are ever-interesting. The recital of them may not be highly colored or exciting; aloof from the gaiety and fascination of smart society, apart from the great matters that make for history, such narratives still deal with the underlying foundations of character if they sincerely picture the reactions of struggling souls.

To be observant of all life around one, and eager for a part in it are characteristics which eventually build up a real life, and in spite of blunders and failures, ignorance and egotism, work out at last a design not devoid of beauty.

Without apology, these memories are offered to such as will, in some quiet hour, follow an average life into its paths of peace.

MEMOIRS OF A POOR RELATION

CHAPTER I

A ROUND-EYED little girl of seven, with two stout pigtails sticking out behind her ears, their terminals resembling shaving-brushes —and all the space between the round eyes and the pigtails packed as full of curiosity as an egg is full of meat, could hardly understand the term "a consecrated widow." In fact, after nearly half a century, the expression has still a baffling quality.

Yet Grandma was a consecrated widow. Everybody said so. I knew that anything consecrated was holy and so in a measure explained Grandma to myself.

She went to church very often, and so did I. The church is the Episcopal Church—in fact, it was the little stuccoed church in Upperville, shaded by old maples. That was the church of whose One Foundation we sang in various keys, the discord and the enthusiasm proportionate to the size of the congregation.

There were other buildings in the village that resembled churches but by some distinction too fine for the mind of a seven-year-old they were not of The Church. They sang "Work for the

Night is Coming," and "Oh! Where is my Wandering Boy Tonight," and "Bringing in the Sheaves," but they did not sing "The Church's One Foundation."

By listening to Biblical stories—in fact, to what might have been called Biblical escapades—and by accompanying Grandma always to divine service, and attending family prayers with great regularity (though this was compulsory), I hoped that one day I, too, might become holy and a consecrated little girl. Indeed, my ambition even went so far as to dream that, with the assistance of Divine Providence, I might one day become "a consecrated widow" just like Grandma, with an organdie cap on, and broad strings tied under my chin, and a sweet sad smile. Small granddaughters would then look up to me as an oracle, and suave clergymen would refer to me as a devout sister and observe that my ways were ways of pleasantness, and all my paths were peace.

It was Judas especially. From the day Grandma told me the story I could not get rid of him. The greatest of traitors could not have risen from the dreadful Judecca in which Dante placed him, the deepest depth of those ever-narrowing circles of the Inferno, to haunt a little girl of seven, as she lay in her small bed in her Grandma's room in an old homestead in Virginia. Yet it was unquestionably Judas.

Having told me the story of his treason, as

given in the Bible, and out-Danted Dante in describing his eternal doom, Grandma seemed indifferent and indisposed to discuss Judas further, though in my anxiety to understand the matter more clearly I often returned to the subject. How could Grandma, who was such a good woman, go on sewing so calmly when such a thing had happened? Twenty centuries mean nothing to a child.

"Grandma," I said. "Don't you think Jesus fooled Judas, too?"

"May!!" exclaimed my grandmother, in a tone that curdled my blood. "May!!"

"I only mean," I hastened to explain, "Judas did not expect nothin' like that—Judas seen Jesus do such wunnerful things all th' time, and he didn't allow he'd let anything happen——"

"May!" Grandma fairly screeched, her face quite white. "Child! don't blaspheme—and," dropping into her usual tone, "don't talk like a cornfield darky."

Therefore I searched the Scriptures myself, spelling out a little more of this terrible story. He betrayed his Master with a kiss. That in itself disgusted me. Men do not kiss each other. They kiss women. I had seen it done, in public and in private—outside the chapel and inside the conservatory.

Judas had bright, black eyes, and a soft black beard. His lips were thick. He was not bald like the Saint Peter in Grandma's Prayer-book, and when he took the money back in such a hurry he was warm from running and there was a frantic look in his eyes. And after that he did the only thing he could do to show he was sorry; he went out and hanged himself and all his bowels gushed out.

The Reverend Doctor Sprigg, conducting service for us one Sunday, twisted his consonants and read it, "All his gowels bushed out." This created some confusion in my mind, but the vivid impression burned into me of the double tragedy, the sordid, lonely sacrifice that preceded The Sacrifice—the sinner's pathetic attempt at atonement for his own sin antedating the supreme atonement of the Sinless One for all.

"Jesus will get him out!" I would moan into my small pillow. "Jesus will get him out!"

And in the night-time, when the big people sat 'round the fire, Aunt Ida and Grandma sewing, Uncle Hal reading "The Baltimore Sun," his great dogs at his feet, Becca and Hill Beverley in the bay window, and my Cousin May softly playing the piano, Judas and I talked his troubles over. His black eyes peered at me through the dark.

Of course Grandma did not know he was in her room. He only came for a minute to say, "Pray for me, little girl." I was glad to see that he was feeling better, and that the accounts of his accident had been exaggerated, and I assured him that Grandma had assured me that

Jesus Christ came into the world to save sinners—and I said to him, "Don't worry, Jesus will get you out."

It is not quite fair to plunge the reader into the gloom of Grandma's theology without at least introducing myself—a bundle of infant unorthodoxy—naming the sources whence I came, and tracing some of the currents that met in me.

Slowly we make adjustments when we come here. First, to the physical world around us, to the air we breathe, to heat and cold, to food and shelter. Then our social adjustments, those first lessons of citizenship learned in the nursery when the two-year-old citizen of the world realizes that his hands will be smacked if he tries to stick pins in the little fellow in the crib. Then through school with its discipline of playground and classroom; that first disconcerting realization that some one will always outdo us and that try as we may we cannot outrank the world.

All the laws, all the amenities of life to the smallest social courtesy, are phases of our second, or social, adjustment.

And then our third adjustment, which is the spiritual, and brings us to the mountain peaks of human life. There we take a bird's-eye view and looking back and down, the vision sweeping around in every direction, we see all the events that have gone before, as the pattern in an oriental carpet, each spot taking its place and all contributing to the beauty of the whole—the white of innocence, the red of passion, the gold of prosperity, the black of discouragement—all working out a definite design.

From this vantage ground I find myself looking back into the years almost forgotten. Perhaps it is well that the events narrated here are seen through the perspective of years and patience and spiritual peace. For Mary Lord is not dead. I cannot lose her. No one can lose a child, or a mother, or any loved one. The physical part, which made them tangible facts in our lives, may have served its purpose and disappeared, but the personality lives on stronger and more beautiful, more helpful and more consoling, if we will but accept it. The companionship is closer and the sympathy more complete. This much I have learned since the child has been away in the body.

The boy came back from France with the Croix de Guerre twice before he was twenty-one, given by the generous French Government under which he served.

The Poor Relation has become spiritually rich and richly content.

Few of us are deliberately and affectionately called into this world. Most of us are mere results of an attraction which reckoned not of us or of our needs. All of us are heterogeneous bundles of inherited absurdities. How bred, how nourished; with what temperament, nervous or phlegmatic; with what body, beautiful or plain; what chance has vouchsafed us as a background; what early recollections sanctify or defile our thoughts; opportunities or handicaps—the stupidity that blinds the eyes, the pride that ties the tongue, the timidity that lets the golden moment slip away—and there's your history!

As a preparation for the problem of our individual duty what can be more serviceable than some evidence from those of our own blood, whose faults and talents have been handed down to us? So where they fell we may rise; where they failed we may succeed. Nothing could make them so happy as to have thus fortified us; nothing could so compensate them for disappointments and drudgeries and disillusions.

I never was refined. It must have been by accident that a spirit so ordinary and plebeian drifted into a body begotten of the blue-blooded, bred under the rule of family pride, fed upon racial traditions and prejudices. As a cornfield darky or a Swiss peasant I should have been quite happy. Grinding poverty was less hard for me than for many. I stood it well in my youth and could stand it again. A delicious and not ignoble curiosity has filled my days with interest, so that I have always responded to the charm of ordinary things and people. Methodist revivals, country fairs, primitive entertainments, crude language, animal odors, rudimentary instincts, homemade clothes, mongrel dogs and coarse wild flowers!

Weeds! And the bloom of vegetables! Blossoms of parsnip and turnip, mustard and radish! All coarse flowers, that take root and grow wherever the passing winds may cast their seed; that find sustenance where rarer plants would starve, asking no care, blooming exuberantly in waste places, bearing generously such fruit as they may,—what is a rare exotic to such a friendly volunteer? Are they not flowers of the grass, whose brief charm touched the harp of David? Did not Solomon witness to their graciousness as they made glad the desert and the waste places? God bless their friendly faces! Lemon-lilies, Joe-pie weed, alder, iris, wild rose, lupine, daisy, goldenrod and briar—they thrive on neglect and multiply under persecution. Prolific and victorious, they have their counterparts in God's great garden of humanity.

We were not always Poor Relations. There was a time when other people were our poor relations, but that was some generations ago, and the traditions bearing upon departed glory do not make it easier to find shoe-leather or bread and butter in the evil days.

At the time that the English blood of my mother's Virginia ancestors was at the boiling point and breaking into revolution against the

The Old Von Minnigerode Forsthof in the Rittergasse, Alsfeld, Hessen.

Facsimile of the Tombstone of Heidentrich Corrigia, 1013. Discovered by Jost von Minnigeroda, 1539, in the Churchyard at Kirchdorf.

stupidity of the German house of Hanover, my father's ancestors, descendants of the feudal nobility of Germany, were alienating their friends, sacrificing their inheritance, and jeopardizing their lives, in opposition to the despotic monarchical government of their own petty German principalities.

They were picturesque and valiant people. Early in the seventeenth century these Minnigerodes, the first scientific Foresters recognized by the German Government, were holding high posts of honor but registering an interest in the proletariat which eventually brought ruin upon them. Their Stammvater, or progenitor, was a Roman soldier, one Don Otto Corregia, ennobled by Charlemagne in the wars against the Saxons "als Belohnung seiner Tapferkeit"[*] and given great grants of land in Germany—among them a village and castle of the name of Minnigerode, one line of his descendants taking that name with that estate. Others, Bochelnhagen, Silkerode, Riemen, spreading over Germany in many ramifications, bearing the red roses and the peacock feathers of Don Otto as their crest, and the inverted fishhook on their shields—even as is shown on the tombstone of Don Heidenrich Corregia, at Kirschdorf.

In Alsfeld, in Hessen, there stands in the Street of the Knights, the Rittergasse, the "von Minnigerodehaus," a quaint old dwelling, flamboyant

[*] As the reward of bravery.

in its decorations, with sculptured allegories and creasy cupids burdening the bad façade; shabby and fallen from all its elegance, inhabited by middle-class Hessians, crowded in among the poorer dwellings which have filled the original acreage of the estate.

This house, built by Johann Ludwig von Minnigerode, Master of the Chase and Judge at Alsfeld and Romrod, in 1687, was called the "Forsthof," or Forest-court. It must have been beautiful in its original surroundings of forest and park, pretentious and substantial even when I sketched it, though the sculptured figure of Justice had become noseless and disfigured, and the coat of arms over the doorway, with its inverted fishhook, somewhat paradoxical amid its poor surroundings. Often have I wandered with my husband and children along the delightful little River Schwalm shaded by stately poplars, and enjoyed the rural life of the village, charmed by the quaint timbered houses with their twin pinnacles, the cleanliness and comfort of the rambling hotel.

Benjamin Minnigerode, born in this house, appears to have been something of a man and made many converts to his views on political liberty between the years 1786 and 1789. The Hessian Government caused his arrest after Louis IX, on November 13, 1789, had approved the recommendation of his cabinet. The accused Benjamin certainly passed out of life, whether immediately after his arrest or later could not be determined. The cause of his death has remained in complete obscurity. It is positively known, however, that in the middle of November he passed away, and it was assumed that he was either murdered or that he committed suicide, in order to escape cruel punishment. This will probably never be cleared up unless some other historical find is made. The archives in the case have been lost or stolen. It is well established that the influence of this revolutionary movement had a very unfavorable effect on the government which did everything against the extension of such propaganda and insisted on some deterring punishment. There is folklore still in Alsfeld to the effect that Benjamin Minnigerode was arrested there and taken at once to Romrod, about four miles distant, there to be confined in a dark dungeon, but that in a place called the Round Meadow, surrounded by forest, he was beheaded, and that the ghost of a headless man in a closed carriage circling around the meadow has been repeatedly seen.

Thus Benjamin brought the beliefs and the activities of several generations to a crisis, discovering for himself a Declaration of Independence, formulating for his generation in little Hessen an unwritten creed which had been slowly evolving in the minds of his forebears. In his part of the world he struck the identical notes penned at about the same time by Thomas Jefferson.

The love of liberty which animated Benjamin Minnigerode was not lost to the world, for his brave spirit animated his more conservative son Ludwig, who, as Director of the Board of Revenue for Westphalia during a most critical period, reorganized the old provinces and, in spite of existing prejudices, curtailed the privileges of the upper classes without incurring extreme animosity, thus demonstrating a democratic mind modified by a wise diplomacy.

He received high public honors, among them the "Commandeurkreutz," but when his son, my grandfather, was imprisoned for sedition at the University of Giessen, it became a matter of conscience with this high old gentleman to retire from public life. His resignation as Hofgerichtspräsident (President of the Supreme Court) in Darmstadt, was accepted, and the highest public and private confidence was accorded him at the time. In private life he found a serene happiness as a writer of graceful verse, a student of philosophy, a lover of horticulture and forestry, branches of science in which his forebears had distinguished themselves.

CHAPTER II

AS for my grandfather, the love of liberty was in his blood and although he was born in Germany and under a despotic government, nature had made him an American. At the time that his grandfather was actively opposing the most arbitrary form of monarchism in Germany, the United States of America was in its birth throes, and with all the world between them, and not a dream that fate would ever blend their posterity in one, my mother's Virginia ancestors, Randolph, Carter, Harrison, and Powell, were then fighting for liberty in America.

Charles Frederick Ernest Minnigerode, law student at Giessen, member of the Burschenschaft (a secret society which took a leading part in the Hessian Revolution of 1834), was arrested on his return from Offenbach where he had gone to supply himself with the revolutionary manifesto first message of his poet friend George Buchner, published in the "Hessen Landbote." Young Minnigerode carried with him large packs of this literature which he hoped to distribute in Giessen, a university town, and the adjoining country. He was placed in a dark dungeon for eighteen months without coming to trial. Finally, when his health broke down completely, he was permitted to reside with his father and brother where he was kept closely guarded by four soldiers day and night. In 1839, about five years after his arrest, the case was "nolle prosequi" with the remark that if the least suspicion at any time arose the old charge of treason would be taken up again. In this respect he fared much better than his grandfather in November, 1789, but he wisely decided to seek the land of freedom and sailed on the first of September, 1839, from Bremen to America.

Sixty volumes of the classics, brought over by this handsome young immigrant, Charles Frederick Ernest Minnigerode—funny, fat little Tauchnitz books bound in mottled pasteboard, are in my possession and I value them very greatly. They are annotated in lead pencil in my grandfather's precise, tight, little German hand, and I can hardly think of a hot-blooded revolutionist of nineteen devoting to the study of the classics so many hours as these volumes evidence. During his imprisonment the Bible was the only book allowed him, and it was then that he acquired his great familiarity with the Scriptures.

My grandfather has been the subject of many more or less romantic stories and as I look back upon him and weigh these reports I seem able to arrive at some reasonable conclusion between the extremes. When he arrived in America, twenty-three years old and penniless, the capital with which he began life was his knowledge of

Marianne, Wife of Ludwig Minnigerode

Ludwig Minnigerode, Wearing the *Commandeurkreutz*.

Robert Carter of Nomini Hall. Copy by Mrs. Andrews of the Original Attributed to Sir Joshua Reynolds.

the Bible, these sixty little volumes of Greek and Latin classics, a very beautiful profile, an unmistakable air of good-breeding, and such education as he had acquired prior to his arrest at the age of nineteen.

In Philadelphia he made a meager livelihood as a teacher of French and German until he secured a professorship at William and Mary College, Virginia, through a competitive examination—and so came South. Here he married Miss Mary Carter and later entered the Episcopal Ministry, to become as Rector of Old St. Paul's Church, Richmond, one of the most picturesque characters of the Civil War. The revolutionary spirit which had involved him in political difficulties at home had grown no cooler, and he threw in his lot with the people of his adoption, whole-heartedly and without reserve. Neither Slavery nor State's Rights, as a political or economic question, was any personal concern of his, but no born Virginian was more passionate in his readiness to sacrifice all, than was Doctor Minnigerode during those bitter years in Richmond.

Neutrality was an unknown word; the matter had but one aspect—the Southern view. Robert E. Lee and Jefferson Davis were among his parishioners in Old Saint Paul's and were his close friends. He followed Mr. Davis to prison at Fortress Monroe and was friend and father to the whole Confederacy, high or low. His career was a vivid, influential and brilliant page in the history of those stirring times.

His intimacy with Jefferson Davis, the ill-fated President of the Confederacy, has been the subject of much controversy, romance, and speculation. Others have told of it in many books of the Civil War period and hardly a history of Davis or of Lee omits some reference to the spiritual advisor of both, Doctor Minnigerode. This quotation from his address on the occasion of the final interment of Mr. Davis' body, at Hollywood, Richmond's beautiful cemetery, will express this intimate relationship better than any words of mine. Doctor Minnigerode said:

> The first time I ever saw Jefferson Davis was when as President of the Confederate States he arrived in Richmond and held a reception at the Spottiswood Hotel. The last time I saw him was a few years ago when we met in Atlanta, Georgia. I was going there to pay a visit to one of my sons, not knowing or remembering that the day of my arrival was the time when, on the occasion of the unveiling of the statue of Ben Hill, Mr. Davis was to deliver the oration. After dinner I went to call on him at Mr. Hill's where he was staying. Although he was resting at the time and excused to visitors, on seeing my name on the card, the kind lady took me to his room. As I entered the door he looked up from the sofa upon which he was reclining; instantly he rose, and rushing upon me, clasped me in his arms, and there, locked in each other's embrace, tears testified to the depth of our joy. At our parting, in a suppressed voice, he said—"This is the last time we have looked upon each other on earth!"

POOR RELATION

Referring to the experiences which he had in prison with Mr. Davis, Doctor Minnigerode said:

Soon after Mr. Davis was arrested and confined in Fortress Monroe, I wrote to President Andrew Johnson,[*] petitioning for permission to visit Mr. Davis as his pastor, and to minister to him. Mr. Johnson deigned no answer. In October following I received a communication from some friends to the effect that they thought the time favorable to again make application. There were ladies acting with me and upon advice of a judicious friend they gave my papers to the Reverend Doctor Hall, rector of the Epiphany and pastor of Mr. Stanton, Secretary of War. He at first was averse to acting in the matter, but the ladies begged him at least to read the petition. He did so and consented to take it to Mr. Stanton, and he got the free leave for me to visit Mr. Davis as his pastor. Mr. Stanton's permit must have been very liberal, for General Miles, then in command, received me politely enough, and did not act reluctantly for more than a day, after which he became very cordial and granted all my wishes. He evidently had asked and received fuller directions from the Secretary. I went Saturday evening on my first visit and spent a pleasant enough interview (here and there his German tongue, in spite of a most scholarly knowledge of English, became a little confused, as in this instance, "spent" an interview!) at the quarters of General Miles, who promised to take me to Mr. Davis' cell the next morning. He waited, however, until the Monday following.

I cannot describe my meeting with Mr. Davis in his cell. He knew nothing of my coming and it was difficult for us to control ourselves. At last the question of Holy Communion came up—I do not remember whether he or I first mentioned it—he was very anxious to take it.

[*]This letter is now owned by Confederate Memorial Association. Confederate Veteran, June, 1924.

He was a purely pious man and felt the need and value of the means of grace. But there was one difficulty—could he take it in the proper spirit, in the frame of a forgiving mind, after the treatment to which he had been subjected? He was too upright and conscientious a Christian man to eat and drink unworthily, that is, not in the proper spirit, and as far as in him lay, in peace with God and man. I left him to settle that question himself, between his own conscience and what he understood God's law to be.

In the afternoon General Miles took me to him again. I spoke to the General about the Communion and he promised to make preparation for me. I found Mr. Davis with his mind made up. Knowing the honesty of the man and that there would be, could be, no shamming, nor mere superstitious belief in the ordinance, I was delighted to find him ready. He had laid the bridle upon his very natural feelings, and was ready to pray. "Father, forgive them——"

Then came the Communion—he and I alone, but with God. It was one of those cases in which the Rubric cannot be binding. It was night. The Fortress was so still you could have heard a pin fall. General Miles, with his back to us, leaning against the fireplace in the anteroom, his head in his hands, not moving; the sentinels ordered to stand still, and they stood like statues. I cannot conceive of a more solemn scene.

Dear evidence of how the bitterness of sectional strife and prejudices have passed, I love to think of General Miles, his back turned on this scene, his handsome head in reverence bowed! He was young then—but only a year ago, I, granddaughter of this Civil War preacher, served on a Committee under General Nelson A. Miles for the Relief of Starving Children in Germany! A handsome human creature, a courtly gentleman, a blameless soldier—he died in his boots. Died suddenly, at the age of eighty; upstanding, genial, good-humored; died, in fact, at the circus, mixing kindly with mankind, his battles fought, his campaigns ended, his many laurels fairly won.

CHAPTER III

A PLEASANT picture of my grandfather's home in Richmond is drawn by John S. Wise, in his book, "The End of an Era"—a most readable book published some years ago by Houghton Mifflin Company. After speaking of General "Rooney" Lee, the author discusses General Fitz Lee, his cousin, and alludes to the wit of the Masons of Virginia from whom, through his mother, General Fitz Lee was descended. That family boasts not only great patriots and statesmen, from George Mason of Gunston Hall down, but remarkable women, of whom one of the most brilliant was Cousin Nannie Mason, wife of Captain Smith Lee and mother of General Fitz. Her spicy remarks, tinged with personalities which forbid their repetition, have become historic, and as I remember her she was the prettiest, snappiest, daintiest, quaintest little old lady ever seen out of the pages of a story book! Her tongue was a two-edged sword and her eyes saw through stone walls.

Miss Jennie Cooper, her niece, was a great belle in Richmond during the Civil War, with Miss Mary Triplett and Miss Lou Haxall, famous beauties, and Miss Mattie Old, a renowned wit. Of the group, far-famed, Miss Jennie Cooper was the only one I knew, for she was living on Seminary Hill when I built the new Vaucluse. She was a high-stepper, profile, hands, voice, all indicative of the thoroughbred, and such courage as thrilled all who knew her. Her father, General Cooper, had resigned from the Union Army to join the Southern States, and his handsome home overlooking the Potomac from the second range of hills beyond the river, was destroyed by the Federal soldiers, as was the colonial mansion at Vaucluse. Those heights above Washington commanded the approach to the city, and the forests and many homes were sacrificed. The Theological Seminary was used as a Federal Hospital and therefore escaped and we are thankful today for any cause that spared the splendid oak grove of that historic institution.

It was Miss Jennie Cooper's mission, as Mrs. Dawson, to reconstruct a home from the ruins of her father's stately mansion and hers was a happy faculty of turning off any embarrassment with a laugh. She could conceal poverty and pain and disappointment under good humor and make the daily drudgery of life as they all had to meet it after the disasters of war, a thing of dignity; she could be excruciatingly funny—and she, who had known the hardest of hard luck, never told a "hard luck story." Noblesse oblige! Gallant and gay, those Masons! Well, this is a digression, but one that is justifiable, and now we return to "The End of an Era."*

"The first time," writes John S. Wise, "I ever saw him (Gen. Fitz Lee) was in June, 1864, in Richmond." (He describes my grandfather's house, for the young cavalry officer referred to was my father—and it was possibly a birthday gathering, father having become nineteen years of age that June.)

> In those days Third Street, leading out to the pretty heights of Gambles Hill, was the favorite evening promenade. The people of Richmond, save such as visited friends in the country, remained in town throughout the summer, for no places of public resort were open, and nobody had the means to go, if they had been open. On summer nights the better classes, maid and matron, old men, high officers, soldiers, boys and girls, strolled back and forth on Third Street to catch the southern breeze upon the hill, cooled by its passage across the falls of the James; to watch the belching furnaces of the Tredegar cannon foundry on the river banks below and to listen to the band that sometimes played upon the hill. While thus diverting myself with a party of young friends one evening, we saw a string of cavalry horses held in front of the residence of a prominent citizen, and as we approached, heard the sound of a piano, accompanied by a male and a female voice singing *The Gipsey Countess*.
>
> The curtains of the parlor were drawn back to relieve the intense sultriness, and the party was visible from the street. A deep, strong voice sang the familiar part of the duet,—"Come, fly with me now"—the sweet answer was returned in female notes, "Can I trust to

*Page 344.

thy vow?" Then the two warbled the refrain together, and the performance finally concluded amid merry laughter and vigorous applause.

The performance was varied by the appearance of a cavalryman with his banjo. He gave them some jingling music which set everybody's blood bounding. Knowing the host we felt no hesitancy about joining the party of onlookers upon the portico and there we beheld Fitz Lee and his staff making a night of it as they passed through Richmond on their way to Petersburg. The house was the home of one of his favorite young staff officers, whose sister was Fitz Lee's partner in the duet.*

In appearance Fitz Lee was short, thickset, already inclined to stoutness; with a square head and short thick neck upon broad shoulders, a merry eye and a joyous voice of great power; ruddy, full-bearded and overflowing with animal spirits. At last the banjo struck up his favorite air:

> "If you want to have a good time,
>   Jine the cavalry,
>   Jine the cavalry,
>   Jine the cavalry!"

Fitz and his staff joined in the refrain with mighty zest making the house ring with their hilarity. This over, they announced their departure for Petersburg, and a mighty hubbub they made. The ladies of the house and the young girls brought food and dainties for their haversacks and wearing apparel for use in the camp; packing of these took place in the hallway, and then followed the farewells.

It was "Good-bye, Lucy" (Minnigerode) and "Good-bye, Mary" (Triplett) and "Good-bye, Jennie" (Cooper),

*My Aunt Lucy, afterwards Mrs. William Hoxton.

and Fitz Lee must have been kin to a good many of those pretty girls. His young staff officer kissed his mother and sister good-bye; Fitz Lee, true to cavalry instincts, began kissing also; this doubtless inspired his young Captain to extend like courtesies to visitors as well as the family, and wherever he led, Fitz followed. By the time their plunder had been placed upon their steeds, and they, with jangling spurs, had scrambled to their saddles, Fitz Lee and staff had taken "cavalry toll" from every pretty girl in sight.

Finally, with many fond adieus and waving plumes, they rode away down Cary Street, their mounted banjoist playing the air and they singing in chorus:

>"If you want to have a good time,
> Jine the cavalry——"

Such a picture of my father, entertaining his beloved commander in his father's house, so near the end of the bitter struggle, is a happy sidelight on the life of our people during that weary time—youth, with its blessed recuperative faculty taking the edge off of suffering, anxiety, danger, parting, death.

My father, "Charlie" Minnigerode, ran away from school in Richmond at the age of sixteen to serve under Fitz Lee; he had seen the cavalryman in a saddler's shop looking at equipment, and had been thrilled as a young hero worshipper by the encounter. Fitz Lee had noticed him and said to him, "Boy, why aren't you in the Army?" And a few nights later the boy was in the Army and those two men slept under the same blanket

Major Charles Minnigerode and General Fitzhugh Lee in Confederate Uniform.

GENERAL ROBERT E. LEE

Portrait by Mrs. Andrews Owned by the Virginia Historical Society.
Based Upon a Death Mask by Clarke Mills.

POOR   RELATION

many and many a dreary night. My father's younger brother, James Gibbon, also ran off at the age of fourteen and entered the Confederate Navy, later to follow in his father's steps and become an Episcopal clergyman, for many years greatly beloved in Louisville, Kentucky.

Father's army record is one of which his children are justly proud. He was not twenty years of age when a minnie ball on the field of Appomattox laid him low—the last bullet to strike a soldier of the Army of Northern Virginia before the surrender of General Lee. Fitz Lee pinned a note on his uniform as they retreated, stating who he was and asking that his father in Richmond be notified of his death.

The feeling which General Fitz Lee had for his young aide-de-camp is well expressed in his report of the operations of the Confederate Cavalry of the Army of Northern Virginia on their last campaign. General Lee says:

> I deeply regret being obliged to mention the dangerous wounding of my aide-de-camp, Lieutenant Charles Minnigerode, Jr. One of the last minnie balls that whistled on its cruel errand over the Field of Appomattox passed entirely through the upper part of his body. He fell at my side, where for three long years he had discharged his duties with an affectionate fidelity never exceeded, a courage never surpassed, wonderfully passing unharmed through many battles fought by the two principal armies in this State: for an impetuous spirit often carried him where the fire was hottest. He was left at last writhing in great pain to the mercy of

the victors upon the field of our last conflict. The rapidly advancing lines of the enemy prevented his removal, and as we turned away the wet eyes and sorrowing hearts silently told that he was no longer in our midst.

Lieutenant Minnigerode combined the qualities of an aide-de-camp and a general officer in a remarkable degree. Personal service to me will be praised and remembered, while his intelligence, amiability and brightness of disposition rendered him an object of endearment to all.

The "mercy of the victors" was greater than they knew. Cousin Fitz, on one occasion when I happened to travel with him from Richmond to Washington, long after my father's death, told me of a circumstance till then unknown to us— that as this poor boy lay in agony on the field, two Union soldiers passed—that he dragged himself from under other dead and wounded to attract their attention and implored them for the love of God to finish the job and put him out of his suffering—that they conferred together—and then one of them said, "Be patient, Johnny-Reb, the doctors are coming—maybe they can do something—" and almost on the point of really shooting him to end his misery, they passed on.

The doctors did come. Federal surgeons picked up this dying boy, took him to their hospital, gave him his chance, cut out the ugly thing which had passed almost entirely through his body, and sent him tottering on crutches back to his mother in Richmond. At twenty-three he married my mother, having been engaged six times before he met her!

I believe no woman ever met the fellow but would have married him. There is a charm about the whole breed—an inexplicable charm! Virtue has nothing to do with it for the Minnigerodes are hardly to be called virtuous, indeed some of us are quite rascally; intellect has small responsibility for it for others far more intellectual have it not. Beauty is not the reason either, for as a race these people are not beautiful. And still it has been possible—even easy—for them to ride on the crest of the wave while better men were floundering in the depths. They have been able to borrow money with smiling faces from hard-working friends who did not know what self-indulgence meant; they have moved in distinguished society where others equally well bred and far more worthy, better educated and better dressed, were strangers; they have been graceful and graceless, debonair and indifferent, impertinent beyond belief, yet always forgiven. A slight trace of arrogance marked them, they had a faculty of grasping "the skirts of happy chance"; they were expert but quite unconscious exploiters of themselves. Their faith in themselves was colossal and carried them far and they were gallant gamblers. To wait and weigh a proposition in cold blood, in war or work or love or trade, was not their way—they played the game!

My father was romantic. He was artistic and

poetic, though these noble gifts ran to caricature. He had no opportunity for study, but Dr. Minnigerode's children all appeared to have a culture which they never acquired by study.

My father had distinction of appearance. The most perfectly shaped cranium I ever saw, the way the dark hair grew on the temples and at the back of the neck, thrilled me with pleasure, even as a little child. As I remember him best the forehead ran up into two points above the temples, that dear, dear forehead! The curly hair was tinged with gray and growing thin; he was a trifle bald in a round spot on top, and at the nape of his neck the hair was still thick and brown, and cut close to keep it from curling. He hated curls.

A wide white brow, large greenish-gray eyes set far apart; a long nose, a mouth that was large and generous but just missed an expression of sensuality, a thin mustache hardly covering it; a colorless complexion, long flexible hands, a tall frame thin almost to emaciation, a marked limp— the result of his severe wound at Appomattox; a restless, nervous manner, an irrepressible flow of wit, an under-current of melancholy that deepened into tragedy as the years crawled on; a genius for business, for speculation, for seeing in a most picturesque way opportunities which others missed because of a too conservative attitude; a trick of nature, which made most men and all women his friends and sharers in the gaiety which was not untouched by cynicism. A man who was a seasoned soldier at the age of eighteen, a man who wrecked his health by the hardships he courted; who, without capital or training, conceived and carried out many brilliant enterprises but failed in the end because a buoyant spirit and supreme self-confidence led him invariably to overshoot the mark. A man who was a rare lover of one woman, too fastidious to waver in his allegiance to her, although so magnetic as to meet with many temptations and so passionate as to demand much love.

This was my father. This was my first love. This, from that first memory of my life, when in his arms I watched the big cloud-shadows glide mysteriously across the sunny fields at Oakley, was my idol and ideal.

As I grew older and saw more clearly, I only adored him more; more when he did wrong, more when others blamed him, more when he blamed himself, as he often did.

The tendency to idealize those whom we love, is by no means so general as is supposed, and the saying "Love is blind" is another fallacy, one which escaped Charles Lamb, among our popular adages. Indeed, love so sharpens the observation that we see the faults of our dear ones often in an exaggerated way and much loyalty is born of this, for when all the world blames, we, who cannot deny, can continue in the love that bears, hopes, believes, endures, all things.

CHAPTER IV

MY mother was a Virginian of the most representative class. Her connections were numerous among historic families. Peytons, Lees, Braxtons, Carters, Randolphs, Turners, Harrisons, Bollings, Hills, Beverleys, Powells, all give to my children the background against which they will paint the picture of their lives. One should know what to expect of one's self in a crisis, having the examples of many lives well lived, of which one's forebears have preserved the history. Also the directions in which one may be likely to err, having reliable information as to racial and inherited tendencies to evil.

My mother was a pretty slip of a girl, one whose life had been peculiarly sheltered, her somewhat stern, but beautiful, stately mother having devoted herself with tragic tenderness to the bringing up of this her youngest child, born two months after my grandfather had dropped dead in the midst of a speech in the State Legislature at Richmond, at the age of forty-two. They did not remain long at their own home, The Hill, at Middleburg, Virginia, after this, but went to Oakley, in Fauquier County, the residence of Captain Henry Grafton Dulany, whose wife was mother's older sister—Ida—famous for her charm, beauty and intellect.

The Civil War found them safe in this haven and many were the thrilling experiences of a handful of women and some little children during those troubled times. Frequent were the raids made by the Yankees, great was my horror as a tiny tot, to see the prints of nails on old mahogany furniture, witnessing to the kicks of heavy military boots; I would hide my eyes at the dark stains on the floor, for wounded of both armies were brought in and laid out in the hall at Oakley, and cared for without discrimination by these Christian gentlewomen; my grandmother and aunt and the little girl who became my mother tore their table linen and underwear into shreds for bandages, and prayed alike for dying friend or foe.

And I would wax wroth at the willful wastes I heard of—when after carrying off or driving away everything available, stores, stock, fodder, the Yankees would take the poor remainder, the broken lots of coffee, sugar, molasses, cornmeal, etc., which the family could so well have used, and stir them into an ungodly mess in the middle of the dining room floor. I never wearied of these stories, tame as they may seem to a later generation.

One old slave, taken from Oakley by the Federal troops, got away from his friendly captors and hustled his terrified self back to Oakley as fast as his legs would carry him—the assumption therefore being that he was a spy and returning with information for the Confederate forces as to his recent observations. Soldiers were dispatched by General Auger to get him, dead or alive, but when they demanded him of Mrs. Dulany, she declined to give any information concerning him. Her husband was not there and so she herself was placed under arrest and conveyed to General Auger's camp as a hostage. She was very young and pretty and there was considerable suspense as to her fate, but the whole matter was a formality; in a few days she was returned to her family having met only with courtesy, having in fact been rather entertained by the experience, and having absolutely gained her point! When she took little Rebecca (now Mrs. Hill Carter Beverly), her baby, on her knees, and asked, "What did 'Becca say when the Yankees carried her mother away?" Little Rebecca, who has all her life been a perfect saint, lisped in a modest undertone, "I didn't thay mutch—I only did thay I wishes they wath all burnin' upth in hell." Many years later at some social function in Washington, as Mrs. Dulany was assigned to a distinguished Army officer who was to escort her to dinner, he remarked: "Have I not had the pleasure of meeting you elsewhere, Mrs. Dulany?" "I believe so, General Auger," said my Aunt Ida. "We met during the war."

That General Lew Wallace, author of "Ben

Hur," had been responsible for the imprisonment of the beautiful Cary sisters of Baltimore, and that Ben Butler in New Orleans had treated our old friend Mrs. Philips in the same fashion; that my mother, at the age of twelve, had run ahead of a firing squad of Yankees pursuing two Confederate spies, had opened a gate for the Southern soldiers and closed it in the teeth of the pursuers, almost being shot for her courage; that neither Yankees nor Confederates would eat cornbread as long as there was a crumb of white bread on the table, were episodes of the war which in different degrees thrilled all hearers.

Grandma kept her "pieces" carefully assorted and rolled in neat little bundles; silks, muslins, print, cloth, all separate, tied up in rolls and labelled—"Bits of Lavinia's wedding frock," "Rozier's homespun breeches," "Bags for May's left hand," etc.; woolens were done up with a little camphor, and lace remnants always in a box. The exquisite neatness of the older generation and their thriftiness in small matters seem qualities hardly human to the modern extravagant mind!

And to me the bureau drawer in which these treasures were hoarded seemed a veritable El Dorado, for was not I the mother of several very shabby dolls? And imagine that day, that thrilling day, long before I was born, when reckless, sassy Yankee soldiers invaded the sacred precincts of Grandma's room in search of loot, ransacked this very drawer, mussing all these honored relics, then turning scornfully away, "Pooh! Only the old woman's rags!"

That Grandma should have been called an "old woman" was blasphemous—old women were not at all like her—old women sold eggs and berries, wore shawls and sunbonnets, were meek and respectful and never wore real lace caps with strings, and little round collars with tiny roses on them, done with real petals made all in the lace!

And "rags"! Those treasures! Those bits of velvets and satins! Those remnants of ancient finery! Those loved and lovely relics of a generation's wedding frocks and party frocks and christening robes! Those mysterious possessions which added just the finishing touch to a ball gown, from which too her own lace caps, and my Sunday hats, and Christmas presents for all her descendants, were manufactured by her ingenious fingers—why, the mere opening of that drawer caused a child to breathe faster, and little peeps into its depths stimulated in all the little granddaughters a love of finery! "Nothing here but the old woman's rags." Ah! My dear patriot! This time you missed it! For counting upon masculine contempt for just such "rags" the "old woman" had tucked away in those bundles many a good bank note!

They say that on these raids Grandma followed the soldiers fearlessly like a sort of religious

POOR RELATION

Nemesis from room to room, shaking a long reproving finger at them and enquiring in her high-pitched Southern voice, if they were not aware that there was a day of judgment coming, in which the righteous Lord would punish their iniquities? Whereupon these scamps of invaders, lost to every consideration even for the safety of their immortal and much imperiled souls, would reply, in voices pitched to a high falsetto note in imitation of her own—"Yes'm—yes'm. Yes, yes, yes, yes'm," while putting up the goods in a thoroughly workmanlike manner.

The thought of their impertinence and ungodliness scandalized me, for Grandma had discoursed with me in a similar strain, very, very often, and I devoted much time to speculation as to just how bad one might be, and still elude the eye of Grandma and the wrath of God. She told me it was easier as well as more profitable, to be good than bad. I experimented with both systems, and satisfied myself that it was not easier, but certainly more profitable, to be good.

My mother, who was a flower-like little creature as a girl, had always specified, after the fashion of young ladies, just the sort of husband she intended to have. Her requirements were not exorbitant, she was prepared to accept him upon two simple conditions—no blood relations, and the possession of handsome legs.

When she was eighteen fate threw my father across her path and within three weeks they were engaged, regardless of his many relations and blind as to his legs. He fell far short of the specifications. His father was a poor clergyman with an over-worked and rather querulous wife; he was the oldest son of a family of nine, all very temperamental, self-assertive young people. Parochial affairs and the administration of advice and consolation to the world at large probably left my Grandfather Minnigerode very little time for attending to the spiritual welfare of his own offspring—and they were not an easily managed group of girls and boys, for whom their older brother felt solicitude and assumed considerable responsibility. Also in the matter of legs, my father varied from the model, for his legs were too long and lean, and one of them was very crooked—he walked with a crutch when she first knew him, and always with a cane. Appomattox was responsible for the limp, but not for the length or the leanness.

The engagement of these young people filled my mother's family with anxiety and consternation. Even the old servants, whom no "freedom" could estrange from the Dulany estate, expressed their concern, and old "Uncle Robert," the time-honored butler, stood deferentially before my grandmother one summer evening as she sat on the porch, while the lovers were strolling on the lawn, and shifting in his nervousness from foot to foot, twisting the napkin on his arm into a rope, he spoke, after the manner of a privileged retainer—" 'Scuse me, Ole Miss; but Ah's bleeged to ax you—Ole Miss, do we-alls people know anything 'bout this here young gent'man, he-alls people, what Miss Ginnie gwine fer to marry? Do he-alls folks b'long to *Us?*"

CHAPTER V

UNCLE ROBERT must have been a twin brother to Uncle Remus, and no dearer delight was known to me than to sit in deep conversation with my Aunt Ida's venerable retainer in the years of which I soon may tell you, when Oakley was my home. He was indefatigable in the matter of cleaning brass, of which there was a great deal in the house, fenders and andirons and old candlesticks that were used in the bedrooms with homemade tallow candles; he had a great many lamps to care for, and was very particular as to the "thief" which was an uneven corner of the wick, and made a mighty smell when lighted, running a tongue of flame above the proper point and smoking the clean glass chimney abominably. As Uncle Robert filled his lamps and trimmed his wicks I sat in a high chair in the pantry, holding sweet converse with him, and young as I was many a sidelight he gave me as to our people. He called us "quality." He told me how my father had "give him consider'ble worriment comin' after your mummer, Miss Ginnie, she was so young, you mus' always be mighty good to your mummer" (he always said "Mummer"), but I loved best to watch him clean silver, of which there was an endless quantity at Oakley; he knew every trophy, and told me of each horse and every detail of each race in which any of "we-all's hosses" had won. These great loving-cups were his special pride, for Mars' Rozier made his mint juleps in them—Uncle Robert never knew which one the young master would select so kept them all immaculate, ranging them, though he could not read the inscriptions, according to date. When he came to the big silver sugar bowl he never failed to remind me that "endurin' of the war, Ole Miss had baptized all the chillun fast as they wuz borned, out of that very sugar bowl—'cause all the preachers wuz to the war, and natchelly she done that herse'f."

He told me all about *Us*. *Us* calls for a chapter—In Virginia we still speak of ourselves as *Us*. Mankind is divided into two parts—*Us* and the others. This small pronoun has a meaning that should be fraught with terror to interlopers but they seem hardly to grasp its portent; they meet us frankly as if they were just as good as we are, though they may hail from Ohio or Maine—remote places mentioned as a courtesy in the geographies, but of no real importance. It is difficult to give these unfortunates a conception of their true status—not of *Us*—only by persistent effort and with a benign compassion and gentleness can we force this knowledge upon them.

As business, duty or pleasure have sent me during later years back and forth throughout our country, the friendly admiration and toleration towards the Southerner surprises and touches me. It is not pleasant to come in contact with those who claim superiority, especially superiority in birth and breeding; and I think it is because fate has left us so little else to brag about, that we do often find ourselves guilty of this lack of taste. Who resents it? No one—people smile, agree with us, offer to our ancestors that incense which is so dear to our own nostrils, invite us to their beautiful parties, marry our poor sons to their rich daughters, buy our run-down dear old Colonial and Georgian houses and restore them, gratefully and gleefully adopting our traditions!

The fact that this State was the battlefield of the Civil War; the proud exclusiveness of our old and rapidly disappearing land-owners; the gallant fight against difficult conditions and economic ruin; the open scorn and contempt for vulgarity; the easy assurance of manner in those who, often inadequately educated and shabby in appearance, are still to the manor born, have built up a sort of romance around the Virginian, and it is largely due to the rest of the world that he is so pleased with himself!

An old lady, whose sacrifices and struggles to maintain in extreme poverty the outer semblance of elegance, put the creed of the Virginian into words. Her young daughter was preparing to make a visit "North." Everything was in readiness; the frocks were freshened and pressed; the scanty wardrobe was enlarged to the limit; heirlooms, laces, cameos, were brought out with considerable ceremony, and the carefully computed expenses for railway fare, tips, etc., were provided; then the final maternal injunction—"Honey, don't you mention you're from Virginia—that would be like talking about money in front o' folks that are po'. We mustn't parade our 'dvantages——"

CHAPTER VI

NOTHING could have been more quaintly insincere than the formal letters exchanged between the prospective son-in-law and mother-in-law, preliminary to my mother's marriage. All were at Oatlands, the Carter home in Loudoun County, and the lover entrusted to Aunt Kate (Mrs. Carter, my mother's sister), a missive directed to Grandma, although a five-minute conversation would have settled the matter.

The correspondence was along the line of Mr. Peter Magnus—the lover expatiated upon his own unworthiness—unworthiness for this especial charming girl, but intimated that nevertheless he possessed qualifications which modesty, perhaps, forbade his mentioning. There were those who knew (the letter hinted)—while his financial resources were limited (whose are not?) he extended to his future mother-in-law a cordial invitation to make her permanent abode under the shadow of his (as yet undiscovered) roof. Grandma replied, also handing her letter to Aunt Katie, in the laboriously polite style of Clarissa Harlowe, admitting that though her "other daughters had married wealthy men, money with *Us* was not the primary consideration"; nevertheless, it seemed to filter through

POOR RELATION

the words that in spite of accumulating for herself treasure where neither moth nor rust corrupt, she would prefer for this, her youngest daughter, some visible means of support. She graciously admitted that she had heard much that was good of himself, and further intimated that though her daughter was a poor girl, she would not come to him dowerless. (But I think she did.) All of this by-play was taken for what it was worth—each referring vaguely and a little grandiloquently to prospects which the other knew to be fictitious, but which decorum required should exist, at least in such a correspondence!

This ruse of substituting notes for a straightforward interview was not confined to my grandmother's generation—mother often did it, where affairs of the heart were concerned. She could detect an incipient love-affair with unerring accuracy and knew no rest until everything was mixed up regarding it! She would leave little notes in the bureau drawers of her daughters, conveying hints, remonstrance, advice, encouragement, as to the delicate situation, and the recipients of these documents would meet the writer of them at breakfast, with no reference to the mysterious communications. But later, if they were willing to share with her the latest news, they would reply also in writing, smuggling the note into the market basket or tucking it under the coffee-pot or pinning it to the pincushion, where she could not fail to find it! With *Us*, these were points of breeding.

Such an epistolary flirtation went on between dear Mrs. Montgomery Corse and her children's governess, for years—each month the situation became embarrassing in the extreme, when the honorarium fell due!

Money transactions between friends are so delicate! And with *Us*, the lady residing in our family and doing us the honor of regarding our home as her home while she devotes herself to the interest of our children, is regarded as a distinguished guest. Dear Mrs. Corse would approach Miss Lucy on the first of the month, an envelope in her hand, coughing slightly—then assuming a playful manner to conceal her agony of confusion, would say: "I think, Miss Lucy, the month has again rolled around and there is a little transaction we must not forget."

Miss Lucy, not to be outdone, would then summon a look of "unfeigned" surprise to her gentle countenance, and answer, "With me, dear Mrs. Corse! How mysterious!"

"Dear Miss Lucy, do you not recall that we had a little understanding by which when you kindly consented to become a member of this household, you were to receive a monthly consideration—hardly what your valued assistance is worth—but still something to express my gratitude in accepting for my entire family such an obligation——"

Virginia Cuthbert Powell (Mrs. Charles Minnigerode), my mother.

THE HALL AT OAKLEY.

POOR RELATION

And so the two dear things, each so tender of the feelings of the other, would bow and bow, and fence and fence, until the envelope changed hands, and for the next four weeks each could breathe freely.

That was the leisurely day of the three-volume novel and the afternoon nap; of the elaborate crochet work, and eye-destroying embroidery; of the verbose guest and the obsequious servant. Pleasant times, upon my word! Impressionism had reached Paris, but was unknown with *Us*. My cousin May painted flowers very nicely, with a painstaking devotion to detail which was greatly admired with *Us*—and letter writing was truly, with Grandma, an art—then why should such an opportunity pass by, as this afforded by my father's proposal?

The wedding took place within the year, at Oakley, dear Oakley. I see my little mother in those sweet surroundings, the house with its generous hall and winding stair, the stately porticos, the swaying fields of corn and wheat beyond the lawn and grove, extending to the very foothills of the Blue Ridge mountains.

He was twenty-three and she was eighteen. They married for love. Love is an excellent reason for marrying. And I detest the sort of wet-blanket who reminds us that love and soft words butter no parsnips! That is another of those popular fallacies which escaped Charles

Lamb. They do better than butter parsnips—
they glorify them.

It is a grave matter for a little eighteen-year-old girl to give up the captaincy over her own life and body and future and to stray off with an improvident youth away from her mother and the good black mammy who had dressed and undressed her, brushed her hair and taken off her shoes for her, every day of all those eighteen years! Away from the generous brother-in-law and gentle sister and little cousins who had all so petted her.

Her story might well furnish an argument against early marriages; against hasty and impecunious marriages; but it does not. Most people tell you that this was not a fortunate marriage. I know that it was. I know what resulted from it—strong stuff; vibrating, stimulating, energetic men and women came from it—is not that enough? If they suffered, then they suffered. But they achieved something. I, the first fruit of this union, know. I know their struggles, sufferings, failures, compensations and triumphs. They fulfilled themselves, they had their love, they expressed themselves in that most marvelous of all mediums, human life and character, which is evolving spirit.

But that blushing little girl who went to Richmond into her father-in-law's family had some rude awakenings.

The first shock came on her first Sunday morning in that house, when her mother-in-law and she had breakfast alone, the reverend father and the amorous bridegroom and the eight younger brothers and sisters all staying in bed late, expecting trays from their mother to their rooms. Life in the rectory of the Reverend Doctor was unlike anything she had ever known in quiet Oakley, where the days were free from devitalizing contradictions and conflicting inclinations. Here were the old gentleman and his constitutionally fretful wife; eight young brothers and sisters-in-law; stereotyped religious exercises. There was the automatic expression of sympathy in the more or less uninspiring sorrows of common people, and the congenial administration of consolation to the more distinguished members of the flock.

There was the bitter gratitude (which is ingratitude) for the gifts and benefits derived from wealthy parishioners, and the gnawing envy that must never be revealed and so torments the inner man, for those worldly luxuries and pleasures in which the clergyman's family, set apart, should not even wish to participate.

The natural reaction was that these gifted boys and pretty girls were continually in scrapes. The bride for the first time came face to face with the love of luxury and in contact with people who did not have the money to do or buy the things they wished, yet without the discipline to deny themselves, or to work for the means to carry out their plans. There was perpetual friction and the bride shed many tears, some of which, I think, tinctured my own whole life.

One day this homesick little creature, looking out of the window of her father-in-law's house, saw a negro boy lead a saddle horse to the door—her own dainty, high-stepping horse, sent from Oakley. She rushed into the street, threw her arms around the horse's neck and burst into tears. Only was she recalled to herself by the little boys in the street calling to each other, "Come a-runnin'—come a-runnin'—come see a white gal a-huggin' and a-kissin' of a hoss!"

Looking back across the years it comes to me with a sense of deep thankfulness that I have lived almost always among the generous and innately noble. Natures based upon what is fine and liberal, in whom the sin that mars us all was still akin to goodness. Love excessive, to use Dante's classifications—not love defective or inverted. When the pendulum swung too far, they erred; they were extravagant because they were generous, and generosity not well regulated easily becomes extravagance. Then they would seem mean, in abortive attempts to catch up to square accounts and come out even after their bursts of liberality. Constitutionally generous, habitually kind, only spasmodically cruel or parsimonious.

I have seen meddlesomeness that bordered on philanthropy, its purpose being friendly; obstinacy, which as it ripened, became firmness of character and self-reliance; vulgarity that is but a reaction from artificial refinement, almost pleasantly human and democratic; vanity, which is a frank appraisal of God-given gifts, and only misleading to such as look not with the eyes of love.

My own has been a stormy soul, saved only by the Power outside itself. Wonder overtakes me as I realize the monstrous confusion which even the most obscure among us could make if we should for a brief season relax our guard upon ourselves, forget the consideration due to others, and the gratitude due to God.

CHAPTER VII

I HOLD in my hand tonight two letters from my godmother. The following was written evidently in reply to my mother's invitation to her to be my godmother, when I should present myself in due time to a world where godmothers were considered desirable. The date is four months before my birth, to the day:

Lexington, Va.
September 11, 1869

Dear Darling Jennie:

Your last very sweet letter reached me just as I was starting to the country to spend several days with some friends, and so I concluded to delay my reply until my return, even though I thought of you ever, ever so much and wanted to thank you and send you oceans of love for the very sweet compliment that I feel you have paid me, and that I will now most willingly accede to, with the hope that I may be enabled by the grace of God to discharge as I ought my duty in the relation that I have already told you that I recognize as one very binding and sacred.

As to my love and affection and interest, that it would have even through that I bear to you and Charley, for I could scarcely feel otherwise toward your child, feeling the warm attachment that I do for you both—but now in this relation a stronger and deeper claim will be given me, bound by a tie as Godmother and child very close and tender, a tie almost as close as blood itself.

P O O R R E L A T I O N

I think I wrote you in a former letter, Jennie, that I look upon this thing as did my godfather, and very differently from that generally done by the world, and as you will see, am prepared (if such in the providence of God ever is to come to pass) to love, and feel a very warm and tender interest ever and always in your child. Our Father grant, Jennie darling, that all may be well with you.

I wrote you last winter that there was something I wished for that particular occasion and which was to be a dress, but I find that I cannot obtain here the material that I would like to have for it and it will take me too long after going to Richmond this winter to make it so as to have it in time, so that I will then give up the idea of it preferring at any rate I believe a gift to my godchild in some more durable form, and that I may be longer remembered by.

I received Lucy's letter some few days since and hope to reply to it 'ere long. I received the sample of sash ribbon and believe I will get Mrs. M—— to take the money I sent her and get me one—I will be so much obliged and send me by mail—also, Jennie, I want a neck ribbon to match in color as nearly as can the sash— I saw some very pretty striped ribbon at Mrs. Barten's. I think one-half a yard will be plenty.

(Here it appears a page is lost)

I enclose three dollars to get the gloves and neck ribbon.

Good-bye, with love——

The other letter is a codicil to a will, as follows:

I give (at my death) to my god-child, May Minnigerode, the sum of two hundred dollars ($200.00) said sum of two hundred dollars to be put at interest, said interest to be used yearly so long as she may live, exclusively for religious purposes, such as books, papers, and such other things as appertain to a purely religious character—such books, papers, etc., to be subject to the choice of her parents as guardians, if too young to act for herself.

I design this my little gift first as a means of thus keeping before her mind in this form, a Constant Reminder that she is not to live for this life only, as also that it may be a little annual Remembrance of the Relation that I have sustained to her in that of a godmother even though I be absent in the flesh. I again repeat my request that it be used exclusively, solely and only for Religious Purposes both for her as well as by herself when arrived at an age to judge with discretion for herself, and my prayer now unto God is that it may become through Him a means of great spiritual benefit to her soul and that I may experience a joy some day in knowing that this my little gift of Love has not been in vain in the Lord.

In the event of the death of my god-child, May Minnigerode, while yet too young to have made suitable disposition of it herself, I request that said sum of two hundred dollars be given in her name to the Board of Foreign Missions. I now offer it in that event unto the Lord to go up as a Memorial before Him in her behalf.

Sallie W. Smith

Benvenue, Fayette County,
Kentucky. April 1874.

Much may be read between the lines of these poor relics of a girl long dead. The simple yearning for a half yard of neck ribbon, that innocent vanity woven in with so much sincere piety.

POOR RELATION

The poverty of the times, the scarcity of everything. The exceptional sense of responsibility.

The little legacy came when I was a small child, with twelve religious books, among them Jeremy Taylor's "Holy Living and Holy Dying," and sermons of Frederick Robertson—the other volumes are scattered long ago, in our many migrations, and I do not recall their names. Also my godmother's gold watch, in which my father as a boy had painted a miniature of the Confederate flag, and her gold thimble. I remember the thrill of pleasure it gave me to have the use of this small fortune "for religious purposes." We subscribed to the "Southern Churchman" with part of it. Once when we were visiting at Oatlands the clergyman's wife came to the house and her dress was very shabby. I eyed her darned elbows and shiny shoulder-blades appraisingly. We were even shabbier than she was, but I nudged my mother and whispered that a preacher's wife ought to have a best dress and maybe my dead godmother would have thought so, too.

After much deliberation we concluded to spend three dollars on material, and did get ten yards of gray mohair for that sum, which I had the pleasure of bestowing upon the astonished lady. This little bequest, so pathetic as we read its reiterated charges to do solely and only strictly religious things for all the years of my life, made a deep impression upon us children, an impression which in my mind has so far borne fruit for fifty years.

One of the fruits of this legacy to me is the bungalow which I call Good Intent and which after my son's marriage I built near Vaucluse, our country house in Fairfax County, Virginia, having turned the larger home over to him. Good Intent is a little memorial to my dear daughter, Mary Lord, who, had she lived a longer earthly life, would have had as pleasant a home on that hill-top as her mother could have given her. But since the many mansions have been opened to her, this little place with its disarming name stands as a tribute to her and her artistic tastes, and has already solved many problems, modest as it is, for jaded nerves and weary bodies are welcomed there to the sunshine and the shadows of the summer days, to the fresh air and the delicious spring water, to the peace and consolation of those quiet hill-tops under the rolling clouds.

There we have built "The Little Theater in the Hills," in a ravine, where alfresco plays and pageants are to many a source of inspiration and recreation. In memory of my godmother and the legacy which she provided for my pleasure and profit, I am giving Good Intent to my little granddaughter, Mary Lord Andrews the third, named for dear Mary Lord; that as soon as she is old enough to do anything, it may be in her power to use Good Intent as I used the income from my godmother's $200.00. Little Mary Lord will be able to loan Good Intent to some family crowded into an apartment, when the summer days come, and to the little children who would enjoy the country where she has so much liberty. She may have delicate babies from the children's hospital there for a time, and I shall provide for her that the money will be in her hands to pay for their care. And she may write her own little plays, as dear Mary Lord did, and produce them in her little open-air theater.

This Little Theater in the Hills, at least, after fifty years, is one recognition of the $200.00 which my godmother left me, so soon after the Civil War, when a very little money seemed a great deal to us in the South, and when the possibility of doing for others was almost cut off by the necessity of doing for ourselves. Then it was that this little sum of money, designated for a specific purpose, made possible a few acts of helpfulness.

In itself the little capital must have been swallowed up in father's disasters; but in its place all that I have has been in one way or another, blindly, extravagantly, unwisely, hard-headedly, but lovingly, devoted to the welfare of my kind, which is to the glory of God, and must be, in a sense which now that sweet lady understands, not in vain in the Lord.

PART II
My Childhood at Oakley

CHAPTER VIII

GRANDMOTHER was Marietta Fauntleroy Turner of Kinloch. Her mother was Eliza Carter Randolph of Eastern View. Her mother was Eliza Hill Carter of Shirley. Pleasant names, calling up pictures of stately old homes and friendly people. And further back, Eleanor Peyton, Elizabeth Beverley, Jane Fauntleroy, women whose painted faces have looked down on us all our lives, and names all woven in and out of Colonial history. My own mother's name, Virginia Cuthbert Powell, is gracious, is it not? I was happy to change my own Marietta Minnigerode for two honest syllables with which a good husband endowed me, as indeed I was willing to supplement my traditions—my only inheritance—with the substantial worldly goods which my husband's grandfather had accumulated in a wholesale grocery business in the early days in Ohio.

We spoke condescendingly of and to "tradespeople" in Virginia when I was young. And I would that my children should bear in mind that such tardy education, and such of the luxuries of life, as came my way, or theirs, came through these sturdy tradespeople.

I was named for Grandma, and she was partial to me. Much of my childhood was spent with her at Oakley, where she made her home with my Uncle and Aunt, Captain and Mrs. Henry Grafton Dulany. It was a calm and dignified life. I have been grateful for it during the anxious, sordid and discouraging events of later years, when memory took me back to that sweet old place: the impulse then given me toward the imaginative and the religious has fortified me against many disenchantments.

The people were cultured and kind, the outer world serene and beautiful, the encircling hills, the noble old trees, the garden, the sun, moon, and stars, combining to make one child happy.

Only a few days ago I dropped into the office of my cousin and trustee, Rozier Dulany, who in my childhood seemed to me the most adorable person on earth (and why limit it to my childhood?) and as I entered his office he looked up, and in his delightful, drawling, Southern way, accosted me with the words, "Gal, you're lookin' mighty young today."

"Well," I said, "I passed my fifty-fourth birthday last week."

Still in the same slow manner, he remarked, "Well, then it has been fifty-three years since I saw you crawling around on the floor at Oakley, my mother and Grandma watching you, as you caught a live hornet and ate it."

"Rozier," I said, "you're the biggest liar that

ever lived. I never did anything of the sort."

"Yes, miss, you did, when you were one year old. I saw you myself catch a live hornet and eat it as though it had been a chocolate drop, and that's what's the matter with you now—that hornet is in your system."

With the exception of my Aunt, Mrs. Dulany, everyone rose in the morning according to his own sweet will; she was early about her business, supervising a large farm and establishment, but the others straggled in to breakfast at any hour—and breakfast and "Uncle Robert" waited. Breakfast? Well, breakfast consisted of oatmeal or grits, with abundant golden sluggish cream; of eggs and chops, and lamb or kidney stew—of fruit in season, at least such as the place produced; and of three or four varieties of hot bread. "Light rolls" always. What had "Aunt Kitty" to do, in heaven's name? Waffles—waffles are very little trouble—and for those who do not care for waffles, corn cakes are at hand—and batterbread, or soft corn-bread (it has many names) a necessity. There was the kitchen to be fed, and what the kitchen failed to consume went to the chickens and pigs, so there was less waste than might have appeared on the surface, in these elaborate repasts.

My Aunt Ida managed the estate in all particulars and with the greatest serenity. She never raised her voice in speaking to an inferior, she never called anyone, or scolded a servant. Sometimes she reprimanded, and her quiet accents made my blood run cold. Both she and her mother spoke in determined and authoritative tones which left no room for argument. She knew all about raising corn and planting wheat and breeding stock and poultry; she knew all about the care of forests, and the proper conservation of timber; she knew all about fertilizers and manure and guano, she knew all about building stone walls and rail fences; she knew all about cooking and preserving and sewing and gardening; and she knew all about God. A remarkable woman.

A lonely child finds many ways of self-entertainment, one source of delight being to snoop. Often one is spanked for snooping. But what is it grown people do, that children are not to know about? What do they whisper about in conservatories? Both of my grown cousins had sweethearts and at an early age I was consumed with zeal to learn the gentle art of lovemaking. We had "parties" at which all the young people for miles around would gather, and from the top of the generous mahogany stairway one peeped till one's eyes popped out, and strained to hear what was not meant for any meddlesome person. The subject of "round dancing" was discussed at great length in that day and generation as a "moral issue," though men held girls off at arm's length, in a manner that would be found highly amusing today.

One of our handsomest cousins had been refused the Holy Communion because he danced after the minister had told people it was wicked. After this disciplinary measure it became the custom for Church members in good standing to sit all night out in the dark driveways, cuddled up in ancient vehicles known as "buggies," while the unregenerate danced gaily under the bright lights and in the presence of the chaperones, thus flouting the Divine Will. For the theologians of all time have been pleased to describe their personal opinions and even prejudices as "The Will of God." Possibly both situations were the will of God. For he has ordained certain exhilaration of mind and muscle, certain stimulation of impulse and imagination. So those who smiled into each others' faces in the ballroom, whirling around in the old-fashioned waltz, and those silent couples hid under the hoods of their old buggies, surrendering themselves to agreeable sensations, were neither of them disobedient to the will of God.

In each generation it appears that the suppression of normal instincts in themselves drives the unhappy priesthood to unwholesome speculations and then to illogical denunciations. Then, it was round dancing; now it is rhythmic dancing, and when the variations on the terpsichorean exercises and arts pall upon the ecclesiastical imagination, there always remains the subject of the Virgin Birth for controversy.

It seems amazing that a subject vested in sacred secrecy among even the most ignorant, and protected by silence and the mystery of darkness, should in the case of the supremest delicacy and importance, be so unblushingly uncovered, so ruthlessly discussed, and by those especially dedicated to a work which honors even the least of them with the title "Reverend." This in violation of all personal privacy and after twenty centuries of time. If Jesus of Nazareth came into this life a bastard and went out of it a criminal, then surely he drew into the circle of his all-embracing sympathy every social outcast. No shame so great, but that in him a friend is found, and brother. Nothing can make him less wonderful. Nothing can make him more wonderful. Please God, the modernists and fundamentalists may cease their arguments, and take His holy Name from the front page of the daily newspapers.

The murmured conversations of my elders and betters were most tantalizing. Just as I would prick up my ears Grandma or Aunt Ida would remember my existence and politely ask me to do a little errand—run, dear, ask Aunt Kitty not to forget the partridges for supper—or, step into the garden darling and gather some fresh flowers for the table. If I made great haste to accomplish my mission I might get back before the expression of pious curiosity and apologetic amusement had quite faded from Grandma's face. But I never heard the point of a really good story.

A certain fascinating married lady was often discussed; it seemed, then, that it wasn't nice for gentlemen to like a married lady. And when Aunt Ida one day enquired of her beautiful son Rozier if he had ever seen this lady give a man a "fast" look, he gazed thoughtfully into his mother's blue eyes, with eyes the facsimile of her own, and asked in his slow dear voice, "What is a fast look, Mother?"

May and Becca were my grown cousins—May witty and artistic—I was a little afraid of her—Becca, perfect. Becca was my divinity. I never wearied of watching her brush her long, glistening, abundant chestnut hair, and the sight of her bare arms and shoulders and bosom, blue veined like marble, put me into such transports of joy that I almost blush to think of it. Her character shone like a pearl against the background of everyday life—To "sins of nature, faults of will, defects of doubts and taints of blood" we others are not strangers; these things never disturbed Becca. The soul of purity herself, she thought no evil of others, yet her mind was without a trace of prudishness.

A lonely child has many unseen playmates; there were little creatures of the barn-yard, the woods and the fields, not so unlike myself, and there were angels and fairies, yes, and devils, which sometimes got into me! At times I was compassed about by so great a cloud of witnesses that I became quite hysterical in the garden all alone making up thrilling stories and reciting them with much oratorical effect.

Long conversations can be carried on between a child and a squirrel, or a child and a bird, and many times after earnest pleadings on my part, a friendly robin has dropped me ripe cherries from the trees. With *Us*, it was not nice for young ladies to climb trees and the fruit was tantalizing in the extreme. Cherries, to a person of seven, are a lust of the flesh. There were two methods of obtaining them without the sin of disobedience; one was to pray fervidly for them, for you must bear in mind I was instructed to pray without ceasing and often did pray that chiggers would not get on me in the woods, or that grown people would not eat all the breast of the chicken—the other way was to appeal to some creature nearer at hand, visible, and with appetites akin to my own. In either case, if I waited patiently, one by one the cherries fell.

Nor did I lack playthings. Fauquier County is famous for its horses and visitors from all over the country have attended its shows and races as long as I can remember at Upperville and Warrenton. Blooded horses were the passion of our people and where two or three were gathered together horse-talk was inevitable.

I had my horses—a stable full of blooded horses. I cut them from the mock-orange hedge, long, lithe, beautiful stick-horses. They were stabled in the lattice-work that concealed the foundations of the back porch, and I exercised, groomed and fed them personally. It is well to see to things yourself if you want them well done. This matter was entrusted to no hired hands, and the sight of the horses, each head stuck out of its diamond shaped window every morning, waiting for me, was my reward. The colts I handled with great care, breaking them myself; after just a little preliminary bucking and jumping, they trotted, galloped or cantered under Grandma's window on my own sturdy legs.

The one difficulty that I had with them was that I could not breed them, and Uncle Hal, who knew so much about such things, could not, or would not, help me.

CHAPTER IX

THEOLOGY was the profession of my father's father, Dr. Minnigerode; but it was the dissipation of my mother's mother, Mrs. Marietta Fauntleroy Turner Powell. Thus not only two strains of Revolutionary blood met in my mother's children, but the theological and controversional microbe attacked them from different angles, making veritable battle-grounds of their immature souls.

My Grandma's personal God and my Grandma's personal maid were important factors in the routine of my childhood, and I fear I relied largely upon the one to shield me from the wrath of the other who, through Grandma as Minister Plenipotentiary, kept strict account of all my outgoings and incomings. The reader has met my grandmother's God; I now introduce her maid.

Martha was a raw-boned, middle-aged negress, honestly black of hue, for which we might well have thanked God. (Grandma did not like mulattos.) Martha was of that fine Nubian type, features as regular as the Greek, and no trace of treachery in the heart. She acted as Grandma's personal maid and as nurse for me in so far as such ministrations were necessary. I can feel her kind black hands upon my naked little back as she bathed me night and morn in Grandma's tub; and to this day I see and smell and taste the little freckled peaches which she brought me as long as the season lasted, in Grandma's little wicker basket. These peaches always had worms at the heart of them—but we found a method of nibbling round and round the stones, cautiously avoiding biting too deep, since many sweet things have worms in the heart of them—thus ignoring the bad and enjoying the good, tasting the sweet and passing the bitter by. Martha and I were a merry pair, laughing over the worms, wondering when a season would come to bring us perfect fruit, speculating as to when the darling little basket would become too disreputable for its owner and be passed on to me as a plaything.

Sometimes it crossed my mind that when Grandma died I might inherit the basket, along with the mahogany work-table and two silver mugs which she had willed to me, but I knew this was indecent, speculating upon Grandma's demise, and I never confided the hope of such a legacy even to Martha.

When I was naughty, did not hem my hems straight, or learn my lugubrious hymns correctly, it was necessary to switch me. Switching was for my good. It rid my system of much original sin and brought me by an almost instantaneous process to a high degree of hypocrisy which so closely resembled piety as to be accepted as genuine repentance. It was the hymns particularly which were my undoing, the sentiment of them was entirely repellant to me, and such reasoning power as I possessed was in open rebellion against them and against Grandma's gloomy, vindictive and unreasonable God.

Such passages as burdened my baby mind!

> I smite upon my troubled breast
> With deep and conscious guilt oppressed:
> To Calvary alone I flee—
> Oh! Christ! be merciful to me!

I did not understand that, but this one was clear and terrifying:

> There is a dreadful hell
> And everlasting pains,
> Where sinners must forever dwell
> In darkness, fire and chains.
>
> Can such a wretch as I
> Escape this dreadful end?

There was no mistaking the purport of these words—the only question was to locate the sinners. Outside of myself, where were they? Who were they? Only the nicest people came to our house and we and they made up the world. They were like us, they *were Us*, and such words could not apply to them. Aunt Ida herself said that a merciful God would never send her son Rozier or her faithful old butler, Robert, to eternal damnation; I shook my little head wisely at the word, for it was reassuring, and perhaps a small niece might be included with the dear

POOR RELATION

Rozier and the faithful Uncle Robert. My Aunt Ida knew God, and I was glad she could acquit him of such discourtesy. Of course God wouldn't. And so there was no need for me to learn those horrid haunting words! But they left me writhing in sympathy for those unknown persons who were sinners and not like *Us*.

> Come child, let us wander alone
> While half the wide world is a-bed,
> And read o'er the mouldering stone
> Which tells of the mouldering dead.
>
> Remember you are not so gay,
> So happy, so young or so bright
> But what death may snatch you away,
> Or some dreadful accident smite.

From these melancholy lines I had gathered that I myself was young and happy and gay and bright, and I solemnly resolved to stay so, and never to be dead, and thus felt somewhat flattered by the dismal verses. I had seen things dead, birds that had been shot, kittens that had been drowned, pigs that had been stuck, scalded and scraped; there were various ways of reaching the state called dead, and the operation of making things dead had a strange fascination for me. When wheels were heard approaching and a carriage full of guests alighted at the door, there arose an instant necessity for making something dead. Then a little lamb would be led to the slaughter, or a half a dozen chickens run down in the barnyard, and after much cackling and noisy protestation and terrified attempts at flight, a relentless brown hand would close around each squawking neck, the body of the fowl would whirl round and round with the dextrous motion called wringing, until the headless trunk of what had been a living thing flopped and jerked over the green grass, leaving dark stains of blood, and then the cook came and claimed them all.

Endeavoring to memorize these metrical masterpieces and to reconcile the sentiment they expressed to the good green world as I saw it, kept me puzzled. The singing birds, the dandelions that could be picked to one's heart's content, the nice hot rolls and Sally Lunns we had for supper, the bonny-clabber and jam, the comfortable old carriages, Uncle Hal's jolly good looks, Becca's voice—Becca's hair—everything about Becca—the kindness of ladies and gentlemen, the respectful attention of servants (which was no more than their bounden duty and service as the Prayer-Book made plain), all these things seemed to proclaim the goodness of God. Yet always somebody was making something dead.

I spent much time in meditating upon these apparent inconsistencies, but it was useless to attempt any discussion with Grandma. Discussion was called argument, and children were only to be seen and not heard, to speak only when spoken to, to abase themselves before their "betters" (everyone older than oneself was one's betters) and to paralyze their reasoning faculties.

And so for my own good I was frequently switched.

On these occasions Martha was summoned and courteously requested to go for a peach switch. She and I would exchange horrified glances, but she would vanish, to reappear with a very wretched little switch, a puny, miserable thing, at which Grandma would glance with withering scorn. "Martha," she would say, "is this your idea of a switch?" Whereupon poor tender-hearted Martha would go out again, bringing back a proper instrument of torture, a nice, long, flexible peach branch, with cunning little knots along its whole length—an instrument worthy of the Spanish Inquisition.

To Oatlands, the home of my mother's other sister (Mrs. Carter, my Aunt Katie), in Loudoun County, always a haven of hospitality, Grandma and Martha and I were accustomed to go for little visits. On one such visit an interesting thing occurred, putting Martha in a new light. The family vault is far down in the bottom of the terraced garden, deep among old cedars and hemlocks, draped with weeping willows, a dark and lonely spot. We children had a naughty way of pounding on the heavy, rusty, iron door, beating a tattoo with our fists and calling to the ancestral dead: "Come out, Mister Carters! Come out!"

One evening at dusk I had gone into the lower

garden for just one more of the luscious Bartlett pears which fell there on the ground, when the deep sounds of a man's voice chilled the very blood in my veins—had he—could it be? No, it was Martin the colored gardener, and presently in a cooing tone which I nevertheless recognized as the voice of my dear Martha came this apocryphal utterance—"Do dat agin, sweet Martin—I likes it." Here, again, was food for reflection. Now what could that mean? But as many of my own indiscretions had been buried in the silence of Martha's tomb-like consciousness, I felt that this mysterious rendezvous at the vault should remain forever sealed and sacred.

It was from Martha I learned that *a man* has something to do with everything.

CHAPTER X

MY clothes were made by my grandmother, and miracles she performed, creating them, as God did the universe, out of nothing. She told me often, for the effect she hoped it would have upon my character, that I was not pretty. It had rather an unhappy effect for it gave me great pain all my life—it took forty years to shake the conviction that such was really the case. A passionate lover of beauty, the sense of being ugly, as she said I was, put me at a disadvantage quite often. Her actions contradicted her words for she spent many hours and much love upon my appearance, making over for me frocks that had belonged to May and Becca, using materials which under her skilful remodeling revived and spent another season or two in good company.

What is not exactly right for grown young ladies with sweethearts may do very well indeed for a little girl who goes to bed with the chickens. My winter mittens were her masterpieces. My cousin Rozier's old pants! Didn't Grandma cut the gloves out from those parts which were not so badly worn, and did not the thumb come exactly right, and were they not the warmest, nicest things in the world, when one picks up chips at the woodpile on a winter's day? Well, you may believe that they were! And there was something so dear and cozy about the thought that they were a part of my cousin Rozier's old pants!

The little calico bags in which Grandma kept my left hand a prisoner were the idiosyncrasy of my wardrobe. Neatly drawn up with a drawstring at the wrist, and changed every day, as my paddies and petticoats were, and the Sunday ones had an edging of tatting, or other homemade lace. Dear, strong left hand with which I earned my daily bread through many a faithful year! With *Us* no lady used her left hand.

One little frock she made me was a longwaisted affair of pale green, with perpendicular stripes of darker green on the bodice, and a frill all around. When Uncle Hal saw it he said: "For God's sake, Ma, don't make that child look like a cucumber."

Without the companionship of other children a child turns to pets or to the make-believe. My tendency was more in the latter direction, a natural perversity, which argued ill for my soul's welfare, so it was suggested. But there were splendid dogs—Uncle Hal's pointers and setters were prize winners, great noble creatures which followed him to the table and lay at his feet before the open fire on winter evenings. He was accused of going to the pantry just before supper sometimes and taking a royal bowl of cut peaches, pouring the accompaniment of cream over them, and proceeding to the dogs with the whole as an offering. I do not believe he ever did it. I saw a great deal and I never saw that.

And there was Bébé—Bay-Bay, as I wrote it— the little lap-dog. I detested Bay-Bay, I was jealous of her. She was in so much mischief and May and Becca loved her. It did not matter about May loving Bay-Bay but Becca loved her too. One day she jumped up on Grandma during family prayers. Aunt Ida always read prayers, and Grandma, Becca and I, and an occasional self-sacrificing guest, were the company. Grandma, in Church or at family worship, invariably responded several syllables behind everyone else. Her high, drawling voice would resound through the church in the responses, "We beseech Thee to hear us, Good Lord"; "Good Lord, deliver us." We were all saying the Lord's prayer together on this especial morning, concluding the little service, the rest of us waiting for Grandma to catch up with us at "Thy Kingdom Come"— Just then Bay-Bay jumped on Grandma. Grandma with a sudden violent gesture to brush the dog away, lost control of her voice which, rising with her arm, uttered in the shrillest possible note of asperity, "Thy Kingdom COME!" whacking at the dog as she enunciated the sacred petition. It sounded bad. I was glad no preacher was there.

Enthusiasm for the dogs was not possible. So many other people loved them and somehow I yearned for the thing that was unloved, that could be all my own. Sometimes I captured a pet, a little tortoise, or turtle, or terrapin, as the darkies called them; a lizard, a chipmunk, a garter-snake, or a baby bunnie (baby bunnies were not hard to get for they live in a warm little hole in the ground); sometimes field mice, and once, from Mr. Cornell, the gift of three young crows. All the pet names in the world were poured into the ears of those baby crows but they hated me. They would not eat, they would not chirp, dejection, utter dejection, marked their attitude toward me and soon they died in my hot little hands.

"Uncle Charlie" was an enormous hop-toad who lived under the carriage step. As long as I remember he was there and just as big. Aunt Kitty said he was there when my cousin Rozier was born. He was a sedate old toad, with all the dignity of established position and he moved slowly, like a bank president. I never annoyed him—I never annoy bank presidents either. Martha told me if I made Uncle Charlie mad he would give me warts. He was exclusive, had no associates of toad or human kind. He lived quite close to the lattice where I stabled my stick horses and I pretended that he was an old negro groom, grouchy as such old retainers are apt to be, but "faithful" like Uncle Robert.

When I gave orders to Uncle Charlie I was careful not to look him in the eye but spoke authoritatively and moved at once away, before he could have a chance to act ugly. I had noticed Aunt Ida do this, speak with decision and go on about her own business before she could see the scowling brow or the protruding lip of a displeased colored pusson. What one does not actually see may be ignored.

I was a very cruel child to grasshoppers and caterpillars. Nature study was not the fashion, or the fad, and no one told me that caterpillars were baby butterflies. I collected grasshoppers as fishing bait for the sportsmen and did it in a horrid way. No one told me it was horrid. I got a big needle and a long, long double thread of strong cotton and walked in the meadows stringing grasshoppers and singing hymns. The little fellows were game—kicking each other and spitting their tobacco-juice on my apron. A yard of them strung like beads was a fair morning's work. Daisies and clover nodded around my knees, Heaven looked on as I sang "Jesus, Lover of My Soul, Let me to thy bosom fly,"— and strung these harmless little creatures without the least compunction.

So Fate walks among men.

CHAPTER XI

THE multiplicity of books for children, and their indifference to them in this day of the moving picture and bedtime story by radio, amazes us as we look back a few years. We had a few volumes of poetry, poor as verse, conventionally virtuous. We had a number of old English books for children, very pious and horrible, which had no connection whatever with the things within my own range of interest. The Bible we had, and Walter Scott. My library was largely in my grandmother's memory and many vivid stories that she told me by the fire are living in my mind today.

Her father, Thomas Turner of Kinloch, was closely identified with the families at Mount Vernon and Arlington. As he had a good old-fashioned family of thirteen children, and his cousins at Arlington, Mr. and Mrs. George Washington Parke Custis, had but one little daughter, it was natural that he should have permitted one of his little girls to spend a great deal of time at Arlington with her lonely little cousin—and that one was Marietta, my grandmother. Sometimes as a little girl she had visited her grandmother at Eastern View, the Randolph home near Warrenton, and her fear of her grandmother must have been extreme. The little girls had "tasks" in sewing assigned to them and Grandma told me that once she broke her needle and was so terrified that she would not tell, but pretended to still be at work with the eyeless needle. She knew that at the end of the hour, when her work was inspected, the fraud would be exposed yet she sat out the wretched period, in her pathetic subterfuge, only in the end to be detected and doubly punished—first, for breaking the needle, then for pretending not to have done so! It is hard to believe that such rigorous training which appears to have put a premium upon duplicity, could have been beneficial to character, but witness the results! I have never known a character superior to my grandmother. On the walls of my Memory Gallery no other portrait is so clearly defined, so masterful in drawing, so full of character. Discipline, devotion, conscience, over-ruled personal interest and selfish desire at every point. Robert E. Lee was another such; her cousin; product of the same society; part of the same system; subject to precisely the same influences, closely related to the same Randolphs of Eastern View.

In telling tales of that old house Grandma would mention with pride that her grandfather, Col. Robert Randolph, had acted as toastmaster when General Lafayette visited Warrenton in 1824. He must have been on his way to Monticello for that memorable farewell visit to Thomas Jefferson. Well, what in the world a "toastmaster" might be, was too much for me. It stood to reason that an Aunt Kitty made all the toast—he could not have meddled with her prerogatives—banquets, and the details of such entertainments were not part of my education at Oakley; and I explained the matter to myself by saying that Grandma, who seldom made a mistake, had done so in this instance, and meant postmaster. I knew something of postmasters, we had one in Upperville. But ever bearing in mind that children should be seen and not heard, I forebore pointing her error out to Grandma, and for many years continued in the belief that Col. Robert Randolph had been postmaster at Warrenton.

On a recent visit to France, a grandson of Lafayette, the Count Louis de Lasteyrie, did me the honor of opening his ancestral château fifty miles from Paris, in my honor, where I saw relics of that great friend of America and souvenirs of the Americans of his day. In the park at La Grange are magnificent old trees planted by Lafayette from seed brought from Virginia—possibly, at least so we were pleased to speculate—from Eastern View itself, as well as from Mount Vernon, Monticello, Gunston Hall, and Oak Hill.

To follow up in a measure the relationship between the houses of Arlington and Kinloch, I must dig a little way into the depths of our

Tudor Place, Georgetown, D. C.

RAVENSWORTH

complicated Virginia genealogy, to which we are brought up, as to our catechism and multiplication table, but which nevertheless baffles a disorderly mind. If I am incorrect I shall find many to correct me for there are a million eyes leveled suspiciously upon such as invade this territory!

However, not to be quite unsupported in my statements, I will turn to that famous column in "The Baltimore Sun" which is authoritative upon such matters and which touches upon three old homes very familiar to me. The first is Arlington, built by George Washington Parke Custis, who was the grandson of Martha Washington, whose only child married Robert E. Lee, at which wedding my grandmother was a bridesmaid. The second is Ravensworth, the home of "Cousin" William Fitzhugh, as I heard Grandma refer to him, who was a brother of Mrs. Custis of Arlington. It was here that Thomas Jefferson often stopped over night on his long rides from Washington to Monticello, and a story is told of one early morning walk in the charmed garden of Ravensworth, when Mr. Jefferson's skilled surgery saved the life of a poor slave seriously wounded by the stroke of an axe. Ravensworth descended from William Fitzhugh to his nephew and namesake, the second son of his sister, Mrs. Lee,—William Henry Fitzhugh Lee, known as W. H. F. Lee, and familiarly as "Rooney." My own mother was a bridesmaid at his wedding with the beautiful Tabb Bolling, of Petersburg, and Ravensworth, still true to ancient usage, remains to this day as remote with its rare family portraits as it was in those old days before "Cousin" William manumitted his slaves and devised this one-third of the original 56,000 acres which was a royal grant, to his nephew "Rooney" Lee.* The third house is Kinloch, home of my great-grandfather, Thomas Turner. Unfortunately the good old "Sun paper" makes no reference to two other distinguished homes in the vicinity of Arlington between which and the estates of Kinloch and Ravensworth there was also an intimate association. One of these is Tudor Place in Georgetown, designed by Dr. William Thornton, and one of the few remaining genuine Colonial landmarks in Washington in perfect preservation. This was the home of Thomas Peter, father of that stately Britania Peter, also a bridesmaid at the wedding of Robert E. Lee and Mary Custis; she married Beverly Kennon, a young naval officer, who was killed March 4th, 1844, by the bursting of a gun on the *Princeton*. She continued to live as a widow at Tudor Place and was buried from the house in which she had been born, on the day before her 96th birthday. As she had been my grandmother's girlhood friend she was fond of me, always calling me by my full name, Marietta. Mrs. Kennon was an erect, queenly type of

*This historic home was completely destroyed by fire in 1926.

woman to the very last. The house is still in the possession of her descendants.

The other house was Vaucluse, a Peyton estate, originally some 50,000 acres, a royal grant to Valentine Peyton who ceded a part of it to George Mason of Gunston Hall, as certain old records prove. This estate disintegrated very early in Colonial history, the home and a large tract of land on the second range of hills from the Potomac becoming the property of the Fairfax family after the death of Col. Francis Peyton, and later, after the Civil War had swept the Colonial house away and slaughtered the noble trees, coming into the possession of the artist, Eliphalet Fraser Andrews, who was able to buy a picturesque tract of about one hundred acres, and who built there, on a new site, a comfortable wooden house with a studio. I, as his wife, and as the lineal descendant of Valentine Peyton, and more or less closely identified by ties of blood and friendship with the historic families and landmarks of the section, was very happy to come into possession of what remained of the old estate, and it was to gratify me that my good husband became a landowner in Virginia.

And now comes the genealogical column of "The Baltimore Sun" of April 23, 1907:

> Among the old Virginia homes famed for hospitality, culture and refinement, were Arlington, the abode of the Custis family, and Kinloch, the home of the Turners, in Fauquier County. George Washington Parke Custis

built Arlington in 1801. The original Arlington was built in Northampton County, Eastern Shore of Virginia, by John Custis, the immigrant, in 1640. This building was burned. John Custis, the adopted son of General Washington, was born at the White House, New Kent County, 1753, died 1788; married on the 3rd of February, 1774, Eleanor, the second daughter of Benedict Calvert of Mount Airy, Maryland. She was of royal descent, being a lineal descendant in the fifth degree of Sir Henry Lee, first Earl of Litchfield, and wife, Lady Charlotte Fitz-Roy. The fourth child of this union was George Washington Parke Custis, who married, in 1806, Mary Lee, daughter of Colonel William Fitzhugh and wife, Anne Randolph, of Chatham.—Only one child of this marriage survived infancy—Mary Anne Randolph Custis, who in time became the wife of General Robert E. Lee.

Another noted house in the vicinity of Arlington was Ravensworth, the residence of William Fitzhugh, the only brother of Mrs. Parke Custis of Arlington. This estate was a principality, being one-third of the original 56,000 acres patented by William Fitzhugh, the immigrant. William Fitzhugh of Ravensworth manumitted his servants and devised his ancestral property to William H. F. Lee, the second son of General Robert E. Lee.

Between the families at Arlington and Kinloch great intimacy existed, the two being closely related. Marietta Turner, the daughter of Mrs. Eliza Randolph Turner of Kinloch, passed her early life at Arlington, in company with her little cousin, Mary Custis, and when the latter was married, June 30, 1831, at Arlington House, to Lieut. Robert E. Lee, of the United States Corps of Engineers, she was one of the bridal attendants, standing with Lieut. Chambers, while her brother, Lieut. Thomas Turner, afterwards Admiral Turner, stood with Britania Peter.

POOR RELATION

And here I will leave the narrative of "The Baltimore Sun," which continues to draw out the later lines, and take up my grandmother's own story, as told to a wide-eyed little girl on winter evenings at Oakley. I had never witnessed a wedding—and the tale of that rainy night at Arlington, when the great idol of our people, Robert E. Lee, married my grandmother's little cousin and playmate, thrilled me. It seems that the young girls of that day cared no more for well-behaved young men than they do today; for, according to Grandma, there was keen rivalry for the pleasure of "standing" or "waiting" with a certain Dick Tilghman—a very great scamp, I fear, but charming; also there was Mr. Chambers, an exemplary young gentleman, but so little in demand, because of his well-recognized rectitude, that none of the girls would have him, and so they drew lots for him! This is inside information, hardly of historic value, but putting a little human touch on those far-off happenings— bringing up again a vision of a group of laughing girls, among themselves weighing the men with whom they were associated, choosing and refusing, girl fashion—girls who long ago grew old and died—whose children all grew old and died— and of whose later descendants few have the time, in such a rushing world, to pause even to contemplate the scene.

And in this lottery as to who should willy-nilly, "stand" with Mr. Chambers, the good young man, my grandmother drew the unlucky straw—and got him! You see the reliable "Baltimore Sun" substantiates the story—and none of us remember now who did get Mr. Dick Tilghman. Uncle Thomas Turner had the rare Britania Peter of Tudor Place as his partner. Apropos of Uncle Thomas who remained in the United States Navy during the Civil War, though his brothers and nephews entered the Confederate Army or Navy, Grandma also told me a little tale or two. She did not approve of his loyalty to the United States Navy. Her brother Charles who had married Margaret Patterson, of Baltimore, a sister of the great beauty who was the wife of Jerome Bonaparte, was just resigning from the United States Navy to enter the Confederate Navy, when he died, and Charles was her favorite brother.

It seems that Uncle Thomas had been desperately in love with a poor Virginia cousin, whose name was Christina, but during his sojourn in Philadelphia had become engaged to a fashionable and wealthy girl whose family would have had no patience with a young Southerner of amorous inclinations and plural engagements. In this dilemma he made his sister his confidante, walking the floor with desperate gestures and exclaiming at intervals to Grandma—who was not sympathetic—"Marietta, comfort 'Tina! Marietta, comfort 'Tina!" From what I know of Marietta I believe she scolded Thomas and congratulated 'Tina.

ARLINGTON HOUSE

KINLOCH, HOME OF THOMAS TURNER

Billiards was a fashionable diversion for ladies and gentlemen at Arlington and Mr. Dick Tilghman was addicted to the tender habit of squeezing the finger tips of the young ladies as he passed them the balls; Mr. Chambers restrained his natural impulse towards such a liberty because he was so proper.

It rained heavily the night of the wedding and the Rev. Ruel Keith, the clergyman, arrived drenched to the skin, so Grandma said. He was a tall man and Mr. Custis was quite below the average height, but as there was no change of apparel for the dripping parson except that of his host, he appeared in somewhat abbreviated habiliments for the ceremony.

Sundays saw the Arlington family all in the big coach driving to Alexandria to attend service in Christ Church; the choice sittings were then in the gallery, and I wondered, as she described these jaunts to me, if the long drive and the view of the Potomac River compensated the little girls for the hardness of the pew and the tedium of the sermon. For sermons then were an honest sixty minutes with no leaning toward mercy and there was no new-fangled method of omitting certain parts of the service. There was plenty of hell-fire in it all and a most uncomfortable session for sinners.

The interchanging of visits between the Arlington and Kinloch families was frequent until the

Civil War came on and the Lees were obliged to leave Arlington. General Lee's letters edited by his son Robert and published by Doubleday Page and Company, in 1904, contain references to the Turner boys who were in the Confederate Army, and to the Kinloch house itself in which the women of his family were guests during the war, from time to time. He appears to have worried a great deal as to their safety, sending many messages to their hosts and hostesses at Eastern View, Kinloch, or Avenel. To one of his daughters he writes: "I am glad you had such a pleasant visit to Kinloch. I have passed a great many pleasant days there myself, in my young days." At this time my grandmother was living with the Dulanys and Kinloch had become the property of her brother, Edward, whose war time diary, recently published in "Americana," shows the mind of a Southern gentleman. His descendants still own Kinloch.

The graves of Mr. and Mrs. George Washington Parke Custis, with the monuments erected by their daughter, Mrs. Robert E. Lee, are in a quiet corner to the southeast of the Arlington house. The inscription chosen is the key to General Lee's attitude toward life and toward humanity. "Blessed are the merciful, for they shall obtain mercy."

Grandmother would never revisit Arlington after its confiscation by the Government and its conversion into a National Cemetery. Up to the time of her death no wives of officers had been interred there, and the thought of her "Cousin Molly" lying there shocked her inexpressibly. "To think," she would say, "of poor Cousin Molly Custis, the most modest and diffident of women, arising at the judgment day, the only woman among so many men, and they all Yankee soldiers!"

CHAPTER XII

ALONG with the April showers came the little new lambs; every morning another group was added to the pastoral landscape—oh, how peaceful, how sweet, as I look back! White spots on the green background of the fields. Stupid, calm-eyed ewes lying beside their newborn babies, busy with their maternal duties. Those lambs a week or so old, frisking about, the perfection of young awkwardness, adorably innocent, laughably clumsy. Often there were twins and one spring when my little sister Lucy was at Oakley, she and I, who never had heard of April Fool's Day, believed in the two-headed lamb that Uncle Hal promised us. He promised us a two-headed lamb; he said it was born last night. No, he did not mean twins, he meant what he said, and he had learned to talk before our mother was born! One lamb with four legs and two heads. When we found it we should have it, and he would be damned if anybody on that farm should interfere.

Here was a dream about to be realized; a pet, a most unusual pet, in fact something quite unique, for our very own. My imagination ran far ahead, as patiently we trudged the pastures seeking the monstrosity that was to be my very own (for I should soon dispossess my sister of her interest in the prize)—my very own, my very own —Uncle Hal would be damned if anybody——

I became more and more consequential as we sought it. "Oh," people would soon be saying, "of course that little girl is the little girl who owns the two-headed lamb," and far as the future stretched that morning the two-headed lamb was my constant companion. Neither of us would grow old, for an old lady could not play with an old, old silly sheep with two heads; we would always be little, and if need be, ravens would feed us. It had been done—in the Bible, or in Walter Scott's "Tales of a Grandfather"—someone had been fed by ravens.

My idea of a raven was vague in the extreme and the thought of locusts and wild honey came to me as an alternative. Locusts did not appeal to me so strongly as did the wild honey—the lamb should have the locusts and I the wild honey, a fair distribution. And surely it would be in my power to direct the lamb in all things, as Grandma directed me and as God directed her. Without a twinge of conscience I counted Lucy out. Lovingly I planned as faithfully we tramped, but heavy became the heart of us as all the lambs appeared to follow the conventional design in lambs, and at nightfall we turned sadly home, having searched more faithfully for this freak than we have since sought for better things, footsore, disappointed and humiliated, for we began to realize that some trick had been played on us.

My little sister Lucy was only fourteen months younger than I and would sometimes visit me at Oakley; these were rare occasions indeed and full of delightful conspiracies in which I plotted against Lucy and we both plotted against Grandma. Lucy, having been less associated with such lofty personalities as God and Grandma, had a fearless faith in her own judgment and did many evil deeds with the most delightful frankness. I envied her then, and envy her now, for the splendid independence, the militant justice of her life. I could get ahead of her when we were little, but no one gets ahead of her now she is big. We invented plays which were enacted under screen of the big box bushes, plays which would have found small approval from our elders. Some of them rival the stories told by Philip Fithian of our little ancestresses, daughters of "King Carter" of Corotoman, and many of them verged upon blasphemy.

Always there arose arguments as to which of us should play the leading part and we compromised by deciding that if I could be the "Lady" and Lucy the "Company," Lucy might be Jesus and I the "little children," for Jesus blessing little children was a very popular game with us. Lucy then, covering her knees with Aunt Kitty's apron, and with her blond hair parted and hanging over her cheeks, would seat herself demurely under the box tree, her merry face as grave and holy as she could make it, while I, endeavoring to represent a numerous body of children, would humbly approach and be blessed, then crawl around the box bush and reappear to be blessed again, thus carrying out the idea of numbers.

Religious pageantry, which became a sort of profession with me later in life, started thus early and with a sincerity equal to that of the peasants of Oberammergau.

When it came my turn to play Lady, I made to myself ample amends for the humility of my former state. I affected the cold haughtiness of the ancient aristocracy and insisted upon my sister's being a po' white pusson to whom I spoke with gentle condescension. Then she would run around the box bush, reappearing next as a particularly unwelcome cousin, who was greeted with the patient tolerance shown to the dreary poor relation. Sometimes Lucy was obliged to represent the Rev. Arthur Johns, and then orders were issued to invisible menials to straightway prepare a repast for the minister. And in all these rôles we mimicked the society around us in a manner little short of masterly.

CHAPTER XIII

THE family at Oakley were great readers. Grandma's line was religious books, especially the sermons and letters of Frederick Robertson, and the sermons of Bishop Elliott, bound in green and gold, a volume as large as an unabridged dictionary. Peter Parley, of similar bulk, was also elaborately bound, embracing every possible subject from the Chinese War Wall to the Baptism of Pocahontas, with full illustrations. La Fontaine's Fables, illustrated by Gustav Doré, fascinated me, and this and the Peter Parley were my favorite volumes, though too heavy for me to lift.

Winter evenings I would lie on my stomach on the floor with them open before me. Aunt Ida was fond of metaphysics and read many scientific books; astronomy interested her and after her busy day, when supper was over, she sometimes took me out on the great back porch and pointed out the constellations that hung so directly over Mr. Cornell's house and the flower garden. She also read novels as her daughters did, and as I was not permitted to do, outside of the "Wide, Wide World" and "Queechy." From these decent productions I learned to "swoon" and practiced swooning with great enjoyment. Of course the mossy bank and the solitary horseman, who should have been slowly riding towards me at sunset, were not practicable, but the swooning was quite easy. Sometimes I went down heavily and all at once like a wheelbarrow of coal, at other times drooped gracefully like a fading lily. This is a confession wrung from the heart of a woman who has never been anything but vulgarly healthy, never once able to bring about a climax or gain a point by means of a timely flood of tears, an attack of hysteria, or a becoming and appealing fainting fit. Grandma, walking alone in the garden one evening, just as God was when he caught Adam and Eve, surprised me during this exercise and asked in alarm what in the world I was doing? I said I was learning how to swoon away, and she said if I didn't stop such foolishness I might get a tuning with the peach switch.

During one of mother's visits my elders were discussing the novels of a young Virginian which I gathered were full of suggestions that little girls can't understand. One of the ladies in the book had pulled down the collar of one of the gentlemen and had kissed him in the hollow of his throat. Well, what was there in that to make such a fuss over? That was not hard to understand. Grandma said no lady would do such a thing; Aunt Ida said the authoress certainly had a vivid imagination. My mother flatly declared that in addition to a vivid imagination the authoress had had some considerable experience.

"She had experience" rang in my mind all the evening. "She had some con-sid-er-a-ble experience"—now, what did that mean?

Darwin's outrageous ideas also were thrashed out at great length as we all sat sewing in Aunt Ida's room. This absurdity I could understand. Darwin said we had monkeys for grandfathers. A monkey had been a pet in a house next door to us in St. Louis when I was six and Lucy was five years old. In my memory he is very large. One day my sister climbed up on the fence to peep at him and just as her little face loomed over the fence he slapped her with his long hairy hand—very like somebody's cross old grandfather. Uncle Hal had once kept a monkey at Oakley, a little black one, which terrified me. His favorite perch was on Becca's side-saddle, a fair leather saddle which when not in use hung across the balustrade of the stairway on the second floor. There this creature gibbered and gesticulated in a fashion revoltingly human; his slyness, his dirtiness, his impudence, his deceit, all disgusted me. But he was terribly like people, anyone could see that with half an eye, especially like delicate babies and old crooked black laborers. I had to admit that there were aspects of the case which justified Darwin's error—a natural mistake; I ventured to point out these resemblances to Grandma, and also to apologize for Mr. Darwin's having dared include her in his calculations. "I suppose he knows that you are descended from Charlemagne and Clovis and King Carter of Corotoman" (the vision of this worthy in his velvet coat and flowing white wig, sent the ancestral ape back, back, out of the realm of the possible); but Grandma was annoyed. Darwin was diverting the minds of men from God, and the fact that his theories were so plausible made them only more dangerous. And Darwin's mother came in here for unmitigated condemnation. If she had attended more faithfully to the matter of her little boy's religious instruction he would not now be upsetting men's minds with his atheistical and blasphemous notions!

And the sewing would go on merrily, the conversation drift to other topics and everyone forget Darwin, until Grandma would come back to him again, proof, as I now see, that her keen intellect had grasped and grappled with his idea of evolution in comprehending sympathy, in spite of herself.

On these rare visits of my mother to Oakley I would be really sick with love. She was so girlish, so pretty! Mother never was "sentimental" over anything, least of all over me, and never demonstrative except with father, and to whomever happened to be the baby. So I had to cheat her if I wanted to get a thrill. I would get a "cricket," as they all sat sewing, and slyly edge it closer and closer to Mother's knee, until I touched her; and then, just as I was surrendering myself to the most delicious sensations, she would exclaim, "Good Gracious, honey! Isn't the room big enough? Don't scrouge me so." *Scrouge!* Scrouging was just what I was after. To be scrouged to death.

My Aunt Ida was thirteen years older than my mother and by the very quality of her mind far more a woman of the world, although it was Mother who had been the rolling stone, travelled far, and seen the world more widely than her sister.

Their points of view were always different. Aunt Ida applied to daily events a certain philosophy touched with imagination while Mother was bluntly direct in all things. One subject of disagreement between them was corporeal punishment for children. Aunt Ida thought a sensible child might be reasoned with. I hoped that I was a sensible child. Mother thought it might be possible, in dealing with one child, to reason; but that in managing eight or ten the quickest way to reason was with the peach switch.

Often in their uneventful lives, sans telephone, sans automobile, sans radio, hypothetical cases furnished themes for animated discussion. Grandma had at different times after the war advanced money to her sons-in-law. Uncle Hal and Uncle George being "land poor" at that time, and my father being all kinds of poor at most times. She now and then referred to these transactions with asperity.

Some people, whom they knew or had read of, had inherited one hundred thousand dollars. Grandma pressed her thin lips together. They would probably waste it. Now, if *she* should inherit such a sum of money—here she reviewed her daughters, all three, through her specs—she would distribute it in certain ways—*if allowed to do so*. Now the chorus—"Why, Ma! You speak exactly as if you were never allowed to do as you think best." Calmly, she continued—she would certainly pay off a number of just debts, for the money would be a providential means vouchsafed her, for that purpose—*unless the money was called for*. Here again the chorus—"Why, Ma, you talk as if your children never let you have a cent"—and, continued Grandma, enunciating each word as though it were a little sword-thrust, "*I would give twenty-five thousand dollars to the Lord!*" "Well, give it to Him, Ma!—by all means, give it to Him," the chorus comes in again—"You speak as if your children had a positive antipathy to your giving your own twenty-five thousand dollars to the Lord!"

CHAPTER XIV

MANY English expressions lingered with us, for instance we called the daily mail the "Post." Sometimes Uncle Hal, driving into the village for it, would invite me to go with him—a distinction which overpowered me, and I hailed the invitation with joy. He had a way of disregarding the doctrine that children should be seen and not heard for he engaged me in conversation during these excursions and appeared profoundly impressed with my opinions. When the tongue of only one person in a household is perpetually bridled, the luxury of being permitted to talk freely is absolutely delicious, and a flood of words, a medley of impressions, an avalanche of questions, broke over my Uncle Hal on these mornings. He seemed edified; his manner convinced me that the rest of the world had not yet awakened to the importance of little girls. There was one drawback to these drives—every pleasure seems destined to have a disadvantageous side.

With *Us* no gentleman permitted any lady to get out and open a gate, no, not even if the lady was seven and the gentleman seventy, not even when the gentleman had proverbially small and well-shod feet on which to carry a high blood pressure and two hundred and fifty pounds avoirdupois, and the lady was as light as a feather and as quick as a cat. No, nothing would do but that he must get out to open the gate, and I—poor me—must drive through it! Uncle Hal's own horse was a steed of mettle with a pedigree, of course, as long as his own, a high-stepper that no sooner felt my feeble hand on the rein than he proceeded to manifest his contempt for me by declining to stop at all. I would wrap the reins around my wretched little wrists, pray till the sweat rolled down my back—and God never helped me—there was, of course, some good reason for that—but He didn't—and I would stand up and pull until almost jerked over the dash-board, afraid even to glance back to the gate where I knew my gallant escort was dancing in the dust, addressing condemnatory remarks to the rocks and the fence-posts and the heavens above and the earth beneath, and hurling uncomplimentary epithets after the rapidly disappearing horse and driver.

The animal, having registered his protest, would trot into the village and stop at the drug-store where the amiable drug-clerk, to whom the performance was no novelty, would jump in the buggy and go back for Uncle Hal. Returning very meekly, abjectly apologetic, with the mail, I would roll up my sleeves and show Uncle Hal how skinny my arms were and try indirectly to convince him that such a little girl couldn't hold such a very big horse, and he would say: "Gal, when there's a man around who thinks himself a gentleman, don't you get out to open any gates."

The post generally contained "The Baltimore Sun," some seed catalogues, a few personal letters and bills, and sometimes the announcement that my mother was going to have another baby. I sensed that this was a thing that she should not do—no one said so—but a sort of guilty feeling descended upon me. What did I have to do with it? What did anybody have to do with it? That was what I wanted to know. One day a letter from my big cousin Rozier, who was in Utah, contained a picture of him with a young Mormon lady sitting on each knee—he sent it to Grandma. Uncle Hal thought it was funny and when he laughed I laughed, but catching a glimpse of Grandma's face I inferred that perhaps it was not funny and I decided not to laugh.

"Grandma, when you were a little girl did you steal your Grandma's rouge?" This searching question is put to me in a clear voice, and a pair of unfathomable brown eyes leveled on mine, by no less a person than my oldest granddaughter, Mary Lord Andrews the third, a person who holds my heartstrings in her dimpled hands.

The question startles me; in that function that once was my conscience something stirs again. My Grandma's rouge! Verily, out of the mouths of babes. A furious contempt for my own belongings,—the beige satin cloak I brought this summer from Paris and the hat to suit it with a long bright green feather, the silver slippers, the few bright spots in my very simple middle-aged wardrobe,—sweeps over me. I believe I blush and that for the moment rouge would be superfluous.

Then Mary Lord Andrews the third who is named for my daughter and is a highly developed personage of three years and a half, climbs hand in hand with me to the attic at Vaucluse where we delve into a box of forgotten books, poor old books all dusty and ragged, which I devoured as a child, and I read to her about my old friend Matilda.

> Matilda was a pleasant child
> But one bad trick she had,
> That even when all 'round her smiled,
> Oft made her friends feel sad.

This evil tendency in Matilda was meddlesomeness. She peered and peeped into things not intended for little girls, lifted the tea-pot lid, stuck her finger in the ink, brought down upon her offending head the wrath of her elders and her betters, and put herself in danger of everlasting hell.

> As Grandmamma went out one day
> Her snuff-box and her specs
> She down upon the table lay,
> Forgetting Tilly's tricks.

Matilda got into the snuff-box, far more disastrous than any vanity box. I recall enquiring of my own Grandma as to this snuff and this little girl's painful experience, and Grandma explained to me that no "Lady" would use snuff. Today I have but to substitute the word "rouge" for "snuff" to know just what my Grandma would think of me!

That a gray-headed grandmother should use rouge! And yet, with pale shades of gray or beige it must be done. A possible deception upon the public in general, though none to an astute person of three and a half, condemned to take a most unwelcome nap at the brightest hour of an autumn day, and whiling away the time by intelligent investigation of her grandmother's bureau drawers, writing desk and closets.

Together we pour over the battered book, which now that I take it in my hands and turn again the old pages, is most familiar. The words have been lying in some pigeon-hole of my brain all these years. Ringing the changes on the graveyard and the wrath of God.

> I had a little friend
> And every day he crept
> In sadness to his brother's tomb
> And laid him down and wept.

Or this:

> Poor little Betsy Smith, she sits
> Day after day alone:
> She had a darling sister once
> But now she's dead and gone.

POOR RELATION

Or this:

> The Brook,
> 'T was here my sister dear was drowned,
> One long bright summer day.

Of the last, Mary Lord Andrews the third demands ocular proof, insisting that she wants to see the brook herself. A dialogue between two virtuous young ladies of seven exposed the complacency of the well-to-do in their attitude toward "the poor." One small girl describes to another the miseries of a family she has visited, and both agree to be noble. It is really too lovely, as an expression of that delicious security and sense of superiority associated with regular quarterly dividends.

> God made them poor: He made us rich:
> The wealth is all His own:
> It was for them as well as us
> The Saviour left his throne.

As "Alice in Wonderland," "The Just-so Stories," Eugene Field and Whitcomb Riley pushed these quaint old verses out of the way, so those favored tales beloved of my children "in the bright fireside nursery clime" have given place to the moving picture and the radio story at bedtime, and the elocutionary efforts ground out on the victrola and gramophone.

Mary Lord the third is the joy of my life, but Fräulein bears down upon us and takes her off, while a mere grandmother bows her gray head in acceptance of the oft-repeated ultimatum: "Fräulein hat immer Recht."

CHAPTER XV

THE Oakley kitchen was dark and smoke-stained, fragrant with mysterious odors. From the roof, in addition to generations of cobwebs, hung strings of onions and garlands of red and green peppers. Also the linings of the chicken gizzards, strung like beads on yucca thongs. Grandma called these "ingluvin" and they were said to yield a new drug excellent for the digestion. Certainly they were uninviting but when Grandma ground them up with her own mortar and pestle and administered the powder to the suffering world, no one was brave enough to protest. As I recall the treatment it is a miracle we did not die from nameless infections for nothing in the range of my memory has seemed so entirely unhygienic as "ingluvin."

The companionship of colored people has always been both an advantage and a detriment to the Southern bred child. There is something so delightful to children about an old-fashioned kitchen with the kindliness, greasiness and merriment of the colored servants of the older type. As one child alone I spent a great deal of my time with Aunt Kitty, the cook, and gathered considerable folklore and filled my mind with many superstitions. There was, of course, a middle ground between grandmother's gloomy theology and Aunt Kitty's hysterical religion. I listened wide-eyed to both points of view and somehow between the two must have found my own faith very early.

On one occasion, sitting in the kitchen, I was greatly impressed with the conversation of a visitor. He was an itinerant colored preacher.

"Yas'm," he said to Aunt Kitty. "I'se po'ly. Las' night I was mighty po'ly. Yo see I thought sho'ly I wuz dyin'. I had such misery in ma breast. I jus' prayed an' I jus' kep' on prayin' and then, when I start to belch I knowed I wuz saved. Yas'm, I knowed when I belched dat I wuz spa'ed a while."

"Dat's de Lawd's truth," said Aunt Kitty. "An' I will say so to anybody, 'cause I don't bite ma teeth for no pusson when de sperret o' Gawd move me to talk. I talks an' I don't overspoke maself neither 'cause de Lawd is with Kitty. I'se jus' crazy about Gawd ma own self an' I'se crazy about Gawd's ministers. Anythin' you wants, Bruder, here in this kitchen is yourn an' you ain't gonna have no misery in yo' chest for nothin' that you eats with Kitty."

To which, in oily phrase, the holy man would reply:

"Yas'm, I needs strengthenen' and refreshin', I does, kase its mah call to bring all tidin's of peace and good will, which is de Lord's word—Wake up 'fo' you burns up! Wake up 'fore you burns up! Them's my tidin's of peace and good will."

The minister continued, after Aunt Kitty filled up a heaping plate and set it before him, to give her a little sketch of himself. He was the seventh son, he said, and he was born twins, so he had seven talents of his own and he had seven talents bequeathed him by his twin brother, who died at birth. Therefore, as he explained to Aunt Kitty, he had more talents than anybody else that ever lived because he had all of his own and all of his brother's. He told Aunt Kitty that he could leave his body whenever the Lord wanted him to leave it and that he often went to heaven to see his mother. This statement both Aunt Kitty and I found very impressive. He told Aunt Kitty that he knew by many signs and wonders that the Lord was with him and this conviction was strengthened by an experience in his boyhood, when he was lying on the grass one day looking up into the sky and a black snake crawled right across his stomach into the woods, turned and crossed again over his stomach, going toward the field, retraced his way and again crossed his stomach going back into the woods.

This seemed, even to me, a very unusual experience and when I went to Grandmother's room a little later and sat on the cricket at her feet, I felt it a sacred obligation to pass on to her the warning that if she did not wake up, she would burn up. I put some very searching questions to her, especially about the snake and the relief the preacher experienced by the process which he called belching. The whole conversation appeared to impress my grandmother unpleasantly. When I told Aunt Kitty next day that Grandmother had received the entire story with great coldness, Aunt Kitty said to me that I had "overspoke" myself and that "Ole Miss" had a way of snapping her mouth to, just like some northern pusson, and that I mustn't take the kitchen talk upstairs or they never would let me sit in the kitchen again when the colored preacher came.

"An' you want to mind out, honey, about overspoking yo'self, 'cause most of the trouble in de worl' comes from folks overspoking theyselves!"

CHAPTER XVI

I HAD but one child to play with—Willy—Aunt Kitty's little black grandson. Never a little girl except on rare occasions when my little sister Lucy came. There was a girl of twelve in the neighborhood, though not on the Oakley estate, but I could not play with her for she was man-crazy. I heard of this unusual affliction by listening to my elders. It seems that this little girl stole any baby that she could lay her hands on and when all the people hid their babies she comforted herself with an ancient baby-carriage on three wheels which she pushed back and forth on the country lanes, singing lullabies which nobody ever taught anybody, and which nobody ever sang to anybody. Her own mother could not put a stop to this foolishness though Grandma said it certainly could be whaled out of any child. The man-crazy little girl affected me very painfully; her wistful eyes haunted me; for the life of me I could see nothing queer about her—and what did the baby-carriage have to do with it?

So I played with Willy. But I know now I had far better have played with the man-crazy little girl, for Willy discussed strange topics. Aunt Kitty always saw to it that Willy minded his manners, for having cooked my mother's wedding breakfast, she was fond of me; she was the personification of faithfulness, and wielded considerable power in the place. If anyone among us, for instance, ever had delirium tremens, Aunt Kitty alone administered such antidotes as were proper, followed by admonitions which left little to the imagination, and she knew just what one felt like the morning after, and how good a thing was a dose of something called Hostetters Bitters.

Willy and I did our lessons together at Grandma's knee and when either of us miscalled a word she would glance sharply over the rim of her spectacles and correct us; the second mistake, and she rapped our heads with her gold thimble. If you have ever experienced the unexpected thump of a gold thimble from the finger of an exasperated lady, you will realize that Willy and I soon learned that it behooved us to proceed warily along the thorny path of learning.

Willy died. It was my first actual sorrow. Someone that I loved was dead. That thing which happened to partridges and rabbits and potato-bugs, which for various reasons had to be made dead, had happened for no reason at all, to Willy.

The boy had been sick a long time. Aunt Kitty had stayed in the cabin, and we had had no Sally Lunns or fried chicken, until Uncle Hal declared it to be a damn imposition, and that these niggers played 'possum, and that the boy wasn't sick, and he would see to it himself, in double-quick time. And he did; he went to the cabin; saw that there was no make-believe, but a little life flickering out; and there he sat, day and night, though it was midsummer weather, beside that dying child. As the little fellow tumbled and tossed Uncle Hal fanned away the flies; Uncle Hal himself, with his own aristocratic hands, bathed the hot little black head with ice-water, and he comforted his poor old Kitty.

I was quite a large girl before I ceased to visit Willy's grave in the far corner of the garden. There lay my only playmate, my humble slave, the long-suffering victim of my childish tyrannies. Long after Oakley ceased to be my home, on the rare occasions when there, I never missed this tribute to an old affection. I felt hurt and sad that the wooden cross with "Willy" on it should have fallen askew. It was all but concealed by rank weeds, proving that in all the world nobody cared, nobody remembered. I would ponder on the transitoriness of things mundane, and then grit my teeth and tug manfully at the sturdy docks and jimson-weeds, finally dissolving in tears and perspiration, because the weeds were stronger than I.

CHAPTER XVII

IF anything could justify the old in seeing visions and the young in dreaming dreams, it might be ham! And if you will pardon this digression, and if I can withstand the pangs of hunger while discoursing on the subject, I will tell you what I know about a "Smithfield" ham, for science will have progressed so far with you that not only no such thing will be known in your day but the very memory of it will be lost! You may trace to your children the brief history of a *Western* ham, a poor machine-bred, machine-killed and machine-cured thing—a round fat pink plebeian ham, ready to be sliced up in a Child's restaurant as a sacrifice to the many-headed monster, the Public; but you can never expatiate upon the flavor of the Smithfield, for it will have passed into history.

If, as the saying goes, the education of a gentleman is begun four hundred years before he is born, so, long before its advent, the Smithfield was prepared for, as is royalty. The "razor-back" is the aristocrat of hogdom. He is a special breed and fastidious in his taste. He demands a large range of oak forest for his ancestors, exclusively their own, fenced in "pig-tight, bull-strong and horse-high," as a fence should be; and for himself, from the day he is weaned, for a year and a half, he expects a diet of bonny clabber, milk, and vegetables stewed with corn-meal into what is called "wash"; then to range the woods and fields, undisturbed, eating acorns with the addition of potato "strings" left in the ground for him, and peanuts of which the choicest "nuts" have already been harvested. The last two months of his life as a hog he is fed upon corn to harden the meat which the acorns, potatoes and peanuts have flavored and sweetened. His portrait presents to you a gentleman long and lean, a good runner, not an ounce of superfluous flesh; a nose made for rooting. He answers to the description "four feet high, four feet long, four inches wide and a nose like a bow-sprit." Early on a bitter November morning he is stuck in the throat and left to bleed until thoroughly drained (the negroes save the blood and make blood pudding), then the carcase is scalded in an immense pot of boiling water, the water heated in the primitive fashion of dropping red-hot cobble-stones into the pot, they having been heated in a log fire on the ground. Next it is scraped, then hung up head down, cut down the middle and drawn; the fat of the intestines goes into the lard, the intestines themselves are cleaned and soaked for days, then boiled, and make for the negroes a highly prized dish which they call "chittlings." "Chittlings" were not despised by a certain little girl either, who hung around the kitchen for companionship, and shared in many a tit-bit from the friendly hands of servants.

Perhaps of all these delicacies the pig-tails were the most savory. You will not be able even to imagine the flavor of a pig-tail, roasted right on the spot of the killing, in the fire burning to heat the water for scalding—Charles Lamb must have known it at some time in his life, for his graphic, heart-felt description of the conflagrations of that ancient Chinese village which made roast pig famous, portrays the precise feeling of all of us who are familiar with that odor, that brittle skin, that rich, juicy taste of fresh pork roasted out of doors and devoured hot from the fire.

The men snipped off the little curly tails for me, the only child on the place, and saw to it that I did not set my apron on fire when I bent my inquisitive little face over the glowing coals to cook them.

The meat remains hanging until the animal heat is out, perhaps twenty-four hours, to chill; the whole hog is beautiful in this condition and now becomes "bacon." The carcase is carved into hams, shoulders and middlings, which are rubbed with salt and taken to the meat-house where they are packed in two layers, on boards, and absolutely covered with salt, remaining so for three weeks.

The chine, or back-bone, and the spare-ribs, are used fresh; the head is cut in two, the lower part, or jowl, is salted with the hams, the upper part, with the feet, goes into the souce-cheese, a jelly made with spices and highly seasoned. From the trimmings our delicious sausage is made, ground up with salt and pepper and sage, and the lard comes from the layers of fat around the ribs, though the razor-back furnishes little lard.

Hog-killing is a season of hilarity for we invite friends in for good dinners of spare-ribs and apple-sauce, or a supper of fresh sausage and waffles— delicious combination! And at Oakley there was, is and I hope always will be, an abundance of tempting accessories in the shape of scones and beaten biscuits, preserves and pickles; corn-bread and sweet potatoes.

The servants especially found this fresh pork a great treat, as their "ration" was so much salt meat in the year, and equally enjoyed the excitement of the killing and the community spirit which is emphasized in work that brings many of them together. The jokes and songs and general fun last through the season which is almost sacramental in its character to them. Nothing goes to waste for they claim the blood, the intestines and the tissue from which the lard is boiled out, which they call "crackling," and use, mixing it into their corn-bread. You cannot believe how good it is!

Three weeks have passed and our ham must be cured. First, the salt is brushed away, and each joint is rubbed with a tablespoonful of saltpetre, preparatory to the smoking. The joints are suspended from the roof of the smoke-house by the rope-like thongs of the yucca—that stately beautifier of the desert which, shaking its million snowy bells over a waterless world, lends itself kindly to transplanting.

A fire is burning in the middle of the smokehouse from a handful of hickory chips in an old iron pot, smouldering as green wood burns with tremendous smoke and little heat; day after day, for fifteen days, this is repeated, after which the meat may remain hanging, or be taken down and painted with black molasses and black pepper, as a preventive against worms, or "skippers."

Here, oh best beloved! hangs this ham for two or three years, and then the last act of its career. There is to be a house-party. It is yanked from its hook, lies in water a day or two, soaking out the salt, then simmers lazily for a day or two longer; never boils, but from the back of the stove gently yields to the operation of moisture and heat.

After the ham is boiled, it stands overnight in the liquor, retaining flavor and juices, and in the morning it is heated again, the skin removed, the surface carefully sprinkled with bread crumbs and brown sugar, cloves stuck in here and there, a few spoonfuls of sherry poured over it as it bakes in the oven for its final tint and tone.

It comes out a miracle. It cuts thin as paper. We handle it with as much care as we would a baby. It lasts indefinitely. We carve as though carving were a high art.

It combines the woods and fields, sun, rain, and fire—all elements enter into it. The nearer the bone, truly the sweeter the meat. When there is nothing left to slice we grind it, using it in croquettes, with fresh meats, in omelettes, in spaghetti; when there is nothing left of it to grind, we grate it, making a cold relish that you dream of—and when the old bone is scraped clean, into the soup pot with it, for there lingers still a flavor that dignifies even beans and carrots.

We plead guilty to the accusation that we love food. Yes, in Virginia, food is of importance. Even today a genuine housekeeper will speak with the tenderest intonation of some special delicacy; the inflexions of voice are almost reverential as she goes into all the niceties of a recipe, and the expressive gestures accompanying the recital are truly pretty. And of all culinary art, the apotheosis is the well-cooked home-cured Smithfield ham.

CHAPTER XVIII

MY Aunt Ida's key-basket was a source of perpetual admiration and speculation for it represented all hidden treasures in the way of fruits, preserves, honey, cookies and other mysteries calculated to tempt the juvenile mind into juggling with the Ten Commandments. It was of leather, very strong, and stitched with a fancy pattern by way of trimming or decoration. It was deep and oblong and showed many signs of long service. It was always with her, in her hand as she went about her daily household duties, by her bedside at night. Rozier's wife still uses it and my Aunt Ida's great grandchildren admire it.

There were many things to be kept under lock and key—the meat-house, where the hams of all ages and sizes hung from the stained old rafters, great tubs of lard and sausage, and shoulders and spare-ribs, salted down for the winter; there was the feed-room, where the grain for the chickens was kept—"tail ends" as the screenings of the wheat was called, and coarser foods for larger stock.

In these times of which I speak it was necessary to keep provisions locked for the farm swarmed with negroes, some of them faithful and trustworthy, but many of them quite demoralized by their young freedom and the impression that the Government, or the Lord, or something or somebody, would provide for them, and that plunder was their privilege, and law or order a thing entirely optional with themselves. Thus they returned, emancipated after the war, to their old masters, many of them living out their lives on the land where they were born, charges upon their former and much impoverished owners.

There was the potato cellar, with bins for different sizes and grades of potatoes; for the potatoes used for the table were not the same as those kept for seed; nothing was wasted and the small and defective, called "strings" were reserved for the stock as winter fodder.

The dairies were exclusively for the milk, with rows of big gray and blue crocks in which the milk was held. The skimming of the cream was a matter of great moment, always supervised by the mistress, and so sweet, and done in a manner so spotless as to put modern sanitary methods to the blush—at least, as it was conducted by my Aunt Ida. All of the cream not required for the table was allowed to sour, or "clabber," preparatory to churning, and the golden butter which resulted from these operations was a work of art, worthy the beautiful herd of Alderney and Jersey cows, gentle and deer-like, which grazed on the rolling fields at Oakley.

The butter-milk, refuse of the churning, was a

highly prized beverage and Uncle Hal, Rozier, my father, and all sportsmen, clamored for it, especially in the gunning season, when they would return from a long, hot hunt for partridges and toss off goblet after goblet of it, thick, icy-cold, lumpy with bits of butter, and served in the great silver trophies, representative of thoroughbred horses at many shows.

What we called "bonny clabber" was the sour milk, hardened, considered by the aristocrats as a great delicacy, but scorned by negroes and the laboring people as "slop," fit only for hogs and chickens. To this day I love it, and no dish that is ever set before me meets with as much approval. A systematic use for the clabber was the making of "curds" or cottage cheese; Aunt Ida had cans, of which the bottoms were perforated in patterns, quite clear to my memory, stars, wheels and other designs, which when the whey had slowly drained away, left the snowy cheese compact and firm in the can, the patterns imprinted upon the mass in what I considered a most artistic embellishment.

Canned fruits and vegetables of every variety were stored in the big store-room, preserves, pickles, sauces, catsups, brandied fruits, cordials, cherry bounce and wines. The mere thought of cherry bounce makes me homesick for the days of auld lang syne! And that mixture of blackberry juice, brandy, spices and sugar, known as blackberry cordial! And for old ladies and little girls, and all virtuous souls who relished a drink which cools but does not inebriate, there was raspberry vinegar—an unfermented decoction of raspberry juice, very delicious when diluted with water in a glass of crushed ice.

The old-fashioned process of canning fruits and vegetables brought whole circles of friends together, as we have read of quilting bees and cornshuckings in other localities and among other classes. A carriage load of cousins would arrive betimes and soon the big back porch, scene of so many courtships by moonlight, was alive with busy hands and humming with conversation. We took the fruits as they were in season, currant jelly, raspberry jam, and especially strawberries with which we mixed one-third of gooseberries to modify the insipid sweet and give a snap. Capping the strawberries was a tedious job and I was allowed to help.

Original sin manifested itself here in greed and selfishness for I tried to pick out the handsomest berries to cap, leaving the little ones and the mashed ones for my elders and betters. When it was practicable, without detection, to swallow one now and then, I did so; and being debarred from active participation in the conversation, this was often possible. If Grandma caught me too often she assigned me to the preparation of the sour gooseberries, which was not a pleasant job, as the tiny stem at one end, and blossom— (or dried flower-stamens) at the other, were very troublesome to remove and hurt the fingers without appealing to the appetite.

If it happened to be tomatoes, big baskets of the fruit were brought in by negroes and tubs of scalding water were all in readiness; it was beautiful to see the perfect fruit yield to the process; the short sharp knife dug into the core, and the thin skin loosened and pulled off as a crimson silk stocking from a rosy foot.

As soon as the ladies had removed the skin from the fruit it was sent down to the kitchen, when Aunt Kitty put it on, let it all come to a boil, and sealed up the jars or cans. Canning tomatoes was an original process in my childhood for this wonderful fruit had but recently made its début into the ranks of foodstuffs; Grandma always referred to it as the "love-apple," and told of its use as a decoration in her girlhood.

Great fun was making "leather" of tomatoes or peaches. The fruit was pared and then stewed slowly into a pulp; this was spread out on flat platters and dried in the sun for about three days; when tough and leathery it was sprinkled heavily with sugar, rolled and packed into jars for winter use, when, cut in chips, it was passed as a delicacy, as a box of Huyler's might be, in our degenerate day.

Evaporated fruits were unknown to us and our peaches, cherries and apples were home-dried. Long planks were laid out in every conceivable place, in the garden, across the corner of the back porch, wherever the sun struck mercilessly upon an unsheltered spot—and there we spread out our sliced apples, seeded cherries or quartered peaches, and left them to the sun. Here they lay for days, covered with mosquito netting to protect them from the insects that swarmed over them, and becoming day by day darker in color and tougher in texture as their juices evaporated. Next into a thin muslin bag they went, to hang up a while longer in the sun, the air still having right of way; lastly they went into heavy sacks and were hung up in the store-room to await the season when fresh fruit was a thing of the past and Aunt Ida would select from the many keys in her basket the key to this treasure house of sweets. I usually found it convenient to be in her vicinity at such times, for the big tins of sugar cakes, gingersnaps and molasses cookies were omnipresent in my soul.

Big eyes give children a spiritual look, but a child can look very spiritual and be exceedingly greedy.

Even the ice-house had a key and the chicken house had a key. No sooner had I exhausted the delights of hog-killing time, which was late in November, than new diversions opened for me in following the ice-wagons. With a knitted josie on under my coat—we did not know sweaters then—and the glorious mittens made from my cousin Rozier's old trousers, I was a member of the party that went out to the pond in severe freezing weather to get in the ice for next summer. The overseer acted as my chaperon; his name was Mister Cornell—especially *Mister*. The men chopped the ice with axes and dragged it to shore with hooks and pitched the chunks into the wagon with their hands.

The ice-house was curiously constructed. First there was a deep well into which the melting could drain away, above which was the ice-house, a subterranean chamber into which they pitched the ice, covering it all with straw. The brick wall, which lined the whole excavation, ran up some few feet above the ground—high enough for a little doorway, and there began the gabled roof, under big trees for the sake of shade in hot weather. This peaked roof of cypress shingles presented a picturesque scheme of color—splotches of moss in every velvety shade of green; there was a chill in the air around it, even in the severest drought, and when the door was unlocked a breath of icy air struck the red face of any inquisitive young person who happened to be peeping in. There was something adventurous in approaching the ice-house. Suppose—suppose that when the door was open, a person went in! Suppose Mister Cornell did not notice this person and locked this person in! How long did it take to freeze to death in August? First, the pleasant coolness would pass into excessive cold. The person would pound on the door and yell, but deep down in the ground, who would hear?

So she would finally say her prayers, arrange herself in a becoming attitude, and with calm dignity give up the ghost and become dead, like Willy. And maybe not until dinner time, when they all were to enjoy peach ice-cream, would they miss a member of the family, and then it would be too late. Where was the child seen last? In the ice-house with Mr. Cornell—and the procession starts hysterically for the ice-house. There—like the young gentleman in "Excelsior," they found her—"lifeless, yet beautiful she lay"—and from that hour no member of that household could ever see peach ice-cream without thinking of the frozen child and bursting into tears.

CHAPTER XIX

TELLING lies is doubtless sinful, but most diverting, and I was quite an accomplished liar. What imaginative child does not invent fables? All the courage in a boy's heart will break out in some fictitious act of gallantry, for life is usually safe and hum-drum, real adventures are few. All the romance in the soul of a little girl will express itself in some invention or exaggeration, and must they both be spanked for their misrepresentations as for malicious lies? This is art!

My lies were usually due to fear—my true lies. The peach switch developed a Machiavellian conscience, and I told some necessary lies so well that Grandma never caught me—the only lies I was detected in were my visions and dreams and innocent communion with my unseen playmates.

But with the other commandments it was different. It seemed most difficult to keep them. Each was explained to me. I could not have any God but the one God, and at that time I did not know how different he was from Grandma's God—or she would have made me have hers for mine. So, in fact, the first Commandment was broken, for I did have a God altogether unlike the God I was told to have; I did make to myself graven images, modeled of mud, chopped out of wood, drawn and painted with such material as came my way—the medium didn't matter. Probably they did not resemble anything in the heavens above or the earth beneath, or the waters under the earth, but I deserved no credit for that, and was it possible God had no more to think about than to watch a little girl and be jealous if she made a picture and adored the creation of her own hands? And how about taking God's name in vain? Why didn't Grandma go out to the stables and tell all the gentlemen and their grooms about that? Wouldn't it be her fault—or my fault—if God did not hold them guiltless? Especially Uncle Hal—I was so fond of him and anxious that God should hold him guiltless. Of course I kept the Sabbath Day holy—so holy that I hated it. There was little to do—after Church half the County came to Oakley to dinner, the minister and all —but I seemed the only person to keep the day holy.

One day I asked our Rector to baptize Violet, my wax doll, given me by my young godmother; but poor Violet was confiscated rather than consecrated, as a punishment to me, and for two weeks locked in a closet; it was warm in the closet and her nose and cheeks melted until she was horribly deformed—she was disfigured for life.

The fourth Commandment seemed very elastic.

Rev. Charles Minnigerode of Richmond During the Civil War.

Rev. Charles Minnigerode D. D.

Everybody did all manner of work on Sunday—ladies went to church and gentlemen stayed in bed, cooks cooked, hostlers and milkmaids performed their functions; only the gardener wore a collar and rested from his labors; he and I bore the burden of that commandment. I tried to honor my parents though I often heard them discussed and small commendation bestowed upon them for their rapidly increasing family. The less I honored them the more I loved them, and as there were so many other old people one had to honor and obey this was a pleasant variation.

I never murdered anything—except grasshoppers, caterpillars and spiders,—but frequently I stole. Once I stole candy. Grandma had left a box on the mantelpiece in the room where I took my nap. I dragged a chair to the mantel, unaware that it was one of those folding camp chairs, and mounted upon it to reach the shelf, only to have it close on my foot and throw me down, terrified and shrieking, for I could not free my foot from the trap. Needless to relate my sin found me out.

When children repeat foul language or are guilty of any little vulgarity in conduct, this, Grandma explained, is adultery. The cure is most efficacious—a hard scrubbing out of the mouth with soap and quinine. It is hardly worthwhile, in view of the punishment, to tamper with this command.

People bore false witness against me every day. Grandma herself bore false witness. And as for coveting—I coveted the breast of the chicken which I saw the preacher eat every Sunday; I coveted the vocabulary of my Uncle Hal, which was adequately picturesque; I coveted the mortgage Grandma held on mansions in the sky, and her immunity from all consequences as to the Ten Commandments. I coveted the sort of parents that do not annoy the rest of the world with their frequent confinements and numerous bills; I coveted the wings of the birds, the red of the roses, the freedom of the winds; I wanted all there was of everything, when I was a little girl!

I found Biblical precedent for all my evil deeds. To ask Aunt Ida for a cookie for Willy when I wanted two for myself, was an easy thing. She thought me very generous and said: "Certainly, honey—get it out of the basket"—and I got two. Though it lay like a stone on my conscience, it never disturbed my digestion and there was the story of the unjust steward who was commended for his duplicity! What he did was a heap worse than to swipe two cookies.

When the first violet of the year smiled at me in the grass, I took it to Grandma. Cousin Ellen Smith was with her. One violet does not go very far among two ladies. It was out of the question to show partiality, there was but one way out of that quandary. "I have brought you-all the first violet," I said—"Gimme yo' scissors, Grandma." "What for?" she asked, looking up from her sewing. "I shall have to do what Solomon done (we often used the dialect of our colored people) about the baby those women were quarreling over," I answered.

One winter day, meeting a colored child without stockings or shoes, I assumed what I believed to be an apostolic pose and spake thusly: "Stockings and shoes have I none, but such as I have give I thee. In the name of Jesus of Nazareth, accept these mittens." When I came in without the mittens made out of my Cousin Rozier's old pants, and underwent the cross-examination (which was really cross) the difference between a genuine apostle and a foolish little girl became manifest. Yet my cousin Rozier had plenty of old pants, as I tried to show Grandma.

Grandma was nothing if not logical.

"Grandma," I said. "Do you know what that means, inasmuch as ye have done it unto one of the least of these ye have done it unto me?"

"Certainly, child. We must think even of the most unimportant people as if our blessed Savior himself were in place of them."

"Grandma, am I an unimportant person?"

"Well, my dear—yes, I suppose you are."

"Grandma, would you switch our blessed Savior?"

Long and earnestly she regarded me through her specs. "I will switch you, miss, within an inch of your life, if you are not careful to bridle your tongue."

The conversation ended right there.

CHAPTER XX

IT was customary at the old country houses for any traveler to stop, *en passant*, to feed and rest his horse, and tarry for dinner or supper; thus many a burly farmer, his trousers tucked into his boots and his beard redolent of tobacco, was our guest at table; often a bishop; sometimes a distinguished student engaged in scientific or historical research; to all of them Aunt Ida was charming. If they happened to strike a poor dinner she was more than usually delightful, and rising from the table their brains were in such a pleasurable whirl that they could never have told what they actually had eaten.

The remotest blood relationship seemed to entitle people to camp indefinitely in other people's houses, and especially in the room that Becca was born in. Very exacting and tiresome people became permanent institutions in a family, being buried after years of residence therein, from a house to which they had come for a fortnight's stay!

Should so much as a confidential glance be exchanged between husband and wife (one of those prayers which are the soul's sincere desire, not uttered, but unexpressed) servants and children soon caught the meaning and small impertinences might fall to the share of the unwelcome guest. So it behooved us to be careful. We pretended with a splendid hypocrisy to enjoy that person's society.

Should a little girl have yielded to the temptation of being funny at the expense of another, results were to be anticipated. This thing happened once. A little girl was seen mimicking a guest. The guest was a colorless, illshapen person, flat of chest and long of nose, and with a peculiarly ungainly walk, yet gentle graces of the spirit seemed to cling to her awkward frame as white and blue morning-glories cling in loving drapery to crumbling structures. The theatrical experiment of imitating her limping gait met with an immediate application of the peach switch.

Should a little girl so far forget herself as to interrupt her elders or reach at the table for the biscuits instead of waiting patiently till "Uncle Robert," who was unobservant and deaf, handed them to her, or push in front of other people when she was in a hurry, or answer back a grown person, or correct a grown person, she was liable to the peach switch; and when Grandma sometimes forgot about it on purpose, Uncle Hal would make his eyes very big and say—"By the way, Ma, haven't you forgotten to switch this gal today?"

There were times when Grandma and her God

disagreed, and this was painful to me and extremely confusing. Neither could be in the wrong, yet was it possible for both to be right? Now, in the matter of old Colonel John. He made a death-bed repentance, a thing I heard Grandma say she never could abide. God expressed no opinion so far as I knew, but acted in a way Grandma thought mistaken. I heard her say that old Colonel John had done exactly as he pleased, indulged himself in every possible way regardless of the rights of others, and had never given God or God's will a thought until he was too old to be bad, and then, at the last minute, when all worldly pleasures and all earthly friends had failed him, had turned to God. I inferred that so far from being angry God was pleased and accepted his tardy recognition, and, so Grandma said, would in all probability let old Colonel John into Heaven to sit with the best of us—those of us who had always paid a great deal of attention to His will. At least this is what Grandma "supposed."

Old Colonel John had not only set God's will at defiance, but had behaved as if he cared very little what was customary "with *Us*." As we were born members of the Caucasian race, we were born members of the Episcopal Church and of the Democratic Party. These were unchangeable conditions. This was all that was meant by "to do our duty in the state of life to which it had pleased God to call us." Colonel John was a born member of the Caucasian race, and of the Democratic Party; but he was a Methodist. I had never, to my knowledge, seen a Methodist, and wondered vaguely what it was—but he, born a Democrat, of his own volition had so insulted the will of God (who was responsible for his being born a Democrat), and so outraged public opinion with *Us*, as to become a Republican; and he had married Grandma's beautiful relative.

Grandma's cousin, even as a very old lady, was vivacious, dainty, alert, responsive and merry; Grandma was statuesque, virtuous, deliberate, rather lugubrious.

Once when Grandma and I were visiting this cousin, and all sewing sedately in our hostess' front room, an unusual noise in the street drew her to the window. "Oh, Marietta," she said, her eyes sparkling as she turned to Grandma, "Come, look—there is a dead horse in the street and they are trying to haul him away."

Grandma never moved a muscle and in even accents answered, "I thank you—a dead horse does not interest me."

"Well, if you could see how funny the men look tugging at him, and ripping their shirt sleeves and nearly tearing their arms out of the sockets, Marietta, and sweating and swearing——"

"Please desist—this child is present."

This child, fired with enthusiasm to witness

these unusual operations in the village street, was sidling towards the window, and as a great concession to human folly Grandma permitted her to get a peep.

And this lady's husband, old Colonel John, so Grandma said, had acted with extreme selfishness towards his wife (who very foolishly idolized him) and had been improvident, and had had an enormous family, and had been intemperate (but no disaster had ever overtaken him), and had rollicked on in his evil ways to about the age of eighty; and then fell ill. So he became religious. He would waken his wife, tired out with nursing him, to smoothe a wrinkle out in the counterpane or do some equally exasperating thing (Grandma said exasperating—his wife never used that word), and his utter selfishness followed him to his last hour; and what was so strange was that his children adored him, and his wife lived only in and for him, and God himself shared in the infatuation, apparently, and overlooked his eighty years of indifference, giving him welcome in the many mansions immediately upon his expressing a desire to be on friendly terms.

And when, during these criticisms, Uncle Hal would ask Grandma what she was going to do about those two thieves and about those servants hired at the eleventh hour and receiving the same wages as those who had borne the burden and heat of the day, Grandma would tell Uncle Hal not to be flippant.

Grandma's sparkling old cousin at last died too, and they say her final utterance was a reference to Grandma: "After all," she whispered, "I am going before Marietta. How furious she will be with God!"

CHAPTER XXI

SOMETIMES I was allowed to make visits to mother's cousins in other parts of the country, and so came to know Cousin Dick. I knew him very slightly, but loved him very much. It was a strange faculty, this love I could feel for "bad" people whom God and Grandma did not love. In after years I pieced out Cousin Dick's story.

I loved him first for his nature stories and woodcraft. Chipmunks were not afraid of him, skunks never intimated in any way that he was not popular with them; snakes, wasps and bees forgot to sting him, and any flower or plant he ever touched flourished exuberantly forever after. There was an apologetic way about Cousin Dick which gave one pain, as though he sometimes questioned his own right ever to have been born. He was very sheepish about the simple things which gave him pleasure, when he was sober; and preserved an apocryphal silence as to things which gave him pleasure when he was drunk. We speculated endlessly upon them; for we loved him, we children, with his profile like Dante, even after we learned that—to quote from Spoon River—the force which made Dante great drove Cousin Dick "to the dregs of life."

Cousin Dick had been expelled from college just before he was to have graduated with honors, and this because he was found out in what was supposed in that Victorian generation to be a disgraceful amour; certainly his irregular mode of life dated from the social ostracism consequent thereupon. It just happened that there had been an epidemic of morality sweeping over the state, and that the University, recently reorganized and anxious to score, took cognizance of poor Cousin Dick's misdemeanor and held him up to public scorn and contumely. His high-bred mother, unsophisticated as were the ladies of her day, went thereafter into what was called seclusion, and soon after was safe in that over-populated locality described as "Abraham's Bosom."

From Abraham's Bosom she must have followed the earthly course of her first-born with startled spirit eyes, as he ran life's mad career "wild as the wave." Scattering his little patrimony, dissipating his vitality, corrupting and degrading his name, and cheapening his talents. Cousin Dick rollicked along with the sinners on earth all unmindful of the angels in Heaven. It must be that the dead learn tolerance for without it their wider knowledge of the world they have drifted out of would poison Heaven itself.

From Abraham's Bosom this dear lady must have wept to see her lovely daughter after years of poor relationdom in the family of a relative, marry—to be married. Such an unsatisfactory way to work out the problem—and after that, to break. Brooding over childlessness; craving the mission of motherhood, inviting it at any price. Finally convinced that she herself is a highborn Jewish maiden and about to become the mother of the Messiah. Note the aristocracy of the hallucination! Of all this world's mothers, she selects the mother supreme, she who was to know the sword thrust through her own heart, the Mater Dolorosa. God knows she looked the part.

In Abraham's Bosom the dead mother must have squirmed to see her baby boy, little Ned, a deaf-mute, sent off to an institution in which, fortunately, he was thoroughly trained to farm labor, and so was able in after years to hold a "parcel" of land and cultivate it for the benefit of all.

Ned was the instrument in the hands of Providence to shelter and feed his utterly irresponsible brother and sister, high-strung and over-sexed, tortured as Ned was never tortured. In his whole life Ned had never laid his hand upon a woman but went the even tenor of his way between the tobacco field and the garden, the kitchen and the pig-pen, in his eternal silence. Scratching along in his soundless world of growing corn and cabbages, Ned knew nothing of the urge voiced in the weird lullabies his sister improvised as she sat under the giant lilac bushes beside the cabin she called home, her great eyes peering out from the mazes of her wild hair, her exquisite features drawn with spiritual pain, as she cradled one hand to her bosom and caressed it with the other hand, as one might a young child. Ned was well content to see Nannie sitting still in the shade. That unrest which men miscall delight meant nothing whatever to Ned. There was no bestial quality in him and no imagination. There was no trace of savagery, yet he was hardly civilized. If he were barbarous some incense of a high spiritual nature must have arisen from his sublime patience and his indefatigable faithfulness. Passion never swayed him. When he whipped a dog he did so with steady determination, but never an extra blow was struck in cruelty. In irreparable impoverishment the boy bent his broad back to his daily burdens, while Cousin Dick roamed far afield in search of what he should never find, and Nannie wept and sung and giggled over the child that was not.

Cousin Dick was sober now and had been for weeks so Ned and Nannie were happy in the rundown home in which the three lived together. The potatoes and tobacco were "perking up a bit" for Ned could work with better heart.

"Land poor" after the Civil War; "brokendown 'ristocrats," in the darkey vernacular; "decayed gentlefolk," in the ghastly English phrase!

What was to be done? The land had been sold off bit by bit and "Po' white trash" were building up the original acreage with comfortable hideous houses. These domiciles were crammed with furniture inside as shocking as the cupolas and porticos were on the exterior, and their prosperous owners were sending their boys and girls to college and building up some sort of new social scheme in which my poor cousins would have been a misfit, even had that early burning secret of Cousin Dick's college days, bared so suddenly, remained forever hid. What had it been after all, but the impatience of young blood, the racial tendency to take what was wanted, and let the dogs bark? The same thing was an established precedent and all his life the boy had seen older men laughing over their port wine together at similar escapades. Well he knew that at many a funeral of the old planters, there stood in silent dignity mulattos, quadroons, handsome boys and girls, there to bid farewell to the earthly part of one who had been, in the fashion of the patriarchs of old, a generous friend.

Cousin Dick went out into the woods alone. Perhaps he found it well to escape Nannie's hysterical tenderness, or the sight of Ned's stupid, unremitting toil. He was always sheepish about this "mooning" around in the woods and would try to justify the simple taste for it by bringing back some trophy, some dry wood, a bird's nest to show his childish sister, some herb of healing property, if only pennyroyal to keep the mosquitoes away, when he stuck it in the tops of Nannie's shoes.

A light step on the bank, the briars are opened a little, and Cousin Dick cranes his neck, peeping and peering into the shadows. He is a long, spare man, filed down by suffering; if it were not Cousin Dick whom we all know to be so good-for-nothing, one might think that a sensitive conscience and tender heart accounted for the wistful expression of his eyes and the sad droop of the cleancut mouth. He is clad in faded blue overalls, open at the throat. Cousin Dick's head was well set, and at the nape of the neck his poor neglected gray hair yielded to a foolish tendency to curl. It curled just like the tail feathers of Ned's old drake. Strange to say he was clean shaven and cleanly shaved; the chin square and firm, and following the line of the throat to his breast gleaming smooth and white between the folds of the coarse blue garment.

Cousin Dick held an old tomato can in his hand into which his long fingers dropped the berries with great fastidiousness one by one. It was very dear of him to go hunting berries for Nannie, and every berry he brought her was infinitely dearer than all of Ned's cabbages and potatoes. Ned liked pork and greens, for he did the work and ate the fare of the day laborer, but neither Nannie nor Cousin Dick could abide 'em! Poor little Nannie was in raptures over the berries until she bit the stink-bug, that hadn't any business in the can. And that was just the way Cousin Dick did everything.

CHAPTER XXII

MOTHER'S Cousin Ginnie had been pretty as a girl, and some one had taken her up North where she caught a rich Yankee beau. After that Grandma said the goose honked high for Cousin Ginnie. But it was not until after she had lived some years in Europe that we found out her head was turned; it was money that turned it. When she came back she was calling herself Eugénie. Grandma said her name was plain Ginnie, and Grandma Ginnied her persistently, though the rest of the connection yielded to the weakness of accepting the more elegant mode of address. Grandma's maid, Martha, said she didn't see why, if Miss Ginnie wanted to be called You-Janie folks couldn't humor her an' call her You-Janie; Martha thought it was sour grapes. Grandma said Cousin Eugénie's fingers had mucilage on the tips of 'em, and that was a puzzling statement. I watched carefully for the mucilage, to which all sorts of desirable things, it was hinted, adhered. But all I could notice were her dainty finger-nails and the lovely shape of her fingers. You could see she never did her own preserving, or pickling, for pickle is even harder on the hands than preserves; especially green tomatoes; they do stain something scan'alous when the soap lathers it all bright green as little girls wash their hands after gathering the green tomatoes. It is the ripe tomatoes that bleach the hands so beautifully, and they do not cost as much as lemons.

Cousin You-Janie let her country cousins make all her preserves and sweetmeats and pickle, and paid them well for their work. They always Ginnied her behind her back, even when they had her Paris hats on top of their heads, but they You-Janied her to her face. To me she and the Yankee husband were the embodiment of grandeur and I did not think her clothes looked as well on the relations as they did on her.

It was difficult to conduct an old Virginia home on the scale of an ancestral English Manor House; the ten or twelve white girls Cousin Eugénie imported from back of Sugar Loaf Mountain, to be trained into English serving maids, were a little dull, Cousin Eugénie said, and could not grasp the idea. They rose clumsily from their knees as she approached, and instead of curtsying they dropped their scrubbing-brushes into their buckets and splashed scrub-water just as the Lady of the Manor passed, and they never addressed her in the third person. It would have been so simple to have stood modestly in the hall until the flow of exalted conversation ceased, and then, dropping a respectful curtsy, and blushing, to have murmured, "Asking Madam's pardon, will Madam speak to the Veterinarian?" But these girls blurted out unceremoniously "Miss Ginnie—You-Janie, the hoss doctor, he says come out in the yard a minute." Cousin Eugénie declined the ministrations of the easy-going and lovable darkies who had brought her up, though Grandma said Ginnie was as full of foolishness as an egg was full of meat; and that many and many a time, when Ginnie was a teething baby, her Mammy, old 'Liza from the lower farm, had masticated Ginnie's food for her, and put it into her mouth morsel by morsel, after the fashion of a mother-bird. It was a pretty howdy-do for Ginnie to turn her nose up at negro servants. Of course it might be a necessity to have white ones, if Ginnie's Yankee husband insisted on calling colored people "Mistah." You-Janie's husband, mistering and mississing them was most demoralizing!

Cousin Eugénie's parties were not successful. She arranged to have special guests seated on the verandahs, while persons whom she called the "tenantry and the villagers" were to gambol on the green. "The country dances are quite lovely," she said, "and are an inheritance from England." We never knew who the tenantry were; Mr. Cornell said they wasn't him; but the villagers were in reality the Braxtons and Fauntleroys and Carters and Pages and all the blue blood under the sun who hadn't married Yankees. These absurd persons declined to gambol on the green.

There are a great many Sunday School teachers and Sunday School Superintendents sprinkled through my memory. The one I liked best was mother's Cousin Carey. Unfortunately he was a very bad man. But not a Miss Nancy. He became a Sunday School Superintendent because he liked boys, and knew boys did not like Miss Nancys. Cousin Carey could take a drink like a gentleman, and played good ball. The boys were crazy about him. Everyone loved him. Mothers said he chaperoned their girls better than they could. Boys did not get mad when Cousin Carey kissed their sweethearts, though young puppy lovers do not enjoy the fatherly manner in which middle-aged cousins paw little girls. Cousin Carey was the champion best man, godfather, pallbearer, vestryman and town councillor. He was the star guest at all parties, young and old.

Then there came on a scandal. A woman told a tale. She asked the vestry to investigate the truth of her statements. How could that sort of thing be investigated? We were very curious, and the Sunday School was in a flutter of excitement. All the men and women were for him, shaking their heads ruefully "because it was so hard for a handsome fellow to escape." The vestry and the town council voted him a vote of confidence; and the ushering, godfathering, chaperoning and pallbearing, went on just as usual.

But one day without warning, up stands Cousin Carey in church and says he is guilty; that he cannot endure the false position in which the misplaced confidence of his friends has placed him; that he is a very evil fellow. Then he tells how he had been asked to escort this person to church—how he had gone for her and been detained—too late for church—remained there! He offered no excuse; if a man has a treacherous inclination, all he need do is be careful; if the tiger pulls on the leash, never let him run. He thanked everybody and said he was leaving town. He had loved justice. He had followed after mercy. He had visited the fatherless and widows in their affliction and had kept himself almost, but not quite, unspotted from the world. Not quite— and so must have been, as he said, a very bad man!

Twenty years later on the occasion of a Confederate Reunion I saw him in a carriage with other old Veterans, bowing and smiling to the populace as they cheered and cheered. He had forgotten the old disgrace, and had been for years an inmate of one of the Confederate Homes.

CHAPTER XXIII

COUSIN NEVILLE got into an argument with Grandma on some Biblical question every time they met. He did not seem to be teasing her but he worried her a lot. One day he spoke of Joseph as a little prig. He said it served him right to be sold to the Ishmaelites, that if he had been sent to West Point he would have had the starch and the conceit taken out of him by systematic hazing. He said he did not believe that Joseph was in as much of a hurry as he pretended to be when he escaped from a compromising situation, that he had heard the old man coming. Well Grandma took up the life of Joseph and went through with the whole story until I was thrilled to the tips of my fingers. The impression has remained indelible. Were I capable of it I would make a great opera of the story; such a motif, such contrasts, pastoral twilight, shepherds, the background of the hill country—and Egypt, gorgeous Egypt. The romantic, dreamy boy, then the grave, sedate ruler. Every ethical, poetical, spectacular, dramatic quality worthy of Wagner himself.

"Neville," said Grandma, "go get me that Bible. Now turn to the next to the last chapter of Genesis." Cousin Neville fumbled around the book, and I volunteered to help him find the place. "Now," said Grandma, "you just read me the blessing of Jacob upon the head of Joseph, and then tell me if a sensible old man, a very shrewd old man, let me tell you, like Jacob, would waste his last breath upon a little prig? No, my dear friend. Joseph was a genius. Joseph was the first true gentleman of history. Fools thought he was a prig then, and the foolcatcher isn't dead yet. Read me the words of that blessing."

And Cousin Neville bent his handsome head over the page, and as he read, his voice showed that the sweeping beauty of the imagery, the deep tenderness of the passage, were not lost on him.

"Joseph is a fruitful bough, even a fruitful bough by a well whose branches run over the wall. The archers have sorely grieved him and shot at him and hated him, but his bough abode in strength and the arms of his hands were made strong by the hands of the mighty God of Jacob. Even by the God of thy father, who shall help thee, and by the Almighty who shall bless thee with blessings of the heavens above and of the deep that lieth under, blessings of the breast and of the womb. The blessings of thy father have prevailed above the blessings of my progenitors unto the uttermost bounds of the everlasting hills. They shall be upon the head of Joseph, and on the crown of the head of him that was separate from his brothers."

This was impressive, but not quite clear to me, and I asked Grandma to explain all that Joseph was to expect as a result of it; but she snapped, rather inconsistently, I thought, that it was a private conversation between two gentlemen, and none of my business.

The night the leather-winged bat got into Grandma's room after I had been put to bed and the lights were out, Cousin Neville caught it under Grandma's slipper and gently put it out of the window, saving me from this devilish creature and then sparing its life. This nobility quite overcame me. I became a hero-worshipper. Seeking in the Scriptures justification for my passion, I lit upon Ruth's adventure with her cousin Boaz, though Grandma's ideas and Naomi's were at variance as to the obligations of a chaperone, and the customs prevailing at that time in Moab were not considered good form in Upperville; wherefore I did not seek a place at the feet of my friend, but relieved my amorous imaginings by declaiming to the box bush in the garden Ruth's ardent address to her mother-in-law. "Whither thou goest," I said, waving my arm dramatically at the box bush, "I will go, and where thou dwellest, I will dwell. Thy people shall be my people, and thy God my God. Where thou diest I will die, and there will I be buried." If Cousin Neville had happened to pass, and had asked me to explain, I think I should have revealed my sweet secret. But he didn't.

P O O R   R E L A T I O N

It always happens so in real life. He didn't, or couldn't, or something.

Mother's lady cousins were able to adjust themselves after the war to altered conditions more easily than her gentleman cousins. The lady cousins "took" boarders in the summers, and the gentleman cousins sat on the porch and conversed with the boarders the lady cousins "took."

At least that was the way Cousin Peter did. He was a pleasant old fellow, had travelled abroad after leaving college, was thoroughly well read and discussed the classics intelligently. He assisted his cerebral processes by the use of tobacco, which he chewed incessantly. He punctuated his talks on Plato's Republic or Homer's Odyssey by spitting from the porch into the tub the oleander grew in. The tobacco juice was good for the oleander—killed bugs.

Cousin Annie and Cousin Peter were cousins. Nobody from a distance ever came into our quiet communities. Our people hadn't the money to travel, and there were few families of our own class in reach who were not related to us. So we kept on marrying each other.

It was rather sad to see Cousin Annie start for a long hot walk of a midsummer afternoon, to drive her turkeys home, while Cousin Peter sat on the cool porch chewing tobacco and talking about poetry with the boarders; but when she returned, breathless and crimson, after an hour's tramp, the real poetry was seen. Old Cousin Peter would rise from his rocking-chair and pull a couple of roses from a nearby bush, and as she approached would meet her saying, "Annie, honey, I just plucked you these little rosebuds to put in your bosom."

"Thank you, Peter," she would say, unfastening a damp buttonhole to stick the roses into her frock as suggested; then glancing kindly around upon the assembled and somewhat unsympathetic boarders, she would add, "I do declare, Peter's the most thoughtful person in the world!"

Cousin Annie made preserves for Cousin Eugénie. She did not have a cherry-seeder, those labor-saving machines were not in favor, because they do really crush the fruit too much; Cousin Annie's cherry-seeder was a small colored boy named Robert.

Robert would sit on the kitchen porch seeding and tasting cherries all day long. A deep-rooted prejudice against cherry preserves has saddened my existence, for the mere thought of them recalls the picture of this dirty little darkey streaming with the sanguinary juice, cherry seed sticking to his woolly head, cherry seed scattered over his ragged apparel, his black fingers popping the cherries open one by one as he extracted the stones, while there swarmed above his head a cloud of gnats and flies.

But there was an indescribably delicious flavor to everything that came out of Cousin Annie's kitchen. I was never asked to dinner at Cousin Eugénie's, but it was rumored that she regaled the élite of the Metropolis upon these Southern dainties which she said the dear villagers prepared for her. All I know is that if they had known what I knew——! The old fat black cook slept in a corner of Cousin Annie's kitchen. There was no place where a servant could possibly take a bath. The ancient timbers were festooned with cobwebs, and cock-roaches, waterbugs, and rats were fearless and familiar.

Nevertheless at an exclusive old hotel in the neighborhood of Trafalgar Square a few years ago (the house was part of the personal estate of Queen Victoria, I believe) I had occasion to concentrate my attention on the depths of the bowl of stewed fruit passed me by an amiable functionary. Marking my delay in serving myself, he leaned forward and peered into the pink syrup anxiously. "Ah, Madam, it is a fly—is it not, Madam?" So even royalty now and then encounters the little housepests familiar in our old Virginia kitchens.

Cousin Buck had to get up at four every morning on account of so many cows; and he couldn't shave so early. Stamping around in stables and cow-sheds, his boots got very bad, and his trousers, stuffed into them at the knee, were stained and smelly. Everybody knew who Cousin Buck was, except the Northern gentleman who said Cousin Buck had not read "Barnaby Rudge," but Aunt Ida, of course, had, and Grandma had, and Becca had, and so I read it. There are things people need not say, and we all thought it very indelicate of the Northern gentleman. No F. F. V. should be compared to Maypole Hugh, who was a great ruffian, Grandma said, and born out of wedlock.

One day Cousin Buck just said his say. He was leaving the milk, when the Northern gentleman accosted him. "Oh, I say!" said the Northern gentleman, "some guests are arriving and will you kindly leave the milk at the back door?" "Back do'? Did you say back do' to me?" thundered Cousin Buck. "Do you know who I am?" "Why, no," said the Northern gentleman, "I thought you were the milk-man." "Milkman or no milk-man, don't you say back do' to me," roared Cousin Buck. "I'm the great-grandson o' Patrick Henry, if you ever heard o' him —that's who I am." "Oh, I beg your pardon," said the Northern gentleman, "and to save me from a similar *faux pas*, would you kindly tell me who the meat-man is?" "Yes," roared Cousin Buck, "the meat-man as you call 'im is a cousin to General Robert E. Lee—that's who yo' meat-man is." And Cousin Buck walked away, which Grandma said was perfectly right.

CHAPTER XXIV

COUSIN ARTHUR was not a blood cousin, but a connection dearer and kinder than many who were. Perhaps of all relatives, the distant one, easily ignored if unsympathetic, is the most valuable; for if congenial, he is then both friend and relative—near enough to feel a quickened interest in one and remote enough to mind his own business.

Cousin Arthur had a genius for philanthropy—that real philanthropy which, true to its derivation, is a love for mankind. He had been in command of the Seventeenth Virginia Regiment in the Civil War, and when Vaucluse, Cameron, Menokin, and other old homes on this second range of hills from the Potomac, went down under the so-called necessity of war, his place Muckross was destroyed, and a Federal fort, Fort Worth, took its place.

After the war Muckross was rebuilt, and the old trenches were taken by wildroses and honeysuckle, and soldierly cedars and widespreading oaks arose as motionless sentinels along the breastworks which zig-zag across all this country. The new home was built over the Federal magazine, which served as an excellent cellar, a rustic bridge spanned the great moat, and peace in fulfilment of promise came to Cousin Arthur. Even as the Psalmist declared, "Great peace have they which love thy law, and nothing shall offend them."

His adoration of his beautiful wife, many years his junior, was the ruling passion of his life, and together, war-worn veteran and exquisite bride, they actually made the desert to blossom like a rose. With her own hands Cousin Alice planted young trees to replace those cut down by the Yankees, gracious trees now memorials of her.

Cousin Alice was never well and spoke in the attenuated drawl of a sickly Southern gentlewoman; her voice was sweet, notwithstanding its suggestion of infinite resignation on her own part and indefinable reproach toward the rest of the world.

Her husband's poor relations were often her pathetic theme, and indeed he had a great many, including some who, like us, had no actual claim upon him. The demands upon him were enough to have exhausted the patience of them both, but frail as she was, she responded as he did, when it was possible. He invented charming ways of making mother happy. At Christmas he would say, "Jinnie, I have no time to hunt up cases of need here, but will you please expend this twenty-five dollars in turkeys for families who otherwise won't have a Christmas turkey?" And mother's radiant face under her widow's bonnet, would haunt the markets, punching and poking the poor naked turkeys, confidentially discussing their leanness or their toughness with the vendors. Our little boy George would drag them home by their necks, lifting them up at first, but as they grew heavier step by step, trailing them along till their "popesnoses" scraped on the sidewalk! The distribution of them among the needy was a joy to mother's generous soul.

Cousin Arthur in his old age had many a good cigar and glass of wine with Mr. Andrews at our new Vaucluse as the two talked over Civil War campaigns. My husband, who knew nothing of it from experience, always beating the table with his fist and speaking with great fire; Cousin Arthur, who went through it all, preserving exactly the expression of calm tolerance which Mr. Andrews himself assumed when some Cook's tourist talked to him about Europe.

Cousin Sophronia was a thin-visaged, dyspeptic person of middle age who lived in Richmond. Cousin John Henry Powell employed her in some small capacity in the school. Having little share in the pleasure and perquisites of the present, Cousin Sophronia dealt largely in the splendors of the past and the bliss of the future, in other words, her pedigree, which represented the past, and her preacher, who symbolized the future.

Her connection with the Gibbon family endeared my sister and me to her, for that gallant Lieutenant Gibbon, who with his lovely fianceé,

Sally Conyers, lost his life in the Theater fire in 1811, was an uncle of my grandmother Minnigerode, and a cousin of Cousin Sophronia's mother. He was a son of Major James Gibbon of the Continental Army, hero of Stoney Point, whose silver tankard belongs to my youngest sister, Ann Gibbon, and because of this connection Cousin Sophronia attended grandfather's church, Saint Paul's. Yet the Monumental Church was built as a memorial to those who lost their lives in this disaster, and she also had leanings in that direction. Thus, in selecting a sanctuary, Cousin Sophronia's mind was, as it were, a house divided against itself.

Cousin Sophronia was mighty glad, she always said, that she was at Saint Paul's that Sunday, October 7, 1860, when the Prince of Wales, later King Edward VII of England, attended service. He was just a fresh-faced boy, she said, and it looked to her as though he had gone to sleep during the sermon. The Duke of Newcastle nudged him once or twice and after the service told him that he had gone to sleep. But she said that he said, "Oh, no! Doctor Minnigerode's delightful German accent made him think of his dear father, and he had only closed his eyes that the illusion might be perfect."

Among the select boarding schools for young ladies was Cousin John Henry Powell's, in Richmond.

Robert Carter of Corotoman: Portrait by Mrs. Andrews after Sir Godfrey Kneller in the Possession of Mrs. Randolph Harrison McKim of Washington.

Ann Carter of Shirley on the James River. Copy by Mrs. Andrews of the Original by Thomas Sully. Louis Storrow Greene Collection.

He was a beautiful creature, not a large man, but perfectly proportioned with the great soft dark eyes and clean-cut profile of the Powells; and his wife, born a Leigh, was a fair match for him.

These two wielded an immense power for good in those early days and stamped many Virginia women with their own rare integrity. Cousin John Henry was very clannish and sometimes we, who could not afford to go to boarding school, were invited for visits to this house. His daughters, Sarah, Betty, Rebecca, and Carrie, gracious, dark-eyed girls, were always very sweet to their poor cousins, and the baby, John Powell, has grown to be one of the world's great musicians.

Among the fortunate boarders in this home of learning was a pretty little Virginia child, younger than I, whose shining eyes, cameo-like profile and abundant black hair, took my fancy. Little Edith Bolling, descended as I, from old Robert Bolling of Bollingbroke. Lucy Bolling, his daughter, married Peter Randolph of Chatsworth and their son was Col. Robert Randolph of Eastern View near Warrenton. He married Elisa Hill Carter, daughter of John Carter and granddaughter of Robert Carter of Corotoman called "King Carter," whose vast estates, peculiar ideas, velvet coat and rippling wig, are familiar to historians and genealogists. Their daughter, Elisa Randolph, married Thomas Turner of Kinloch and these were Grandma's parents.

This little far-off cousin, this little lass of long ago, became "the first lady in the land," as Mrs. Woodrow Wilson. In the hour of the world's sorest need, her personal beauty, quiet mind, perfect tact and gentleness of character, were to the foremost figure of the time, and the most authoritative leader of men, an oasis of refreshment in a desert of anxiety.

On December 14, 1918, that day which for the first time in history witnessed the arrival of an American President upon a foreign shore for the purpose of participating in a readjustment of world-relationships, it was she whose little feet first pressed the soil of France; her husband, with the habitual courtesy of an American gentleman, standing aside, that she should precede him as they stepped ashore at Brest.

One autumn day Woodrow Wilson rested here at Vaucluse with us, on my own land, calling at sunset for his wife. The spot where we received him is today marked with the trees he loved best, the common American beech and dogwood, and the memory of his visit will remain an ever dear one to my children's children.

CHAPTER XXV

CHAPTER TWENTY-FIVE must be by way of parenthesis for I cannot resist sharing with you, whoever you may be, this rainy October day in the country, the welcome patter on the big skylight of the Vaucluse studio, the only room in the house where we have already an open fire, and the delightful companionship of Mary Lord Andrews the third, Helen Tucker Andrews the second, and Carter Randolph Andrews, quite new and the only bearer of that pleasant name.

My publishers have admonished me, in the most fatherly fashion, to *work* over this manuscript if I expect to do anything with it; and dutifully I struggle to obey; but the difficulty is that nothing I ever do really seems like work. One is conscious of fatigue after any exercise mental or physical, and doing memoirs with one finger on the portable Underwood, is both; but there is fun in it that outweighs all consideration of the cost. In such broken time as belongs to a grandmother, left in charge of all her grandbabies while their parents are off on a little trip—their daddy showing to their mother the battlefields of France so familiar to him a few years ago—serious study is hardly possible, and yet concentrated effort, really, is not called for, here; this is merely a report of certain facts and the reactions of an egotistical child to those facts and their accompanying conditions.

Grandmothers today are not the arbiters of destiny they were in the days of which I have written. They must be adroit indeed to establish any influence. Hence my own unbounded sense of importance at having weeks and weeks with Mary Lord Andrews the third, Helen Tucker Andrews the second, and the one and only Carter Randolph Andrews. These three young ladies are at this moment disposed round my chair, on the floor beside the fire. Happily it is Fräulein's "day off" and I do not care if that undaunted disciplinarian gets a thorough wetting to dampen the ardor of her Teutonic efficiency. Of course you understand that it is a delicate matter for a mere grandmother to disagree with an expensive Fräulein, and if by so doing the grandmother should offend, there would be a situation to face that would terrorize a more valiant soul than I. But today we are free; we do everything Fräulein forbids. We took a long walk instead of a "nap." We ate the things she does not allow—raw milk, not boiled, and not skimmed; thick slices of bread with butter and brown sugar, instead of toast. The milk toast Fräulein had prepared was bestowed upon "The Widow." "The Widow," by the way, is the black and white tabby cat, whose mate, the old Tom Cat who has lived so long in the barn, vanished mysteriously some time ago. Since his departure the conduct of "The Widow" has not been above reproach, but when she fastens her lustrous pale green eyes upon us we find ourselves tongue-tied as to her indiscretions which are many and various. Infidelity toward the memory of her honored spouse being in our opinion far less criminal than the hypnotism she exerts to lure our baby wrens and robins to their doom. She is beautiful, "The Widow," but she is not a consecrated widow by any means.

Mary Lord Andrews the third is engaged in building a card house of souvenir postcards. Helen Tucker the second is inspecting a large catalogue of Sears, Roebuck and Company, in which a number of legs with no ladies attached, as advertisements of beautiful silk stockings, cover one page, and lovely ladies without legs, advertising hats and blouses, adorn another page. Helen Tucker the second being not quite two years old expresses no astonishment at these mutilations, but Mary Lord the third says it is sad to see pieces of people, and where are the ladies who belong to those legs? And where are the legs that belong to these ladies? She is interested in the Sears, Roebuck catalogue, and I feel her active little brain is at work upon some scheme to defraud Helen Tucker of it without interference from me.

Carter Randolph is nine months old, a thing

of beauty. She is in the high chair, tied in with a diaper. The blazing logs astonish her, and an empty spool passes from one hand to the other with great seriousness. To get it safe from the right to the left and then back again from the left to the right, is a triumphant achievement over which she gurgles deliciously.

I am making some nightgowns for Mary Lord Andrews the third. Upon closer acquaintance with my granddaughters I find them fair without and a little ragged within. Carter Randolph's belly-bands are awful, torn by the safety pins beyond repair. Them I patched with nice soft flannel, only to be told by Fräulein that they are now too small, and must be "aufgehoben" for the next baby. For Mary Lord the third I have made a dozen dresses, fearfully and wonderfully made, no doubt, for I never have been a needle-woman—they look pretty good to me, and I sincerely hope will find favor in her mother's eyes. Thus sallying forth into a new field of enterprise, how can I rewrite the "Memoirs of a Poor Relation"? Apropos of which, Mary Lord the third explains that when she begins to wear the new dresses I have made her, Helen Tucker the second may have her old ones, and Carter Randolph may have Helen Tucker's old ones. And, Grandma, who will have Carter Randolph's old ones?

And as she asks this pertinent question she raises her melting brown eyes to mine from the pages of the Sears, Roebuck catalogue, now

POOR RELATION

open in her lap and held there secured by her two dimpled elbows, while Helen Tucker strains to reach the high chair in order to rob Carter Randolph of the empty spool.

PART III

LIFE IN NEW ORLEANS

CHAPTER XXVI

THE end came suddenly to this my quiet life—the summons to join my parents and their other children. My father was going to start in business somewhere else. I was going away from Grandma and from Oakley. Grandma admonished me as to how helpful I should be to my mother and what a good example I should set my younger brothers and sisters. She said I must give them the benefit of my own religious teaching, and I said that I certainly would. Thus I started out from the very beginning on the wrong track. The adjustment to a house full of other children was suddenly demanded of one who had lived only among adults, and whose understanding of children was most imperfect. Yet it was high time that the change should be made.

It seemed a wonderful thing to be going to them, to be a sort of little mother to them, to be the companion and adviser of my own mother, to help her with whatever she might have to do, and to give her my blessing in her frequent confinements. Dumbly and obscurely I had resented the criticisms which met her on these occasions from those whose confinements were less frequent, but who, as I soon learned, had only her welfare at heart.

It never struck me that I was putting myself on a pinnacle. As the oldest of this large family I felt my importance, and when it slowly dawned on me that the younger ones did not look up to me as the embodiment of all wisdom, my astonishment knew no bounds. Mother did not want my blessing upon her confinements but merely wished me to be a nice little girl and not put on airs. Nobody wanted me to explain things to them; they all seemed to know enough.

And then, for the first time, I learned that I had an "unfortunate disposition." And for the next fifteen years I and my unfortunate disposition ran the gauntlet together. No one loved the things I loved—they seemed silly. These things and I were misfits; my love for poetry, my idealistic tendencies, were all subjects of ridicule and "quixotic" was my mother's word for all my thoughts and aims. After the passing of those fifteen years, (in fact in less time, for here and there some one else turned up a little queer like myself) the term was changed, and instead of hearing of an "unfortunate disposition" I heard of "magnetism"—and later from artists and poets of "temperament."

Glorying in my responsibilities, believing in myself, and setting my face, almost unconsciously, toward my duty, (I know now that I did this) I made myself utterly obnoxious to the very people I most longed to serve, whose love I coveted beyond all things. I was just eleven, and the most absurd little creature ever born.

Father had opened an office in New Orleans and there the clan assembled. Once Grandma came down to be with mother in a confinement and have an eye on us, and we were much amused at her commentary on the fields of ripe cotton, which from the train window she could not see very clearly—"This pestiferous ox-eye daisy!" she said. "It has possession of the fields here, as with *Us*. *That* we may thank the Yankees for—ox-eye daisies were never known with *Us*, until the Yankees brought the seed down with their hay during the war!"

This fourth boy was a very delicate baby, the seventh child; and while the old lady was devotion itself in her care of him, carrying him for months on a pillow, she would apostrophize him in a manner far from flattering. "If you were the first child, and beautiful," she would say, "you would die; being the seventh child and as homely a child as I ever set my eyes upon, of course you will live."

My mother was very tender-hearted. She often had reduced us to tears long before we knew the meaning of "abolition" by a recital of her own conversion as a little girl to that unpopular policy. It seems that her Mammy, whom she adored, had one little boy—as bad a little black imp as ever grew up on a plantation. This little boy was exhorted and rebuked in season and out of season, he was thrashed with something heavier than a peach switch at the discretion of anybody and everybody, "to make him good"; but he remained a thing of evil, and the threats to sell him became finally a reality—he was pronounced incorrigible, and sold. Mother was looking out of the upper window, of the old home at Middleburg, Virginia, The Hill, as a strange white man, who was different from our own people, sat in a one-horse wagon at the door, and her Mammy's bad little black boy was ordered to scramble up to the seat beside him— then mother's ears were pierced by a terrifying scream, and her Mammy, her own Mammy, fell on her knees in the dust at the back door clinging to the wheels, praying aloud, dragged a little way in the dirt, raising herself and running, running, running, after the wagon way down the road, as the trader and the bad little black boy disappeared in the distance. Her own Mammy, whose hands comforted her in all of her troubles and whom now she could not comfort. All she could do was to promise her Mammy that when she was a big lady and everybody in the world had to mind her, she would never let little boys be taken away from their own mothers, never, never; and that when she was a rich big lady she would buy this bad little black boy back; and then she punctuated her promises with big kisses on her Mammy's tear-stained face.

When Lucy and I were little, mother often read us poetry. Tennyson's "May Queen," and later, "Enoch Arden." I seem to feel our small selves at her knee, and the horribly agreeable sensation of woe that crept over me and the lumps that rose in my throat; I would be compelled to cough frequently, and would justify myself for so doing by complaining of a slight cold; the lump would grow unbearable, pride still battling to keep it down, a terrible love for my mother and a desire to lay my head on her knee and howl because of all the misunderstanding and pain and religion and faith that was too much for my small nerves—then my little sister would suddenly burst into a loud boo-hoo, and I would follow suit, and as we all united in an orgy of lamentation mother would know that the reading had been instructive and enjoyable.

CHAPTER XXVII

OUR first regular schooling was in New Orleans. We attended a private school conducted by a Miss Atchinson in the basement of an Episcopal Church, quite near our home. Lucy and I were in the same classes; though I was fourteen months older it was she who had the master mind. I arrived (when I did arrive) by intuition; she, by reason. I achieved (if I did achieve) by luck, or bluff, or impulse; she, by concentration.

Miss Atchinson was a woman of good breeding but highly nervous, and very possibly addicted to the use of some stimulant. She had a great faculty for imparting knowledge and would never spare herself if results were probable; but with dull, indolent and unambitious pupils she was unmerciful; to say that she made no attempt to control her temper might be saying too much, but she did not control it. Her method of punishment was to use a leather strap on the hand of the culprit, and she sometimes went quite wild during this pastime.

She had a wiry little under-nourished body, a face in which anxiety and ill-health had chiselled many a line; her color was that of a chronic dyspeptic, and her hands and wrists were veinous, bony and very ugly. We understood that she had an invalid mother at home, and it was quite evident that the passion of her life and all the tenderness of which she was capable centered in a very pretty little niece, at school with us. This child also was highly temperamental, recited poetry in a very admirable manner, and balked at no thrill or gesture which the elocution teacher suggested. Breathlessly, the whole school listened when she declaimed and the glow of satisfaction on Miss Atchinson's face should have encouraged some of the other young ruffians with whom she had to deal to try to please her.

My little sister, "Our Third Girl," was unusually pretty and never much of a student. A mite of a child, at this time, she was an object of especial severity with the teacher. I shall tell of one episode, not to incriminate Miss Atchinson, but to show a side of my mother's character.

The little girl was kept in one afternoon and commanded to finish a piece of work; whatever it was, the child may have become nervous, and done less well than usual at that late hour of the afternoon, detained in the basement rooms alone with the teacher, always fagged out herself at the end of the day. Lucy and I had lingered as long as we dared, but when ordered away, had gone, leaving our little sister, with many misgivings, to her fate. About five o'clock after a two-hour seance, the sexton of the church, who had been gardening in the grounds, brought the child home to mother in his arms, in a fainting condition, her baby arm beaten with the leather strap to a bloody pulp. He had become alarmed, hearing Miss Atchinson's violent voice and finally interfered.

She followed him, suddenly sobered, and in a state of pathetic remorse and grief. The forbearance of my mother, who could have ruined this woman's business, made a deep impression on me. Mother removed our pretty sister from the school, as too young for such strenuous discipline, but left her older children, making no report on the matter, on condition that Miss Atchinson abolish physical correction in the school for all time.

We little know the sort of minds that take control of our children, and lasting injuries result from some such abuse. Episodes obscure and forgotten, to which may be traced distrusts and embarrassments of later years; idiosyncrasies of conduct which so puzzle those who love us. As George Eliot somewhere has said, these peculiarities of character are like the knots and excrescences on old trees, unbeautiful reminders of wounds received in youth.

CHAPTER XXVIII

IN New Orleans we had a large house with a side garden. There were live-oak trees, beautiful, gnarled and twisted, rich in their glossy foliage; there were fig-trees, lots of fig-trees and they were easy to climb and yielded their fruit to the touch of a child's hand. Lucy and I played housekeeping in them, or she would get astride a horizontal branch and go riding while I would recline gracefully in a crotch and beguile the time with recitations from Byron.

Japonicas, sweet-olive, jasmine and hibiscus bloomed for us there. Their perfume comes to me across the years. It was a dear garden to dream in. Lucy and I did not know that we were Poor Relations, in fact, as this was one of our spasmodic periods of good fortune, we were little Ladies Bountiful to other children whose mothers were not as gentle and whose gardens were not as large as ours. Mother always said that she had so many of her own, a half a dozen extra young ones made no difference.

In a remote corner of the garden was a latticed outhouse, possibly at some time used for fowls. Father had his empty bottles thrown into it and there we would sit by the hour on hot afternoons, enjoying the shade of the place and fascinated with the outlandish names printed on the bottle labels which we would spell in good-natured rivalry, imagining that we were learning foreign tongues. "Château-Y-Quem," "Liebfraumilch," "Curaçao," "Johannesberger Auslese," etc., and the warm sunshine sifting through the cracks in the roof flecked our pinafores with golden splotches.

It was in this edifice that we committed an unpardonable act of vandalism, cutting off a long loose lock of hair from the head of our brother Charlie. Mother loved curly hair, but as I explained to her, this was a vanity and Heaven gave her only straight-haired children for the discipline of her soul. She struggled to train one curl on the top of Charlie's head and called it "Charlie's roach," and it was Charlie's roach which Lucy and I amputated.

One afternoon a Mr. Christian, from Richmond, was shown by our father over the place; my sister and I in our retreat heard them coming, for we were engaged in the aforesaid pastime of "spelling bottles." "What have you here, Charlie, chickens?" asked the visitor. "One sort of chickens, our first and second girls," said father, as he opened the door and revealed his offspring and his bottles. "Hem! Pretty good showing in the way of bottles, Charlie." "Too good," father answered, with a little sigh. All of which seemed very stupid talk to us.

POOR RELATION

Tho' far more ostentatious in my religious observances than my brothers and sisters, I must admit that my mother's other children were not devoid of religious faith. "Our Oldest Son," even he of the lost roach, demonstrated this in a notable degree after mother had instructed him in the story of Shadrach, Meshach, and Abednego in the fiery furnace. Did he repudiate the story? Oh, no, he accepted it in unquestioning faith, and went at once "under the house" (houses in New Orleans are built up a few feet, a lattice concealing the vacant space beneath), and started a nice little blaze in an old watering-pot. As the house was of wood, and old, a perfect opportunity was offered for the demonstration of Divine Power. God saved us, too, for mother saw the curl of white smoke just in time. The noble child who had given this beautiful demonstration of faith, was spanked.

Upon frequent occasions Lucy and I were spanked. One day "Our Oldest Son" who was not very old, followed along to enjoy the diversion of listening through the keyhole to our loud lamentations. Mother marched us in and closed the door. After the entertainment, opening the door suddenly, she caught our loving brother with his face against the wall, a delicious expression of appreciation still upon his features. She took possession of him without ceremony and gave him a more personal knowledge of her disciplinary methods which suddenly turned for him from comedy to tragedy.

The difficulty of making my mother's children good, oppressed me. I was already good myself. Grandma and the grace of God had made me good long ago. I was determined to pass on to the others all I had received from God and Grandma and with the identical inflexions of voice I repeated my grandmother's axioms and precepts.

But witness what happened. Mother's children treated the young evangelist with scorn. The ethics of quiet Oakley did not apply to them. The prophet was without honor in his own country and among his own people.

I must have been insincere. I must have been priggish and hypocritical, for these were honest little children. Their resentment only convinced me of my own superiority, for now I was being persecuted and reviled for righteousness sake. So I just determined to keep it up and to insist, whether or no, upon bearing my mother's burdens for her, and thus fulfilling the Law of Christ.

No wonder I repelled my mother. Such a child would drive me to drink; turn my hair white in a single night like the prisoner of Chillon.

She said it would be better not to read the Bible at all, than to see myself like Joseph, with all my brothers and sisters bowing down before me. Why not? They bowed down before Joseph!

P O O R   R E L A T I O N

It was an intense disappointment that no one wished to be made good. I could not understand it. If those to whom I had been sent repudiated my teachings, I would see what could be accomplished in the way of sowing a few seeds by the wayside, though I could not actually go into the highways and hedges, not knowing where they were.

The board fence around our garden was thick and high as the walls are in English suburban towns—no inquisitive passer-by could get a glimpse of our tennis-court or flower border through the smallest crack; but a clear voice, raised to its highest note, could penetrate far beyond this fence, and who knew but that some virtuous thought might reach the attentive ear? So I would station myself close to the fence and there recite whole psalms and hymns and spiritual songs, firmly believing that some passing sinner would pause outside and that he would go on his way regenerate. Was not the Bible teaching clear on this point? Were we not told to go into the highways and hedges? Were we not told to entertain strangers? (No doubt they were vastly entertained!) Were we not told that the stone which the builders rejected would become the chief stone of the corner? What was the story of that rejected stone? Had it been thrown about under the feet of the builders, had no one recognized its value, had it been shoved and kicked about, in everyone's way during the construction?

Did it bear upon it, perhaps, a sculptured cherub, something like me? And then when the corner was to be finished, had a section been missing? Had all laid aside their work to search because the completion of the great whole could not take place until that bit was found? And then did someone see among the weeds and litter, the rejected and forgotten stone, and trying it, perhaps in idle experiment, find that it was the only one that could finish out the design?

So I haunted the fence, chanting the twenty-third psalm and other passages of the Bible and Prayer-Book, and I think with as true a missionary spirit as ever set an enthusiastic pioneer into the wilderness to preach the gospel.

Nobody understood why I did this, and I was ashamed to explain; Mother used to say, "There is that child plastered against that fence screeching psalms and hymns at the top of her voice—she has a very unfortunate disposition," and she would go about her business, shaking her pretty head, wondering what she had ever done to give birth to such a peculiar child and concluding that I resembled my father's family. But those unregenerate ones, going about their probably sinful business, had heard the clarion call to righteousness, *they knew;* they could have told mother a thing or two, I reckoned! And so the evangelist was pleased to look wise and self-satisfied and mysterious, having a nice little secret with God.

Servants hated me and gave all the tit-bits to

Lucy who had never heard of the Prisoner of Chillon. They went so far as to hold me and let her beat me, when mother was absent, a thing I found most surprising. Always, I reasoned, my sister's better nature would rebel against this thing. That nobleness which lies in other little girls, sleeping but never dead, would certainly arise in majesty in her to meet my own. It never did.

From Miss Atchinson's school we were sent to a school for older girls from which we were expelled. I have forgotten why. But as Grace Carter was expelled too, the authorities must have been in the wrong—for Grandma and mother both found Grace Carter always right.

CHAPTER XXIX

THESE first years in New Orleans appear to have been one of our intermittent attacks of prosperity, and one impression of them is that a great many men came to our house and that father's "stag dinners" were frequent.

The library was furnished in dark red leather and there were many books. It was a roomy, pleasant, free-and-easy loafing place, and a child could curl up in a big arm-chair with a volume of Scott or Dickens and forget the troubled world. Sometimes there was a close queer smell in it, an odor suggestive to me ever since of Confederate Veterans—of Cousin Fitz Lee, General Beauregard, our fat cousin Jim Tucker, Old General Jubal Early, and a Chaplain, Mr. Jones, and Governor Nicholls. Many of these old friends had young nephews or cousins in search of a job, and after each party a new man would be taken into father's office "to learn business."

Whenever there was a Confederate reunion, or any Confederate officers passed through New Orleans, father had a party. From the staircase we could get a peep into the dining room through the transom and great was our amazement at what we would see. Once Cousin Randolph

Tucker, who was a member of Congress, rose in his seat, stuffed all the table-napkins up under his waist-coat, building himself a huge stomach, and then proceeded to mimic a clergyman, who, it seems, had expressed himself as opposed to what he called Higher Criticism. "Folks what wanted to air they l'arnin' claimed the word 'soul' come from a Greek work, and also meant essence, an' this nonsense he could squelch from the Bible itself—essence was what you smell out of a smelling-bottle, and what sort o' teachin' did a sinner git from that?" And Cousin Ran, still imitating the preacher, then quoted passages from the Bible, substituting the word "smelling-bottle" for the word "soul"—"Why art thou so cast down, oh my smelling-bottle—and why art thou so disquieted within me?" and, "What shall it profit a man if he gain the whole world and lose his own smelling-bottle?"

That wise men can amuse themselves in so brainless a fashion, which intelligent children would despise, and which disgusts women of their own age and rank, did not impress me then—nor can I claim that the grand old passage of the Scripture lost in dignity or meaning from such attempts at wit. Yet I longed to see a smelling-bottle and to know what an essence might be, and for many days the words rang in my ears. "What shall a man give in exchange for his own smelling-bottle?"

On another occasion at a brilliant dinner party

Cousin Ran's star performance was as an Italian opera singer. He left the table and in the adjoining room pinned his coat tail back to represent what was called a swallow-tail, rumpled up his hair and returned, mimicking a grand opera singer whom he had recently seen in New York. His wife was Cousin Laura Powell, my mother's first cousin, a famous beauty, and the mother of children in whom her beauty and dignity were combined with their father's wit and brilliance. She seemed to enjoy her husband's buffoonery more than anyone else.

Cousin Mary Lee, the oldest daughter of General Robert E. Lee, enjoyed New Orleans life a[nd] made a round of visits there every winter. S[he] was a most extraordinary woman and will [be] remembered by many of my readers. She [re]sembled her father in appearance and would [have] been handsome as a man but as a woman she [was] homely and untidy, arbitrary and often merci[less]. She was a passionate hater of everything N[orth]ern and to her death an unreconstructed rebe[l].

The men of the Lee family have followed [the] example of General Lee, been faithful and l[oyal] citizens of the United States, and served t[heir] country to the extent of their ability as pro[fes]sional men or private gentlemen, but the wom[en] have shown animosity toward the Federal Go[v]ernment which neither time nor argument coul[d] alleviate. They have been as arrogant as the men were modest. The bitterest expressions that I have ever heard have fallen from the lips of Cousin Mary Lee, and yet there was never a question raised during her long life as to her exalted and authoritative position.

It was her custom when travelling abroad, and she was a great globe trotter, to notify consulates and embassies, principalities and powers, that she was coming, and when she arrived she rarely failed to receive the attentions which she considered were her due. The story was told of her that on a visit to Wiesbaden or Weimar, or one of the smaller German principalities, no invitation was sent her for a court function and she expressed herself very roundly on the subject, that the daughter of the greatest military genius of the nineteenth century had been unwarrantably neglected. Within a few hours, the story ran, a messenger approached, bowing at every step, and bringing to Miss Mary Lee an official invitation addressed, "Miss Grant."

General Kitchener was her devoted and lifelong friend. On one occasion at Constantinople, Cousin Mary Lee, rather shabby and unattractive, insisted on joining an excursion to Egypt which had been arranged by persons who did not know her and excused themselves from including her in the party. A telegram from her to General Kitchener was answered by a special vessel sent to Constantinople for her at his orders. Unbounded astonishment was occasioned in the minds of those to whom her company had been unwelcome. "What in the world is she—merely the daughter of a defeated General—that General Kitchener should take such notice of her?" A brilliant woman of New Orleans, a woman of exquisite beauty and national distinction, replied, "That is the reason; she *is* the daughter of that defeated General."

On her visits in New Orleans cousin Mary honored my father's house for weeks and weeks, her presence greatly flattering to him as a Confederate soldier, but rather difficult to mother who found that cousin Mary's arbitrary ways and luxurious and irregular habits made the household arrangements difficult. The entertaining necessary for so distinguished a guest and the numerous calls to be received, added quite a little to mother's responsibilities. She was very fond of father and recommended to him several young men to be taken into his office to learn business.

At a luncheon in Washington, many, many years later, I sat next to Cousin Mary Lee. She made it a rule never to attend a luncheon that was not given in her own honor and she was not partial ever to entertainments for ladies only. The masculine quality of her own mind interested men who always paid her great attention and for whom she openly showed a preference. She was apt to be cross at women's luncheons and on this particular occasion, when I sat next to her, she was very cross to me.

"May," she said, eyeing me very severely, "I

understand that you are an active Suffragette. What would your father think of that?"

"Well," I said, "my father must know that I did a man's work in providing for his large family after he was gone and perhaps he would approve of my having a man's opportunity and recognition."

"Well," said Cousin Mary, folding her hands upon her large stomach and leaning back in her chair, "I think that it is ridiculous. My own experience has been that a woman, if she is reasonably attractive, can get everything she wants from men without a vote."

Another cousin of mother's, a frequent guest at my father's house in New Orleans, was Cousin Kinloch Fauntleroy. He lived somewhere "up the river"; and the river being the Mississippi that is an indefinite address.

Cousin Kinloch was a Methodist minister and was said to have been the ugliest man in the Confederate Army. I could not see that he was ugly at all. I would have loved to be "ugly" in just the same way. He was very tall, and mother said that in spite of his freckles and being so cross-eyed, she would know him for a gentleman in the desert of Sahara.

Cousin Kinloch stammered in a most fascinating way. It was terrifying too, to us children, for it seemed as though he would die in agony over each word; it could only be compared to having the whooping cough for life. Yet when he conducted family prayers for us, as he did on mother's invitation whenever he stopped over with us, he never used the book but poured forth a torrent of eloquence from which every trace of his impediment had vanished, and held me spellbound with his beautiful rhetoric and saintly fervor. It was a privilege to be God's child and Cousin Kinloch's cousin, and very wonderful were the feelings that possessed me at such times.

With Cousin Fitz Lee and some other chosen spirits (spirits is good), father sometimes went on a spree to New York, and there in the Opera House on one occasion he met the Yankee surgeon who had saved his life after Appomattox. He had often tried without success to find and thank him. The announcement having been in the papers that a party of Confederate Veterans would occupy a box at the opera, this Doctor Carter recognized my father's unusual name, and presented himself between acts, asking for Major Minnigerode. Father at once arose—"That is my name, Sir——"

"I think I had the honor of carving a minnie-ball out of you, Sir, after the battle of Appomattox——"

"You did, Sir—and here it is," said father, reaching into the pocket of his dress-suit, and producing the talisman. Naturally there was some fun after this encounter.

There was much hilarity on slight provocation, and mother was always very solicitous before a party and very tender with him after one. The Lost Cause lost a good deal of its Romance upon close observation of these ex-heroes.

CHAPTER XXX

MAY of each year would find us all en route for Virginia, and until November, we would stay at Oatlands,* near Leesburg, as guests of Uncle George and Aunt Kate Carter. These journeys were wonderful; there were no Confederate Veterans, and no anxieties. We had enormous baskets of lunch to last three days, and we had cards and paper-dolls and books; porters and conductors were kind for father was a liberal tipper; fellow-travellers were patient when babies cried; we had the drawing-room where the little ones could nap; stars shone into the upper berths at night, and flaring pictures with lurid lights marked the stops along the way. By day the world unrolled itself to greedy eyes at the window, bayous and palmetto and hibiscus and alligator changed to mountains and mighty pine-trees, or to endless fields of cotton. This was the way to study geography, as my own babies remarked long years after, in their annual European wanderings.

It was at Oatlands that that memorable corre-

*Oatlands was bought in 1902 by Mr. and Mrs. William Corcoran Eustis, from Mr. Stilson Hutchins, to whom my uncle sold it some years earlier. Its present owners have cared for the place most beautifully, making necessary restorations without radical alterations, till house and garden have regained all the charm which had been sacrificed to war and change. It is one of the greatest houses of Virginia.

spondence had taken place between my father-to-be and my grandmother. It was at Oatlands that I had overheard my dear black Martha murmur mysteriously to the gardener. Two of my mother's babies had been born there, Lucy and Fitzhugh Lee. To Oatlands were welcomed at all times, all who were troubled.

The original tract was a royal grant to Uncle George's ancestors, and the building is a fine example of the Georgian Manor House. It was built about 1800, Robert Carter being his own architect and contractor as Thomas Jefferson was at Monticello, making his own bricks which were laid by his own slaves. In Uncle George's day its high stone porch and spacious halls were over-run with the children of his wife's relations—especially ourselves.

How we romped among its priceless heirlooms! Portraits of long dead Carters and Randolphs, Willises and Taskers looking down upon us from the walls. Old India and Canton and Minton china rattled in cupboards to the accompaniment of our wild feet. Books and prints of which none of us knew the value, lying open to our iconoclastic touch. On rainy days we overhauled portfolios containing Boydell's engravings of Shakespeare, Nash's "Historic Homes of England," Hogarth's "Rake's Progress" and other true Museum pieces, leaving them scattered over the floor of the octagon drawing-room for Aunt

Katie to pick up. We scrambled into four-poster beds at night, in the early morning figuring out the elaborate carving of the bed-posts until it was time to rise. We ransacked the mysterious attic, trying to force each other through the round cat-holes in the doors, pulling old finery out of the musty chests, frocks, cloaks, linen and brocade falling almost to pieces, but of exquisite design. Anywhere but in Virginia such bits for the sake of their color and patterns would be in Museums—the Kensington Museum in London is full of just such fragments framed in narrow frames, under glass and hung along the stairways. There students of design are to be seen making faithful and affectionate reproductions of the patterns, which reappear in the tapestry or wall-paper, the brocade or chintz, of a later generation.

We read old letters, far too sacred for us to have touched, going into paroxysms of laughter over the stately and formal phrases. Once mother ran her hand way back into the pigeonhole of a desk in daily use, and brought forth a little package wrapped in crumbling brown paper; it contained a seal ring of rare workmanship, which no one within the memory of the household had ever seen, and on a tiny slip of paper, written in the fine old-fashioned script, "Wear this for the sake of one who loves you, but whose name you will never know." So one of those Mister Carters, reposing in the vault down in the garden, had been the hero of a mysterious romance!

Oatlands, Loudoun County, Virginia, a Carter Estate.

OATLANDS

The books at Oatlands were truly burdensome. The family were not great readers, as at Oakley, and there was little use made of the thousands of inherited volumes. Old calf-bound books into which no eye had glanced for many a year were taken indiscriminately to the attic, and tumbled there a prey to rats and mice. So little did we know their value that often we children tore out the title page in sheer idleness.

A few years before her death, Aunt Kate gave me two folio volumes of Josephus, published in 1795, in Baltimore by Pechin and Co., the inside of the calf-skin covers marked by a slip, "Case Shelf — 3 — 3 — Robert Carter"—I value them greatly. In sending them to me by express she also put in a nice fat turkey, omitting, however, to wrap him up, so that the two big books, lying heavily upon him, crushed his breast-bone quite out of line, thereby offending the cook whose duty it was to restore him to something of his pristine symmetry and prepare him for the table.

Another wonderful volume which I bear in mind was a massive Bible, which three of us children could barely lift. It was like a little trunk, with its wooden back covered with calf skin and its queer clasps. If my memory does not trick me, it was printed by Queen Elizabeth's printer, Christopher Barker, and it may have been one of those rare volumes which I came later to hear of as the "Wicked Bible" because of the omission in the Seventh Commandment of the word "not," by reason of which it reads "Thou shalt commit adultery." The luckless printers, Barker and Lucas, were heavily fined for their typographical error, in 1632. This treasure was presented to Mrs. Phoebe A. Hearst by my Aunt Katie, who had in her a generous and devoted friend.

These volumes had belonged to Uncle George's wonderful grandfather, known as Councillor Carter. He owned many acres of land and hundreds of slaves, and with the foresight of George Washington, Thomas Jefferson, George Mason and William Fitzhugh, and many of the most thoughtful land-owners of earlier times, had registered in his will his protest against the institution of human slavery, setting free upon certain conditions, many of his slaves. If I remember correctly, every able-bodied male coming of age was to be given a wife, three acres of ground and $100.00, with his own liberty. Economic conditions made it necessary for his descendants to restock their plantations with slaves, no other labor being available.

It is obvious that the emancipation of the slaves and the collapse of our whole social system after the Civil War, the depletion in men, the wreckage in buildings and forests, the years of neglect of agriculture, the penniless condition of the best element among us, and their unfitness for manual labor, would mean ruin for a long time.

Uncle George and Aunt Kate remained in the same great house after the war, every day as it dawned calling upon them to lead a forlorn hope; sixty helpless negroes came back at one time, after having run away with the Yankees, and settled down again at Oatlands, living on Uncle George, raising enormous families, working or not working as they pleased, that being their understanding of "freedom." One old fellow, dying in Washington, bequeathed his remains to Uncle George, who borrowed money to go for the body and brought it to Oatlands for burial. To this day their descendants live on the place, to the third and fourth generation.

We children stuffed our stomachs full of grapes and peaches, wandering unchidden through terraced garden, generous orchard and stately grove. We dearly loved the colored children, and tyrannized over them without mercy.

Those who could swallow the warm milk, as I could, went to the cow-pen, (pronounced "cuppen"), at milking time, and drank the foaming fluid, blood-warm, as my children since have drunk the goats' milk in Switzerland. No wonder there was little need for doctors or for what we called "physick."

In November we organized a regular Union against the turkeys, as rivalry was keen in the matter of chestnuts. Grace and I were the ringleaders, we would get up long before day, October and November mornings when the air is quite nippy, and hie us to the trees, sitting down with our backs against the giant trunks and waiting there until it was light enough to see to pick up the nuts. We were armed to the teeth against our enemies, the turkeys, and no sooner did their confidential gobble-gobble-gobble fall upon our ears, than we fell upon them and routed them gloriously from the field.

The history of Aunt Katie's life, spent in the community which she entered as a black-eyed bride, is one of fortitude and charity. The war changed conditions immediately, leaving her young and not very experienced, to solve tremendous problems. Oatlands with its immense acreage, its swarm of ignorant and dependent negroes, suddenly emancipated but homeless and positively refusing to leave the place, fell to her management.

Uncle George had not only the kindest heart in the world but the sort of training that unfits a man for effort or to assume responsibility; and woman-like, she tried to spare him. Neither of them could be harsh or exacting with their fellowmen; their first thought always was *not* to take advantage of the other side in any sort of transaction, and consequently they suffered on all sides from the time-serving employees and inefficient labor.

Aunt Kate was a genius in the extraordinary

direction of justifying any rascality practiced against herself and of finding excuses for the wrongdoing of others. Her charity covered the errors of the selfish and frivolous as it forgave the sins of the ignorant and vicious.

Brilliant and distinguished visitors were constantly there. Her less fortunate relatives made the place their home; there were additional houses on the place, permanent homes for such as were in need, for the big house over-flowed. There was always room for one more, by the fire or at the table. As the years passed and her beautiful head whitened, difficulties increased, and few of those whom she had so faithfully served were able to come to the rescue. The burden of the great place wore upon her, until they sold it at a sacrifice, settling down with the most adorable simplicity to live on a smaller scale in one of their pretty cottages of gray stone on the premises. To this a wing was added, and the Lords and Ladies portrayed by Reynolds and Copley and other masters, gazed in undiminished dignity from the humbler walls. I copied for her the Reynolds portrait of Councillor Carter, when she sold the original to Mrs. Phoebe A. Hearst.

To her there, as in the big house, came all the troubled of the countryside; for them she was wise, economical, shrewd, far-seeing; but for herself, never. She was judge and jury, doctor and accoucheuse, banker and peacemaker; she was adored and robbed, she was the good angel and the victim. While her feet were in the turkey-pen or garden, her thoughts were in the clouds.

She lived like a chapter in the New Testament—the utterly impracticable, impossible New Testament. She *did* it—lived it—the life we others read about—the life of the Sermon on the Mount and the XII chapter of St. Paul's Epistle to the Romans. She was the man of the New Testament, who, compelled to go the one mile, bearing the burden of the stranger, as was customary in the East, voluntarily went the other mile, doing always more than was asked of her or could have been required; loving others always better than she ever loved herself.

CHAPTER XXXI

OUR Cousin Grace went back to New Orleans with us, to go to school. She was two years my senior and her proficiency in all things domestic was the bane of my existence. When anybody was going to have a baby—as some one always was—lo and behold!—Grace knitted an afghan or crocheted a sack for the newcomer, and thus her praises were sung by a grateful and admiring chorus.

She made muffins that were marvelous and preserves that were miracles. Goaded by the hymns of praise in her honor, and green with envy, I attempted once to make some cucumber pickles. I peeled my cucumbers and cut my fingers. I set the sliced fruit in alum overnight and stung the wounds I had made. Next day I scalded myself horribly while cooking the stuff. When it was done it was lovely. The color was good, the slices of lemon showed so prettily against the dark green—I kept the jar on my mantelpiece for fear some one would steal it before Grandma could see that I, May, had really made some pickle, and caressing it early one morning as the product of my own culinary genius and a thing to be loved, I dropped the jar on the hearth. I was as Rachel weeping for her offspring, and would not be comforted after this tragedy.

Perhaps because she had been unaccustomed to much money, perhaps because she had grown up among inherited heirlooms and had had no opportunity to select her furnishings, mother had no artistic taste and no bargaining instinct, and when she bought things they were not well-chosen. Her selections of bric-à-brac were, as I recall them, dreadful, and her clothes were only redeemed by her own prettiness. She loved color, and one electric blue satin dress was very vivid. She wore with it a white poke bonnet with a long pale blue feather and lace strings tied under her pink chin, and we knew no one ever was so beautiful. Dear, straight-forward little mother!

She never bothered with metaphysical questions—on one occasion when Aunt Ida, discussing a book called somebody's "Physiology of the Mind," observed that the subtlety of the distinction between right and wrong was so deceptive one could really not distinguish 'tother from which, mother instantly responded—"Then I'll tell you how, sister, when the difference is as subtle as that, just do what is disagreeable and that will be right." A thousand times in my life this simple statement has held me true.

In this direct fashion she decided that when Lucy and I were about ten and eleven years old she would put us into corsets and have us confirmed. "The girls," she said to father, "had

better have corsets this spring and be confirmed."
There was no discussion of the matter whatever.
We felt consequential as regarded the corsets and
the confirmation assumed in my eyes a rather
tender significance owing to the fact that Willy
Callahan, a boy attending Miss Atchinson's
school, would be confirmed at the same time,
and I liked him, notwithstanding his freckles.

Yes, I liked him long before that auspicious
evening when he and another youngster called on
us—our first visit from boys, an event which
plunged us into great excitement. It was Saturday, and we children entirely unsuspecting of such
distinction, were amusing ourselves when the doorbell rang and these two swains appeared. Lucy,
for once in her life, paid tribute to my fourteen
months seniority, and rushed madly over the house,
screaming, "Boys! Boys! Boys to see Mamie!"

In view of the fact that this Willy Callahan
was to be confirmed, I found my mother's suggestion very agreeable. I would be confirmed. I
supposed the thrill that the thought gave me was
piety. I certainly was not able to analyze my
own sensations, but they were distinctly agreeable, though vaguely disconcerting. After we
were confirmed it struck me that Willy Callahan
might go into father's office and learn business.

Willy Callahan certainly became entangled
with my religion, in spite of my efforts to disassociate the subjects. He would not stay out—
and then I remembered the little girl at Oakley,

who was man-crazy. She had been about my present age. The empty baby carriage that she trundled up and down the road—the contempt people had for her——

Oh, but this was a funny world! Everything seemed so mixed up—men and religion—baby carriages. Out of the air came to me black Martha's voice at the vault—and now I would not repeat to myself the thing I had heard her say.

So this thing was running all through the world—rawboned black servant maids and negro gardeners—lonely little girls with empty baby carriages—the photograph of my beautiful Cousin Rozier with two Mormon ladies in his lap—and the expression of Grandma's face. My mother and her seven children—Willy Callahan's freckles, and the confirmation class—the corsets our mother bought us, and the boys who came to see us. What could it be?

About the same time that mother decided to put corsets on us and have us confirmed she concluded that we had talents. She selected music to be my sister's talent and art to be mine. I had always scribbled, as children do, and at Oakley had attempted to illustrate the whole Bible, making Nativities and Crucifixions of true pre-Raphaelite type. These talents having been assigned to us, we must cultivate them; we could not bury them in a napkin—(oh, the joy of hearing a Biblical phrase!)

POOR RELATION

So Lucy had piano lessons from Aunt Imogene, who was the wife of our Uncle Willy (Father had brought Uncle Willy to New Orleans to go into his office, but not exactly to learn business) and I was entered for drawing lessons from the local painter, Mr. Molinari, and the sculptor, Mr. Perelli. Mr. Molinari was florid and fat with dark eyes and long black hair. Mr. Perelli was old and sallow. They set me to draw an ear from Michelangelo's David and kept me on it until I hated Michelangelo and David and Molinari and Perelli. I wore the paper out in the shadows, stumping things in that Mr. Perelli told me to do, and rubbing them out as Mr. Molinari commanded. I sassed them now and then and they wrote notes to Mother and I was made to apologize.

Making apologies was a regular business. My tongue, so long under restraint at Oakley, broke all bonds, involving me in endless complications.

Most of my apologies were to my Aunt Imogene. She was our Sunday School teacher, but what in Heaven's name could anybody teach me along that line? She always selected me to recite that most intricate and unnecessary explanation of the Lord's prayer, beginning, "I desire." She would put her little head on one side and look at me and begin; "My good child, know this: thou art not able to do these things of thyself," and I, weary of the foolish words and anxious to show off before the class, would tell her the prayer required no explanation and was easier to understand than the explanation given in the catechism.

I loved to shock her. I applied my own reasoning faculties to the story of Moses, Miriam and Aaron, and insinuated that God had been unjust in striking Miriam with leprosy just because she objected to Moses having married an Ethiopian lady. How would Aunt Imogene like it if her brother did the same thing? But her brother, she would say with the greatest earnestness, was Mr. Gordon of Lynchburg. He couldn't marry an Ethiopian. In his case it would be a horrible misalliance. But racial and geographical conditions made it very different with Moses.

And having delivered myself of this ugly talk I would go home with a heavy heart, to prepare the phrases for the inevitable apology.

Aunt Imogene naturally came fluttering in to Mother like a disturbed little thrush, wondering what in the world she could ever do with me? I knew. A taste of my old friend, the peach switch, would have been the thing.

And then when I had the measles, this dear mistreated lady exposed herself to the contagious disease for my sake, sat by my bed, wrote for me the poems I composed, and broke down forever all my resentment and insolence by her heroic devotion.

CHAPTER XXXII

BENNY COOPER was a playmate of ours at school; and I, who never knew how to play properly, shoved him one day against the stuccoed wall of the church in which our school was located and cut his lip open. It was an ugly wound from the sharp angle of the wall, blood was all mixed with sand from the stucco and I was terribly distressed. I knew no peace, and gave my mother none, until she furnished me a bowl of jelly to take to my victim. Along the way to his house I cogitated as to how I should address Benny's august, and I feared infuriated, mother; finally deciding that when she entered the room, I would say,"Mrs. Cooper, I presume?" I drilled myself faithfully in this courteous salutation, yet almost choked and died over it when a majestic female loomed before me in the darkened house. I see her quite distinctly. She assumed colossal proportions to my feverish mind. A face like a horse, untidy hair, and a tall figure clothed in a gray calico wrapper. I made the obeisance which seemed appropriate, as low and respectful as the bowl of tremulous jelly, in my equally tremulous hands, permitted and through chattering teeth forced the phrase —"Mrs. C-C-Coo-per—ah—I p-p-pre-sume?" The superior female admitted that she was Mrs. Cooper; my deferential manner seemed to mollify, if not to amuse, her; she was forgiving and hospitable; upon delicate inquiry on my part, she vouchsafed that, as I feared, the Doctor's bills would be very large; and it was apparent that the resources of the household were modest; this was one of the times in my life when I longed for a little money of my own. I had incurred a debt, for it was truly an obligation, and these poor people were to suffer because I was clumsy.

An incident of our school life while Grace was with us will demonstrate my mother's conception of the courtesy due a guest. Each day when we returned from school, Grace and my sister and I put our books away in a little closet under the stairway. One day Grace discovered her penhandle crushed in the door of the closet which had been slammed upon it and she reported to mother that I had broken her pen. I held out stoutly that I was not guilty, and I was not; but mother only taxed me with an additional fault in contradicting a guest, stating that it was impossible for Grace to be mistaken in her assertions, and ordered me to apologize. This I flatly refused to do.

This occurred at three o'clock, just after our return from school, and I thought the incident closed until I realized at dinner that mother was not speaking to me; nervous attempts on my part to be recognized in the conversation, failed utterly, and the weight of her displeasure lay heavy upon my soul—and appetite. Nothing is so contagious as unpopularity. I have often noticed with a sickening soul how we resemble barn-yard fowls which attack any one of their number already sick or bruised or bleeding. All that evening I wandered miserably about doing battle in my obstinate heart for my small rights. The next morning at breakfast I perceived myself under a boycott—but dragged forlornly to school.

Returning much cheered after a successful day, I tried to kiss mother, having for the moment forgotten the boycott; ignominiously I failed to accomplish this affectionate purpose—and another wretched evening followed. On the third day my pride was completely broken—my truth and honor forfeited to my need of comfort and companionship—gregarious little animal.

Passionately I threw myself upon my mother, lying glibly; admitted guilt, deplored my miserable hypocrisy, apologized to everybody and begged everybody to love me, in spite of my unfortunate disposition and all.

My mother was grieved not only at what seemed to her a rudeness to a guest, and lack of courage in the first place, but hard-headed persistence in a falsehood, and it was with an anxious face that she talked the matter over with me, urging me to more honorable conduct—and the touch of her, and the sweetness of her, paid me

well for the wrong I did to my immortal soul—
so love lures us to a lie.

A child cannot live but under its mother's smile and there have been times with all of us when a kiss in the present was more to be desired than endless æons of blissful eternity. And yet these small injustices do tear down character.

Our Cousin Grace as a knitter of sacks and afghans for all the family babies was not only popular but very wise regarding the interesting processes by which the small wearers of these creations were brought into existence. She was two years older than I and a girl of so much character and sense that we would never have dared approach her with questions which were beginning to torment ourselves.

Providence sent us a friend for our enlightenment—a handsome and precocious girl with whom we were at school. She may not have been pure-minded—neither were we, if natural curiosity as to the initial processes is to be considered impurity. Our family was still increasing and we had but the vaguest and most uncomfortable comprehension of the whys and hows. We had been hardened to complaint and criticisms from mother's friends, who regretted her increasing cares more than they feared sharing her responsibilities, which, when the necessity arose they did share lovingly.

This girl—her name was Ella—undertook our

initiation in a manner far from delicate but as we had a burning desire to know the facts, and no grown-up would tell us, we accepted Ella's version, coarse and cruel as it was, and envied her her omniscience and her acquaintance with communicative chambermaids.

Mother's trusty maid found us closeted in conference, Ella expounding to Lucy and me for the hundredth time, matters which it appeared "were none of our business." That is what mother said when we were dragged into her presence. She blushed furiously during her scathing rebuke of us, and then I as the older mustered up my courage—"Mother, we will promise you never to ask anybody, or read the Old Testament, or hunt up words in the dictionary, if you, yourself, will just tell us—just tell us once, Mother—now—if what Ella says is true. Is it true?" Dear mother; she sent us away unsatisfied and crestfallen and ashamed. Grown-ups, then, it seemed, knew and did things they were ashamed of, and we who had travelled at their bidding from some strange world invisible and inapprehensible, to this, were not to know the road we had travelled!

We shook our little blond pig-tails sadly, avoided Ella as if she were a pestilence, and I resolved that when I got some little girls I should tell them all I knew, and never let life frighten or torture them with its impulses and terrors and vague joy and sorrows.

In the nasturtium, in the wren's nest, in the

baby pony, my little ones have read the story. A pony is rare and precious, harder to get, more valuable when got, than a baby robin. It is not to be trusted in a thin shell, as a little chicken is; the chicken-mother can have a baby nearly every day; if she loses one or two of her brood, she still has a dozen to love; but the pony-mother lived through almost a year of patient waiting, and carried her baby with her till it could stagger after her on its own uncertain legs. When she was carrying it we did not drive her hard, or let her trot uphill; she gave her strength to her baby, and fed it when it came; it could not scratch for its dinner as a little chicken can—and so my small son and daughter learned this fairy-tale of life and love—the boy, with excellent sense, remarking that it was a good thing that the lady-mother could carry her baby where her own arms could shield it, and her watchful eyes see whatever might come near—how awful it would have been if she had been obliged to have it on her back—wouldn't her head be always turned, to see if anything was following her to hurt it? Wasn't it safe under her heart, so helpless itself? Yes, God had been very sensible in making these arrangements.

Butterflies, in the very act of mating, were brought to me one summer day, by my babies. No, not twins, not a freak, not a double butterfly—see, the body of this one is broad, there is room for the eggs—and this one is the father-butterfly, for everything, even maple trees, have fathers—and because this father-butterfly has found his little mate, and can give her the germ that will make her little eggs alive in her, good children will have butterflies to run after on summer days! And, of course, a word in season on behalf of the much mistreated caterpillar was here found appropriate.

In these revelations the purpose was to save the children from their own blind instincts, to give dignity to a dangerous theme, to present sex-love to the mind as a sacrament, not a self-indulgence, to spare perplexity, when the imperative summons comes.

A woman's happiness and usefulness depend largely upon her sex life, these facts should be clear while still impersonal, before the dawn even of curiosity; once instinct has spoken, the child dare not ask, the parent is apt to be reserved—then on one flounders, sometimes to disaster.

We coach our girls most carefully in the niceties of etiquette, the proprieties of dress, the doctrines of religion; but remain absolutely silent on the great subject—man.

It was as I lay hid in the bathroom after this foolish humiliation, with my head stuck into the space between the laundry basket and the bath tub (a favorite place for the working off of ill humors) sobbing myself sick with chagrin and disgust, that Mammy found me. She came to find. Her heavy black hand roused me. "Honey," she said, "Don's you carry on like dat. 'Tain't nothin' but natur! All chillen is et up wid curosserty. Only you mustn't go to peramberlatin' an' identifyin' 'bout sich matters yet a while. Some day you gwine marry some nice white gentman an' fin' out all dem indentifications. But you musn't worry yo' Mummer; now—get up—go on, wash yo' face—jes' like Mammy tel you."

So Ella taught us about babies and Mammy taught us about nature.

CHAPTER XXXIII

THE story of our life in New Orleans would be incomplete without a mention of Mammy and Old Fannie. Old Fannie was our cook and a very picturesque personality. She weighed about two hundred pounds, was a light mulatto, with a broad, friendly face and the merest excuse for a nose. When we came home from school Fannie feasted us, and as many other children as we pleased to bring with us, on hot biscuits and slow black molasses. We would sit in the sun in the back-yard or on the cellar door, each holding in his lap a plate swimming in that delicious treacherous molasses. Fannie was addicted to several weaknesses of the flesh, if tradition is not misleading, and of one of these I may speak without offending the decency of the most scrupulous. It is queer that we differentiate in the discussion of crude human appetites, the sins of gluttony and drunkenness being permissible subjects of conversation, and in Fannie's case, even choice topics, because when drunk she was so screamingly funny; but of her original views as to the conduct of life nothing definite was ever mentioned, mere hints and innuendoes furnishing us food for speculation, until having arrived ourselves at years of indiscretion we pieced two and two together and figured out the numerous romances in the life of Old Fannie.

She took father's WHISKY—(can you believe it?) when his back was turned, and replaced the liberal potation with water; but as two things which he disliked extremely were a full decanter and an empty decanter he rarely missed that which Old Fannie had purloined. When unduly exhilarated Old Fannie would crawl under the house and sing hymns and later if the yard were full of children, she would delight us by jumping over the tennis-net, a good jump for two hundred pounds. Mother cast a disapproving eye on Fannie's other acrobatic exercises and we were told that if we wanted "to see Old Fannie be funny," we must insist upon her jumping over the tennis-net, and omit other features on her programme.

I had an especial tenderness for her because she never held me in mother's absence for my sister to wallop, and often invited me into the kitchen. Others she drove from the door of that Shekina with wrath and contumely, but now and then extended to me the hospitality we coveted. Once I attempted to make a sponge-cake under her critical eye. The result was very serious for the cake was a failure and she shook her big head over it. Old Fannie murmured, "Et teks a pure heart to mek a spownge-cake; no pusson ain't got a pure heart can't mek a spownge-cake." The failure was humiliating but the cause of the failure was devastating. Yet it would always crop up and do harm—waste good material—disappoint reasonable hopes—injure other people, this thing of not having a pure heart. And how could people help it if they did not have a pure heart? And Old Fannie took on an added dearness in my eyes, in spite of the whisperings as to her Cave-man ethics—for the proof was there—she could make sponge-cake!

As our fortunes failed Old Fannie stood staunch, reducing her own wages, stretching the food by means miraculous, and augmenting the work she was employed to do by much that was not expected of her.

Faithful and funny—with an adage or a charm or a "conjure" for any situation. Mother's headaches were due to the fact that she threw the combings of her chestnut hair out of the window, and the birds immediately pounced upon them as dear soft linings for their nests. For every hair used in this way, a headache! Black cats had caused many of the disasters of history.

Why we called her Old Fannie I cannot say. With the eternal youthfulness of such as acknowledge no moral code and are spared the tragic conflict between the law of the flesh and the law of the spirit, and who, devoid of the sense of responsibility which burdens others, never age, Old Fannie remained perpetually young. She looked about thirty, but there was her son, Myjim—Myjim himself was thirty. His mother must be fourteen years older. There was also a person of indefinite status known in our kitchen as Mister Fannie. Mister Fannie was the cause of no small controversy between Old Fannie and our Mammy.

Fragments of animated dialogue that moved rhythmically from cordiality to asperity and from asperity to vituperation were wafted out into the balmy air of the garden, even penetrating the little bottle-house, where my sister and I would pause in the spelling of long foreign labels to prick up our ears and listen.

Old Fannie perhaps recounting the sufferings of Myjim, who was afflicted with a strange disease called "the stretches"; he could only lie in the bed and yawn and stretch; he suffered no pain whatever, except distress at the thought that his mother could not afford this expensive malady, and worked for all her family; Myjim's appetite was good, and he mos' in gen'ral enj'yed a seegar.

Some demurrer on Mammy's part might here have evoked a more explicit diagnosis of the case; for Old Fannie would continue the tale of Myjim's woes, with the account of how his wife had conjured him—grounded up the dry skin of a snake, she did—mixed it with his vittles—somethin' been a goin' up an' down in him ever sence—inside o' Myjim's insides. 'Co'se he done seen a doctor. All sorts doctors. The Yarb-doctor (herb-doctor) hissef say som'in' sutney is inside o' Myjim—he didn't say jes' what.

Mammy, ironing the baby's diapers, would intimate that it might have been better if Myjim had never been borned; Old Fannie had had no business whatsoever having Myjim; she ought o' knowed that her own self. And then Old Fannie would call Mammy an old maid. And Mammy, so black she might have spit ink, comfortably fat and immaculately neat, would make what was if not strictly a threatening gesture, one that was impressive and oracular—"Ole maid? Ole maid? Thank you, ma'am—thank you. I iz. I iz. I tell you I *iz* a ole maid. Dat name's mah glory's crown. 'Ooman, deys all sorts ole maids—my kind an' yo' kind. Dey is Gawd-fearin', selb-respeckin' old maids, an' other kinds I ain't a-specifin', dem kinds as is hair-hung an' breeze-shooken over Hell. The Lord he loves ole maids lak me. You know 'bout dem wise virgins. Well, I done said mah say." And she would sweep from the kitchen with the diapers ironed and in a great pack under her arm, muttering about folkses what got white an' yaller an' black back of 'em, an' who-all's mothers mus' 'a' flew de coop——

Mammy was a genuine aristocrat. In her old age she struggled hard with a spelling-book we had thrown away, trying to learn how to read her Bible. She was a Baptist, though brought up by Episcopalians—her "call," she said, "Was to go into the water, and she found her Jesus in '59."

When we children asked her why she had not gone to school as a little girl, she shook her head and said it wasn't fittin' in dem days for a slave-child to go to school; that when she had begged her ole mistress to let her learn to read, she had been told that it was against the laws of "Vaginia"—but that at the same time her ole mistress had told her to look the world in the face and try to do her duty, and never to tell a lie, and that if she could remember those things to do them she would never lack for friends. And suddenly springing to her feet, both hands extended over her head in a passionate gesture like some priestess of the jungle, she would exclaim, "An' *dis day!* Dem words is true! An' *dis day!* I praises an' blesses them remains (meaning the memory of her mistress) what iz but dus' an' ashes!"

Very big-eyed and quiet, we sat listening, thrilled by these recitals. Mammy had been sold twice. Once to a gentleman, once to a trader. The latter, as she stood upon the block in the public market, ordered her stripped, that he might observe whether or no she showed the tell-tale marks of beatings—thus depreciating her value.

"An' there I stood," she told us for the hundredth time, "fair as a lily and brown as a berry," and after his inspection the slave trader remarked that she must be a damn good nigger or have had damn good masters—to which Mammy reported her own reply as having been one of great finesse, "I have belonged to gent'men, Sir."

Folding her arms across her ample bosom, she would then throw up her head, registering "scorn" and tell us that she had looked on that po' white Yankee man and advised him that day that he had made a good purchase, but cautioned him that if he ever had one lick—so much as jes' one lick—give to her, he would have throwed his money in the dut. "Now is yo' time, Sir," she said, "but maybe it ain't a-goin' to last forever," then suddenly dropping her voice to a dramatic whisper she murmured confidentially, as if still in fear of a secret service officer—"an' it didn't las' forever—fo' Gawd, it want so long fo' he wuz blowed up with gun-powder a lot of 'em wuz a-settin' to kill Mr. Lincoln with."

Thus unconscious that it was history, politics and sociology that we were learning, Mammy's loyalty, her pathos, her wisdom, went in, in good measure and pressed down, to the minds of a half dozen little F. F. V's.

CHAPTER XXXIV

WE were learning a great many things. Franklin Edwards had been a gardener at Oatlands and father brought him to New Orleans to be in his office and learn business. He was a valuable addition to our household. Instead of following him around the garden as we had done all our lives at Oatlands, we now invaded the little room mother had assigned to him and sought his advice as an oracle on algebra and other knotty problems of school work.

He was a hard student, this quiet, rawboned boy of seventeen, as patient with us now as he had been when we dulled and misplaced his tools or plagued him in a thousand ways as he weeded his garden, while we tagged after him like sheep under the trellised grape arbors or in and out along the hardy borders.

Now he plodded away evening after evening alone, practicing penmanship with his big stiff fingers, clumsily mending his clothes, reading, or working at mathematics or bookkeeping.

Frank was on very confidential terms with father, knew things we did not know, and was already in his quiet way trying to stem the tide, with loyal devotion holding off the evil days.

I do not know when my pride of blood gave

way but I think this boy set me thinking. If humble birth was no handicap to him, breeding and manners must lie deeper than the accident of inheritance. There must be fountains further back than we could trace, to send such a gentleman as he, to be our friend.

And so Franklin Edwards taught us democracy.

Mother's Cousin Horatio Whitridge Turner had married a fashionable New Orleans girl and they concluded that Lucy and I were old enough now to eat shrimps and oysters, whether we liked them or not. No doubt they knew about the corsets and the confirmation and the boys who came to see us and the things Ella had told us; young ladies often found it necessary to eat things that they did not like and we were almost young ladies. So we went often to dine with them and gulped down the unwelcome delicacies until, just as Cousin Horatio had declared, we did learn to like them. He also thought we should learn to dance. My thoughts went back to Oakley, and to our cousin who had been denied the Holy Communion because he had danced—and I saw that my sister and I were becoming immoral, but if that was necessary in order to be stylish, we should submit.

And so Cousin Horatio taught us to eat shrimps and oysters and to dance.

Cousin Mary Lee, as I have said, visited us for

weeks at a time and was careful to teach us that Southerners were superior to all mankind, that Virginians were superior to all Southerners, and that the Lees were superior to all Virginians. I cannot recall that she ever said that but it was obvious. No other Virginians travelled around the world like royalty, as did Mary and Mildred Lee, and Cousin Mary of course knew what she was talking about.

So Cousin Mary Lee taught us to despise the Yankees and to revile and ridicule the name of Abraham Lincoln. I married a "Yankee," and forty years or more had passed, since her instructions, when on the invitation of the State Republican Committee, I, daughter of a Confederate officer, was asked to read my own lines on Lincoln, at a great banquet in Washington, on Lincoln's birthday.

We had elocution lessons and I could say yards and yards of poetry and delivered "Locksley Hall" with great effect. My sister's masterpiece was "Young Lochinvar."

And we had a smattering of French, from an old lady whom we cruelly tormented. So our educational equipment consisted of Aunt Imogene's music and the Molinari-Perelli sort of art; of the bit of French; of the elocution, which was a liability; the ability to eat oysters and shrimps; to dance the polka and the heel-and-toe; and the ordinary rudiments of schooling. We had learned to hate Yankees and to wonder at the high breeding of the obscure country boy. Ella had told us things about babies, mother had had us confirmed and put into corsets and endowed with artistic talents, boys had begun to come to see us, and now we were to put up our pig-tails and let down our skirts and be "ladies."

And here am I, arrived at fourteen years of wisdom, Willy Callahan gathered to Yesterday's seven thousand years, and a genuine suitor looming upon the horizon. A cousin of ours came to Oatlands from the West and fell in love with me. This grown-up man, eight years older than I, fell in love with me. Grandma said it really appeared that he was a marrying beau.

He was said to be rich. Anybody who had anything was said to be rich, with *Us*. Rich is an elastic word. And this desirable person was casting approving eyes upon me!

One is eaten up with importance under such circumstances. No heroine of romance had achieved more than a bona fide lover, at the age of fourteen. Oh, how glad I was that my hair was tucked up!

Lucy and I wore knitted capes that season; they were one of mother's philanthropies, and had been knit by the dear old lady who taught us French. My sister's was sky-blue, and mine was salmon-pink (or was mine sky-blue and hers salmon-pink? I must ask Lucy). They reached to our knees and were finished with knotted fringe. In the afternoons all the young people went out walking, two and two, girls together, for there was but the one beau—and think of the irrepressible pride of me, with my victim!

On such occasions Stanley's long bony fingers would fumble around in the salmon-pink (or sky-blue) fringe, until they encountered and fastened upon my little stubby ones, and we would think love a very holy and wonderful thing.

Stanley wore a pompadour in those days, and being fresh from college he sprinkled his English with Latin words which made a profound impression.

A year passed before we were again at Oatlands and during that year this swain came, as a faithful lover should, to visit me in New Orleans. I fear he turned my head, for Grandma, writing to me from Virginia, cautioned me against pride and vanity.

It is quite apparent that I, regardless of the fact that our whole family were quartered month after month in Aunt Kate's house, eating her bread and accepting her care, had so little judgment and so little sense of the fitness of things, as to try to show off at my cousin Grace's expense. A pleasant guest! Grandma herself made a habit of saying to Grace, "My dear, why do you never open a book? Your cousins are very intelligent and well-read." Then she would say to us, "Why do you girls not cultivate useful and practical habits, like Grace? Your mother is very poor, and it would help her if you loved to keep house and sew." So as children we girls glared sometimes at each other, and each reviled and scorned the accomplishments of the other.

We outgrew all that and have valued each other for years. As for men—Grace was very popular and had two beaux to our one. I cannot remember teasing her about men, but of course I must have done so, and Grandma must have heard the fact discussed.

This letter speaks for itself:

My darling May:

Before seating myself to my work this morning, I must write you a few lines in answer to your letter. I was so glad to see from your mother's last letter that they were beginning to form some plans for the summer. Your Aunt Kate, I know, has her heart set upon your coming to Oatlands; she is devoted to you all and feels it will be hard for her to get through the summer without you, and your Aunt Ida is anxious that some of you come here at once. Rozier is still here, and May will be here early in June, to remain until cold weather, but that leaves one vacant room, and I heard her say that she hoped as many of you will come as that would accommodate.

There is one thing I want to say to you, my dear child, and which I do not want either of you to mention, that is, be careful never to tease Grace about anything, especially about young men. It is not pleasant for anyone to be teased; you, my dear child, do not like it yourself. Grace thinks that your sister and yourself are much smarter than she is, and that makes her a little sensitive. So, my dear child, don't tease her about her hatred to reading, about men, or anything else, but my dear child, please don't mention to anyone that I have written you this caution. I know you are devoted to Grace; I never heard you speak of her but admiringly in your life.

Dear May, I hope it will not be long before I see you. I do so long to see you. I hope your mother will come to see me before she goes to Oatlands. Please, my dear child, don't mention that I wrote you about teasing; take your old grandmother's advice and give up the habit; it is so apt to make a person unpopular, and I think you deserve to be popular, and I want you to be so. God bless you, my darling, always realize that the advice I give you proceeds from my love to you and my desire that everyone else should love you too.

Your devoted grandmother,
M. F. Powell.

Oakley, March 14th, 1885.

Here, beyond all doubt, my "unfortunate disposition" had been much discussed and poor grandmother had tried to counteract the adverse opinion, and prove an alibi for her namesake and pet.

CHAPTER XXXV

AT some time during these years in New Orleans, there was a great flood of the Mississippi River and the levees broke and terrible inundations of the plantations resulted. The flood swept over the low-land, bearing everything before it, farmhouses, levees and trees almost submerged. Small frame buildings and cabins were ripped from their foundations, torn wall from wall, and were seen bobbing like broken cigar boxes up and down in the rushing torrent. Father said that there were crazy cats squealing horribly on the roofs. Colored women and babies were strapped to rafts, going rapidly down stream to almost certain death. Father saw some men clinging to the topmost branches of trees, and hundreds of cattle and hogs drowned and their carcasses floating along with the rest. Some cabins stood firm, and poor, frightened people crowded together on the roofs as the water continued to rise.

Father had not told us that he was going. He had a mania for doing dangerous things and never was hurt. Full-blooded, broad-shouldered fellows died of pneumonia or from other exposure to wet and contagion, and Father went through it all unscathed. He had gone on a relief boat sent by a newspaper—"The Times-Democrat," I think—and the vivid picture of disaster which he brought home to us caused my very bed to reel and jerk and bob and topple under me for many nights after.

We were all hero worshippers and our father was a hero. So was Mr. Waters, our clergyman. He did not look like one, he was so mild and neat, with a very small voice indeed. It was he who had prepared my sister and me and Willy Callahan for confirmation, and we knew then that he was a hero. A hero has a great influence. He never preached about God's anger or hell fire or unpleasant things and never bellowed at you as some do to wake you up. He leaned forward very earnestly over the pulpit and spoke gently, and his only gesture was to put the tips of his fingers together in a very precise way and extend his two hands thus united toward you. He wiggled them gently at the wrists. Perspiration never came on him while he was preaching and he never tossed his hair back from his brow— perhaps because there was none there. A text that comes to me across forty years of sorrow and worldliness is typical of him. "They went and told Jesus." A very simple statement, a most natural action. It is a great comfort in times of doubt or distress to tell someone who will comprehend. Jesus does. And those who took their griefs to him found consolation.

The thing that revealed the Rev. Henry Harcourt Waters as a hero was not in a sermon. It was merely the pestilence that destroyed in the noon-day. A thousand fell beside him and ten thousand at his right hand, but it did not come nigh him. It was one Yellow Fever summer and he was already on his vacation in Canada. He never raised his voice in speaking, or used an exclamation point in a letter; he was deliberate and sincere; and now he just packed his bag and took the first train for the stricken city. Rich and poor, white and black, Jew and Gentile, knew his face as he devoted himself with that same simplicity of manner to going in and out among the dying. That was all. There were other clergymen in New Orleans at the time—perhaps I should not remember it—who hurriedly forsook the stricken city. One of them was made a Bishop later. Mr. Waters had confirmed Lucy and me and Willy Callahan. He knew how I behaved to Aunt Imogene about Moses and the Ethiopian woman. He would not want me to remember about this clergyman, but I do.

Changes were gradually taking place behind the scenes, but childlike, we were unconscious of them; Frank Edwards and Mother knew, and anxious conferences took place between the two as to Father's business and his habits. He was open-handed; all that he had was at the disposal of his friends and upon these terms he had many friends; a generous table, good cigars and good liquor, drew the rag-tag and the bob-tail of the

Lost Cause as well as the brilliant and valiant who were my father's peers. The poorer the old ex-Confederates were, the more imperative the obligation of offering such consolations as he could; surely no one can hold this against a soldier!

But his health and habits grew worse from this manner of life and his business suffered. The brilliant deals he might have made had his head been quite clear and his nerve steady, went amiss through some carelessness or oversight. Discouragement and anxiety and the disappearance of the hordes of hilarious friends, preyed upon his sensitive nature; he became very morbid. He was away from home too much, going off on business trips which resulted in nothing but expense—Frank Edwards would follow him and bring him back to Mother. Dear, faithful, quiet Frank!

After several wretched days for us all, illness would overtake him, his stomach was delicate and a spree always ended in an illness; then Mother would pet and nurse him, we children would be wild with joy because he was so funny —laughing ourselves crooked at his witty remarks and his mimicry of everybody, of the doctor who prescribed, and of the preacher who preached, of us, and of Mammy, and who not?

We are a race of men-spoilers. All of the women of our connection have spoiled their husbands, and why not Mother? So, she turned on his bath, always, and spread his robe, and would then call him. During these sicknesses she brought him his meals herself, and the moment he heard her foot-fall on the stair he would stop reading a novel, or delighting us children with his nonsense, and begin to groan; so with each step her solicitude increased, and by the time she reached his bed-side his imagination and theatrical exercises combined had convinced them both that he was suffering acutely.

Father was a Dickens character—a combination of much that was noble and something that was mean—pathetic, ridiculous, heroic. But he was everything. He was everybody. I have seen him on the street make a most graceful salutation, when two persons, strangers to him but friends to each other, met with pleasure. This sympathetic mind is very dear, and I saw it in my little girl, one day in Switzerland, when she came to me, a tiny tot of six, "Muvver, what makes my foot hurt me so when I see a little bare-footed peasant child stump its toe?" I thought, then, of my father—he spoke in my child.

On Mardi-Gras he always filled his office with guests; people came all the way from Virginia for these parties and many old friends were assembled on the balcony which overlooked the line of the processions. The last spring of our stay in this old town it fell to me to act as hostess, for neither Father nor Mother could be there. Cousin Custis Lee was there, Col. Venable and Mr. Christian, Professors from the University of Virginia, and Col. William Preston Johnston, the President of Tulane University, also a few stars in the theatrical world and other people I can not recall. In my grave little way I tried to do the honors, passing mint juleps and cigars and introducing and welcoming guests, and explaining how sorry my father was to be unwell, and how sorry my mother was that because of his indisposition she could not have the pleasure of being with them.

And soon came an end to the Carnival Balls, the early breakfasts in the French Market, the little trips to Pass Christian, the theater suppers at the old St. Charles.

Trades-people became importunate and in New Orleans that is significant. For trades-people were patient in New Orleans; polite, humane, their bills one might say were written in the milk of human kindness, for they knew the atmosphere of the place; humble persons like tailors and grocers maintained a soothingly respectful attitude forty years ago. So, when these long-suffering people began to plead for payment it meant bankruptcy. We gave up first one servant and then another—the dreary details are superfluous.

At last the crash came. Some Western Rolling

Mills failed, Father was one of their largest creditors, he was left with nothing to cover his own obligations, and so went to bed.

Mother and Frank Edwards closed matters up. The summer had been so dreadful that the failure hardly made things worse. In a way it was a relief, as it might be to drop from the edge of a precipice to which one had been holding for many hours. We knew at least where we were, and there was a definite thing to be done.

We did not understand where any money had been coming from for the daily expenses. Franklin Edwards brought it to Mother, who supposed that in some mysterious way the firm earned it; he must have been doing work on a salary outside and have handed over to her his own earnings. Mother was not a financier.

This summer marked my début into the ranks of bread-winners. I was fifteen, the oldest of eight, and another coming.

CHAPTER XXXVI

MOTHER had an account at Holmes and Company, the Lord and Taylor of New Orleans of those days, and a Mr. Sanders, a floor-walker who probably had a little girl at home, was very good to me. It is strange how good one is to little girls for the sake of one little girl at home! All that summer this man seemed to me a divinity, for I bought palm-leaf fans by dozens and painted on them birds and flowers in hectic colors—Mother and I said that I "decorated" them—and after binding them with ribbon to match the flower or bird, I took them to Holmes and Company in my arms and this angelic person sold them for me. They were really effective and seemed to suit the summer days in dear, smelly, hot, flowery New Orleans.

As for Willy Callahan, I had forgotten him, and even my Cousin Stanley paled into insignificance as I thought of this noble floor-walker. My gray eyes closed at night upon the vision of his stately form and flowing mustache, and after dreaming of him all night I wakened with the thought of him and it made the heavy midsummer days easier to remember his friendly eyes, as I bent over the work on my knees, the odor of oil and turpentine in my nostrils, my attention riveted to the point of the brush, my little back aching, and my heart full of gratitude and hope.

On the last delivery of the evening Holmes and Company's wagon would leave an envelope addressed to me in his beloved hand, enclosing money—real, wonderful money—there is no exhilaration equal to that. If a few lines from my benefactor accompanied these emoluments I was thrilled unspeakably and read between them all that my imagination was pleased to invent.

   Dear Madam:
      Please find enclosed $4.50 (four dollars and fifty cents), sale of six hand-painted fans at 75 cents each.
                       Yours truly,
S/   Holmes and Company

I was old enough to appreciate that there was nothing compromising in this missive and to admire the chivalrous forethought which made it so formal and business-like, but I would say "dear Madam" over to myself a million times, until it became a sort of sacred chant. The "S" itself became a term of mysterious endearment, and surely "brightened the corner where it stood," and as I painted the fans the following day I beguiled the time thinking of all the tender words beginning with that letter—sweetheart—sympathy—soul—Sanders—sunshine—that the word "silly" never occurred to me in this connection may be surprising!

Thus Romance and Finance walked hand in

hand and I entered the ranks of the Wage-Slaves like a conquering hero.

Mother and Franklin Edwards settled up as best they could, late in the season; there were sacrifices and compromises but those could not be avoided. The "Dago" from whom we had bought fruit and ice and vegetables besieged the door pleading in truly temperamental manner for some settlement of his historic account; sometimes all his sons joined him, weeping, gesticulating, tearing their shirts open over their hearts as though to reveal their inmost emotions; especially Pasquale, who always brought the ice and always gave us "lagn-i-appe" and was a great favorite with us.

But had not Pasquale become our enemy? He had. Therefore Mother's small boys, unconscious of the real situation, met his hysterical entreaties with scorn and ridicule from the top of the high fence around the garden. Franklin Edwards arranged with the Dagos finally to accept a set of Minton china as payment in full. They wept apologetic tears when they took it from us, in real Old World chivalry.

Other bills were paid in similar ways. Mother did her best. Alexandria, Virginia, was selected as a point between New York and New Orleans, Father building air-castles about the business he would conduct in both cities. He had been a commission man between the factories and the railroads, dealing largely in equipment and railway supplies. All at once the manufacturers and the railroads began to deal directly with each other and the middleman met his Waterloo. Incidentally, Alexandria was near to Mother's relations. And thus we returned to Virginia, bringing nothing with us but a few additional children.

PART IV

Alexandria, an Old Town on the Potomac

CHAPTER XXXVII

ALEXANDRIA, VIRGINIA, where we next found ourselves, is a quaint old town on the Potomac six miles south of Washington. Before Washington was, Alexandria was known as Beall Haven, or Belle Haven, and figures under that name in a delightful book by Mrs. Burton Harrison. It had indeed a beautiful harbor and was a famous shipping port long before the Capitol ever lifted its dome over Washington. It took its name from a family of Alexanders who at one time were owners of the Arlington estate and of much land in the vicinity.

In Colonial times, as the nearest city to the plantations along the river, Alexandria was of much importance. George Washington as a young engineer, laid out many of its streets; he must have had the dream of a great metropolis, for he made scant provision for parks or gardens. The old streets are paved with cobblestones laid by the Hessian prisoners, who in their own country were accustomed to roads which rival the roads of ancient Rome; these of Alexandria are of admirable workmanship in spite of the inferior material; the round cobbles still hold their own, death and destruction to generation after generation of vehicles! In jolting over them year after year one can but think of those mercenaries and the strange circumstance that the hire of them paid by England to the Kurfürst of Hessen was the foundation of the great Rothschild fortunes, for the old Kurfürst placed the money for investment with a Jewish broker in Frankfort by the name of Rothschild, whose descendants have since practically controlled the finances of Europe.

To this ancient burg upon the river our parents brought us, but for us it had none of the interest then that it has for the artist and the historian. Our young eyes never even saw the old hand-carved doorways, which architects came from afar to reproduce, and we cared nothing for mahogany panel or spiral stairway. The narrow little disreputable streets and alleys running downhill to the river, and the old mossy roofs and stained chimneys piling up against each other, beloved of artists, had no charm for us.

We had been rooted up again, the familiar live-oaks and fig-trees had vanished forever, the circle of friends was broken, there seemed little to compensate us for the loss. This was a dreary place. We hated the sound of the ferry boats, chug-chug-chugging on the river.

The Poor House was on the outskirts of the town, an old mansion hemmed in between the railroads, a house of distinction long ago and during the Civil War a famous tavern. I formed a great aversion to that place and as the oldest of this very large and impecunious family regarded it with some anxiety.

A ramshackle hotel surrounded the once elegant Carlyle House in which Cousin Arthur Herbert had been born. It faced the river, a terraced garden sloping to the water, where later the city's coal-yards and lumber-yards are found. Even in its degradation this old garden could start some pleasant fancies, as gray and blue eyes looked down upon it from the back windows of the Mansion House. The cheap and vulgar life of the Hotel created a tragic atmosphere around this stately mansion in which many significant conferences took place during the Revolutionary War, and from which General Braddock started out to Fort Duquesne. Its very existence was forgotten until Mittie Herbert, lineal daughter of the house, undertook with love and patriotism to restore it. Little by little it has been redeemed and stands a precious monument to her patience and to the generosity of a few public-spirited persons. She has accumulated rare furniture of the period which visitors to Mount Vernon stop and admire; its great mahogany balustrades and wonderful cellars provoke profound respect for the sincerity of the old builders.

But we looked out over it upon junk-shops and lumber-yards and car-barns, and dingy, dirty, dilapidated hovels and thought this place a dreadful place!

The ferry boats and big steamers, the small sailing craft, delighted our four boys, who, as often as possible, sneaked out and were captured on the wharves among the loafing negroes that infested the river-shore.

From the front (Mother had a front room), on Fairfax Street, we saw a row of junk-shops and the market and the police station. There were also vendors of second-hand clothing and menders of old furniture.

Monday mornings our four little boys would escape us and go into the police court to hear the tales of woe which were utterly unfit for them but if a fatherly policeman so much as shook his "billy" at them they scampered away like mice.

A block to the left was King Street—the thoroughfare. Indicative, perhaps, of an improvident mind, the first thing my sister and I did was to have our photographs taken on King Street, to give to our relations.

Frankly, our relations did not want our photographs. We were not strikingly pretty girls and our spasmodic movements, our ups and downs, the superabundance of us, numerically, were all so many thorns in the flesh, so many anxieties and compulsory responsibilities, to the people who really loved our mother. Mother had one hundred and eighty first cousins, so, you see, we were worrying a good many people. Fortunately, they were not all living at the same time. Some had died before others were born, but the children of her own uncles and her own aunts, actually number so many. Mother's mother was one of thirteen children—the Turners of Kinloch, and her father was one of seventeen—the Powells of Llangollan.

Our advent into the realms of Poor Relationdom had been earlier than at that time I realized. This Hegira into Virginia, sickness and debt and uncertainty attendant upon us, made the position clear enough. One's rich relations do not leave one long in doubt. To help, and at the same time to forbear to advise, is a rare degree of charity. Those who come to the rescue expect the pleasure of exhibiting their astuteness, and so the path of the poor relation is full of pit-falls. One kind relative thinks one way, and one another, and when services have been accepted from all, and various theories are advanced as to the most judicious conduct, someone is sure to be disappointed.

We have a great way of declaiming that gratitude is so rare a virtue. But what is gratitude? If you are good to me, the chances are I love you; if you are good to me and I cannot love you, what would you have? Some deference, no doubt, and some respect for your opinion; yet logically, are you entitled even to that? In carrying out your ideas have you not had the satisfaction your money or influence paid for? You help me to get an education, or pay my doctor's bill, but boss me because of this assistance so that my soul is weighed down with the burden of an obligation I am unable to cancel. And so I come to hate you. I feel your disapprobation if I spend a little money for something which does not appeal to you, but is to me the breath of life. I hear your thought—if she can afford to do this sort of thing, surely there is no occasion for me to deny myself to make other matters easy.

And are you kind to me, if after paying my confinement bills, you urge me to put my baby in an orphanage? Are you kind, if after sending my son to college, you almost force him into an uncongenial profession? Are you kind when there is an ostentation in your helpfulness, and I feel myself, so to speak, dragged at your chariot wheels?

Mother was ill in this miserable place; Father had no occupation and his active mind was the prey to anxieties of many sorts. A little baby named Roberta Randolph had died and my mother's grief for months had been pitiable in the extreme. I did not know that with seven children left, one could so sorrow and we were glad another was coming to fill her empty arms.

A relative of Mother's, who was kind in his own way to her, made no effort to conceal his dislike for my father and Father hated him for this impertinence and for the frequency with which he kissed my sister and me—now fifteen and sixteen years of age.

The greatest pleasure to us were the daily visits of our cousin, Robert C. Lee. He was a brother of General Fitz Lee, and combined the Mason wit inherited from his mother with that wonderful gentleness of the Lee men. He had a pretty voice and a repertory of quaint old songs; I can hear him now, "And a voice from above—'T was the voice of her God—I love thee—I love thee—pass under my rod." He was a sort of fallen angel. Much that was noble he dragged into the dust. But there was a beauty that survived. No dissipation quite degraded him. All who remember him will bear me out in this. Later, we rented his mother's house on Washington Street. Lucy, who was a good sport, made some girl friends, and boys began to come to see us. We were entered at Cousin Rebecca's school. It was the Arlington Institute for Young Ladies.

CHAPTER XXXVIII

TWO years had passed since I had first met my Cousin Stanley, and during that time he had come both to New Orleans and to Alexandria to see me. We had theater tickets and ice cream and flowers and candy galore, for as the old ballad says, "What other lovers did, did he." Mother was very fearful lest the oldest and least pretty of her girls should miss a good match. I was anxious to please her and to be good to him for he was kind to me—never urged a decision upon me, agreeing that I was young, and that he could be patient. My reluctance was not to him but to the connubial state on principle. It did not appeal to me. The more I thought of the inevitable climax the more repugnant the whole idea of marriage became. There is a time for all things. The time for this surely had not come. My mother and I disagreed.

My two sisters were pretty and our house became quite a rendezvous for boys.

Then the twins were born. Mother was desperately ill. The twins were girls. One of them was destined to breathe the air of Alexandria for but a few days. The tiny creature was carried on a pillow, could take no nourishment, and in a few days died. Died early one February morning on my knees. I had sat up all night before a little discouraged fire with this unconscious scrap of humanity on my lap. I had studied its emaciated small countenance at first with profound pity, then with a sort of resentment. There is something foreboding in that hour of the early morn which sees so many come and go—the hour of birth and of death. That hour before dawn, which is to the day what March is to the year, the vital forces at their lowest, before a renewal of strength and warmth and light.

The poor little fire flickered and died in the grate, as the spark of life in the babe. And, I, sixteen years old, stirred by strange, and I think, terrible emotions, wanted to die too. The experience sickened me; the claw-like hands of the child clutching my own strong finger sickened me. The thought of Stanley sickened me. I was cold and hungry, the night had been a very long one.

It was not well to be cold and hungry and cynical and weary, and sit passively holding a dead child in your lap in the early, early morning, at the age of sixteen.

I wanted light and sun and flowers, I wanted to know and see, I wanted to do good—I *was* bearing someone's burden then, and fulfilling the law of Christ, but not in the way I would have chosen! I wanted what I knew I never could have—beauty—I wanted beauty desperately, that morning, to be praised and kissed, to fulfil myself, to create something strong and splendid. I did not want to sit in the chilly morning alone, with a dead child stretched on my knees. Death at that moment had little of mystery or of dignity. Was it *Love* that produced this imperfect thing, this little weary body and fleeting spirit? Does Love come to this? There was no beauty to me, then, in Love or Death.

The business was supposed to be going on in New Orleans under Father's partner, and a branch office with Frank Edwards in charge was opened in New York. No business was done in either place for the railroads had begun to deal directly with the manufacturers, and the middlemen were out.

My father needed me, more and more he turned to me. Mother adored him always but I adored him and understood him. He tried her patience, and the irregular income, and the debts and duns, and the checks that no one wanted to cash, and the swarm of children, all taxed her beyond endurance.

We sold a few pieces of family silver—we drew drafts on Frank Edwards. None of us earned anything, we didn't know how. Father needed stimulant constantly and Mother could not distract him from it; she was too care-worn to try; but the love did not wear out.

Visitors besieged us. Those who do not know

the habits of our section of the country, or the traditions with which my generation grew up, can hardly believe what a tax the unexpected guest becomes (angel though he may be), there are so many of him. Dear Mother would glance out of the window and observe, as one might observe an approaching rain, that someone must be coming, for the express was bringing in two large trunks. Often when there was a "hop," boys and girls tumbled in until every cot and sofa was occupied and two or three in each big bed.

CHAPTER XXXIX

OUR boys and girls visited all over the country, staying with relatives or friends, arriving at meal times without notice, and naturally we, too, kept open house; and we were not the only ones whose furniture was shabby and whose bills were unpaid and whose happy-go-lucky ménage ran itself. To stem this tide, to hold ourselves to ourselves, to require our young ones to exercise a self-denial which would have eventually cut them off from all harmless pleasure, would not have been wise or right, and Mother let things drift. Once I, as the least hospitable and least aristocratic of us all, attempted to calculate how much additional expense this open house entailed in one week (for butter and sugar alone were items if bills were ever to be paid) and I found that in six days forty-five meals had been merrily consumed by droppers-in. Three or four extra people at each meal seems not many; one of us would bring home a friend from school, others would beg that a game be not interrupted for so long a time as it would take their friends to go home—why, lunch is on the table; come right in!

What a laughing and scrambling there would be! What a scamper to the bathroom or to the pump in the back-yard, to wash the grimy little hands. What reaching and passing of plates and what a really beautiful self-restraint on the part of the hosts and hostesses, until the guests had been served. Among whom were men now quite distinguished, for future bank presidents and members of Congress played marbles in Mother's back-yard. Sometimes it would flit across my penurious mind that less butter would be needed if we had cold baker's bread instead of hot batter-cakes or waffles, but a suggestion of this sort actually pained Mother who wondered how a Yankee streak had got into one of her children. Mother herself sat smilingly at the head of the table, no evidence upon her rosy face that the neck of the chicken or the gristle of the beef-steak were not her especial preference.

Also, as to school. In our day the public school was impossible for folks with pedigrees. We sent our boys and girls to Cousin This or Cousin That, or to any dear old lady of our own class who had no visible means of support, rather than to the public schools to trained teachers. All sorts and conditions of children were admitted to the public schools and with *Us* that sort of association was not to be thought of. When somebody in the country sent a basket of preserving peaches to Cousin This or Cousin That, she gave a holiday; when a little sewing was necessary on her own scanty wardrobe, there was a sewing lesson; when she was cross, she pinched and slapped; and when questions were asked in the line of study which nonplussed her, she looked very knowing and said she preferred that a pupil should find that out for himself. Mother paid such people to teach her younger children and felt that the fact that the free schools were the better schools had no bearing on the case. "We will economize in some other way—certainly not on the children's education."

Our Cousin Rebecca was a figure in the town, in appearance and in character, not to be forgotten. She was an intensely romantic person but so unprepossessing in appearance that no man ever had looked at her with the eyes of admiration. In her girlhood she wrote dainty verses which in her old age she volunteered to show to favorites among her pupils and I had the privilege of reading them often. The theme was the dear old theme and the rhymes those hackneyed syllables which tell us of maidens sitting in the bowers mid blooming flowers and April showers, whispering yes. Cousin Rebecca's maidens always whispered that significant monosyllable, "yes."

She had a brother-in-law who was a widower, upon whom she seemed to have cast a partial eye. She alluded to him frequently, with a coy little manner which was unspeakably pathetic. If, in spelling class, the word "onyx" appeared, Cousin

Rebecca would pause—tell us what onyx was—
and then, "Well, gy-irls, my brother-in-law has
a very beautiful onyx clock on the mantelpiece
in his bedroom."

Then overcome with maidenly modesty at having mentioned any furnishing of a gentleman's
bedroom, she would add, "During the lifetime
of his wife, I became familiar with the interior
of the bedroom." Which of course made it all
just as nice again as the most scrupulous parent
could wish.

While my sister and I were in boarding-school
under her I had the permission of my parents to
correspond with a young gentleman—that was
the term of my day. The young gentleman was
my Cousin Stanley. There is no doubt but that
much of the passion which slipped from the point
of Stanley's fervid pen underwent the scrutiny of
Huntas, the austere virgin who was Cousin
Rebecca's handmaiden, then fell under Cousin
Rebecca's spectacles, and finally those of her
father, Cousin Charles; young love is hardly able
to endure such analysis. She also confiscated and
devoured the candy Stanley sent, because it was
against the rules for the girls to have candy—but
she would give me the card, with its legend,
"Sweets to the Sweet," which Stanley thought
an original sentiment.

Cousin Rebecca was "small town" and in many
ways trite and undistinguished; we felt superior
to her for years; we, her pupils. Now I see what

a great woman she was—her personal oddities are lost in the realization of her goodwill and faithful service—the wisdom we ridiculed comes back, endorsed by hard experience. Her insatiable desire to acquire knowledge, and her authoritative expression of well-founded opinion, were most wonderful, and at the age of eighty she would go to the Capitol and listen for hours to the discussion of important questions.

Lucy and I were at Cousin Rebecca's when Father died; Mother owed her several hundred dollars, which no power could ever persuade her to accept, even when his life insurance was paid. Her school was the best in the section, and some conscientious work was done by teachers and pupils. It is true, work ran to a smattering of many subjects rather than to thorough knowledge of anything; we did chemistry without a laboratory and astronomy without any observation and we learned French from women who loved the language and knew the history, literature and life of the country from reading, and who had a good basis of grammar and idiom, but no idea of the pronunciation whatever. Cousin Rebecca was sentimental and so was I, and thus a real love of poetry and art was fostered in my mind; looking back I am glad to credit to her many true appreciations and artistic perceptions which have helped me along the way. She was a remarkable woman and a good friend.

What could we do without old maids? The

type is vanishing, as the good old mammy is, and the self-reliant, efficient, bachelor women, who are afraid of nothing, balk at nothing, will not help us poor mothers out as did the conventional old maids of the last generation. They were very dear, with their starved motherhood expressing itself in solicitude for our offspring; piecing out where we fell short, doing things that we forgot, loving, praying, sewing, teaching, nursing, explaining, filling in so many chinks for our children.

I have memories of the type, always there when needed, never obtrusive; there were a number of unmarried relatives scattered around in different homes during my childhood, filling these positions, gracious and uncomplaining, towers of strength in the hour of trouble. It is a loss to the rising world that today this element is busy selling real estate or practicing law or reporting for newspapers or running cafés or doing massage —anything rather than to lend a helping hand and eat the bread of dependence in gratitude.

Perhaps the disappearance of this class is due to the altered home life; in that era of domestic productiveness, when distances were great and intercourse with country neighbors occasional, it was a pleasure to have as an inmate of the home a well-bred relative, and the pleasure was mutual; all worked together for the provision of all. Bread and canned goods and preserves and cheese and wine and dried fruit and syrup were all made on the place; clothing for a whole family was made twice a year. Certain drugs were prepared at home, the poultry alone required one person's whole attention—there was a community spirit.

Now, if you are motoring twenty miles to go to the theater, you will find it difficult to get a servant, much less a relative, to sit alone through a long evening, listening for your baby. This obliging person has vanished from view, has changed with changing times and prefers a Government salary, and to go to the theater herself, and you must listen for your own baby or see that there is no baby there to be considered.

The day is gone forever when the unmarried woman sits at a brother's fireside, gathering up the crumbs of love that fall from his children's table. I should think the world would build her a throne, and beg her to come back.

CHAPTER XL

THE three years' love-affair with my Cousin Stanley came abruptly to an end when I was seventeen; I had engaged myself to him with many misgivings, and he had come on to Alexandria from his Western home. He was kind to me and I wanted to be good to him but the state of engagedness was bitter; I could conceal from no one my reluctance to be left alone with my suitor. Father did not often run counter to Mother in any matter but here he came to the rescue and urged her to let me alone as to this marriage. So Mother and I had a confidential talk one night, when Father was away, and she asked me to sleep with her. She told me, her first-born, under the cover of darkness, how a woman feels when she wants to be the wife of a man—she told me of the moods of which I had read, of palpitating hearts and throbbing pulses— (so all this was real)—and asked me if I felt conscious of any excitement when Stanley came around? No, I didn't. Well, then she supposed she had made a mistake, and I was at liberty to break the engagement. I felt a return of self-respect though I realized I should be left to grow into an old maid like Cousin Rebecca, and turning over, slept the sleep of the righteous, or something resembling it.

The following day was Saturday and Stanley was giving a theater party; it was a question whether to tell him then, and spoil his party, or wait a better opportunity. We did not often go to a theater. I decided to go on with the theater party, which would have been good fun but for the oppressiveness of my own conscience, and not until Sunday morning did I find the courage to speak and then resorted to the cowardly custom, old with us, of writing a note.

Stanley, who was a Roman Catholic, had been to early mass and when we Episcopalians started to Old Christ Church, across the street, he was seated at the piano, his head thrown back, singing lustily. He was singing "Tantum Ergo Sacramentum." I handed him the little note and wended my way to the sanctuary.

When we returned, he was packing his trunk. I helped, sad and lachrymose; we mingled our tears into the depths of his festive apparel. He would fold a shirt and gulp; I would roll a pair of socks and sob; I was thoroughly ashamed, as Stanley had got some sort of "dispensation" from the Pope or someone, to marry me, a cousin; I felt Popes should not be trifled with. I had promised to have all my children baptised in his church; it seemed rather late to change the plans.

Mother was sepulchral. And here I was, growing old—already seventeen—in a cold and disapproving world. No theater tickets. No candy. No flowers. No envious glances from other maidens. Two very pretty younger sisters. I felt I should probably never marry now and yet I was happier than for many a day. For three years this thing had shadowed me with a vague discomfort, a sense of helplessness and shame.

More and more I estranged myself from the others, avoided the young people and clung to my father. They thought I was stuck-up. I was not. The atmosphere was tense. My soul was on the rack. He could not sleep, and sitting up all night, wished me to sit up with him. Night after night I have read "Pickwick Papers" aloud till morning broke.

Sam Weller and Mrs. Bardell have worked overtime for me—my husband too was a Dickens' enthusiast, and the week of our marriage saw me return to my old friends, those caricatures which bring the weaknesses and greatnesses of humanity so clearly before us. Personally, Dickens bores me—I blush to say it—but in reading aloud with the male of the species, it will be recorded that women usually read what the listener enjoys, rather than matter of their own choosing. What difference does it make? To see a man settle down contentedly in an easy chair before a fire, and listen to a tale he loves, as he smokes a cigar and toasts his toes, is a pleasant thing.

So the hours wore on 'til the gray morning light as I and my father lived through the night's insomnia. Anything to gratify or divert him, anything to distract him from that one ruinous craving. Ten, eleven, twelve, one, two, three, would strike, and Sam Weller never rested.

Another diversion was the writing of voluminous business letters to railway magnates all over the world. We often used a code and wrote telegrams galore to Mexico, London, Berlin. We would use up whole pads of telegraph blanks in an evening which the morning found in scraps in the waste paper basket or strewing the dining-room floor like autumn leaves. If my slowness irritated him, I wrote faster, and soon my pen had wings.

He would pace the length of the room, back and forth, back and forth, his uneven step and tap of the cane he always used marking time as he dictated, while my little pen scratched along as rapidly as he could frame his sentences. Sometimes he stopped at the sideboard—I never objected—then resuming his march and steady flow of terse, clear, admirable English. I never questioned, I never remonstrated—I merely sat there and drove the pen all night long.

Mother and all her brood were sound asleep.

In the luxury of my life today, I glory in the memory of these hours with him. We truly belonged to each other, we needed no explanations, no apologies. Wrong is wrong and cannot be called right, but love is love to the bitter end.

I should not have loved a mediocre father. I

Mrs. Andrews, in Costume of Mrs. Jefferson, Used During the Campaign to Preserve Monticello.

The Mansion House, Alexandria, Va., Built Around the Colonial Mansion of John Carlyle.

OLD CARLYLE HOUSE, OVERLOOKING THE POTOMAC.

liked the stuff of which I was made—I knew long before he spoke, what he would say, and long before he did it, I knew what he would do. So I haunted him by day and cheered him by night, and stored up wealth for the soul of me against the evil days.

Mother and I would quarrel over him—she could not understand these nocturnal performances, which really were not wholesome experiences for a growing girl; but I knew their value, and they had a rare joy for me which few things in life have had. Yes, Mother and I had bitter arguments, yet the hunted miserable look in his eyes lured me, charmed me, to him; Mother loved him, but I both loved and understood.

What a terrible love is that love! That a woman, longing to hold her man to her, to endear herself, to compensate him for all the slings and arrows of outrageous fortune, to restore his faith in God and his confidence in himself, continues to devote her body to his momentary physical desires, long after passion is forever done with, for herself, and at a so dreadful cost to herself and her offspring. Could this loving and devoted heart have set aside the household cares to be with him, the situation had, perhaps, been saved. There was an elasticity, a recuperative power in him, that with one more chance, perhaps had set him right. Dear Mother! She could only keep on having babies.

Something was always weighing on my heart,

as though I had swallowed a big cobblestone. A vague sense of guilt and disquiet.

Something was going to happen—and I, who could have relieved the situation by marrying, would not marry. Would not marry Stanley, at least.

Vainly I looked about for some solution of the problem and despairing for myself, bethought me of my sisters. They were young, it is true, but some of our ancestors looking down from the walls of Oatlands had had a dozen children by the time they were twenty-eight and, according to Copley, their figures were as slim and girlish as could be.

Opposite us in Christ Church sat a pew full of good-looking great-grandsons of Thomas Jefferson. I measured them with a mental yardstick, six-footers, and their father a banker. I observed them keenly, but never saw them manifest the least interest in our girls. Lucy could sing, Ginnie was pretty. The descendants of Thomas Jefferson were deaf and blind! Yet there were enough of them to go round and they might have rescued us all!

These square-shouldered financiers little dreamed that a day would come when their vis-à-vis in Christ Church would be a leader in the campaign to preserve the home of their illustrious ancestor, making speeches, directing campaigns, even broadcasting by radio, calling upon Americans to honor themselves in honoring

POOR   RELATION

Thomas Jefferson. Being officially received by the President of the French Republic, in his name! There was one of these boys that I selected for Lucy. He looks exactly like his great-grandfather.

Yet, I would have married, I would have stolen, I would have sold my soul, I would have died, for my father.

Shabbiness for myself and the little children I never felt. A rabble of small boys are not expected to be dandies. Women, if they do not feel well-dressed, can and do stay away from public places—but you cannot hide a man.

I felt it keenly when my distinguished-looking father was not well equipped. He was unlike the rest of the world, his fine head, his long, lean hands, his laughing, sorrowing eyes.

I noticed how threadbare the velvet collar of his overcoat had become, and took stock of my assets. I had few negotiable possessions, but I did have a watch. The one which my godmother left me, with the twelve religious books, and the two hundred dollars to be used for strictly religious purposes, and the gold thimble. Father had painted the Confederate flag on the face of this watch, and I loved it more for that than because of my godmother. I could sell that.

We had a friend, a frayed and threadbare little person, of whom Mattie, the solitary retainer of our house, remarked, "He is de jumpinest pusson 'bout other folkses business—ain't he got no business o' hisn?" And to him I confided my inspiration as to the watch. In a few days he brought me thirteen dollars and fifty cents.

My godmother's legacy to me was far-reaching in the good it did, for out of that money Father took me on my first visit to the Corcoran Gallery of Art.

He knew pictures. He drew well, he also wrote fluent verse. In his boyhood he played wild pranks with pen and pencil, illustrating the manuscripts of his father's sermons late Saturday night, the old gentleman unsuspectingly opening them in his pulpit on Sunday, and barely escaping disaster. But in neither verse nor illustration did Father do any serious work.

But his faith in that talent which had been more or less wished upon me and his love of English literature and knowledge of classic poetry, stimulated in me a love for them; yet I had no spark of what is called ambition. That has always remained outside my calculations. What I did most ardently desire was to be helpful and comforting to him—to earn money—money—money.

The revelations which study brought to me came later, gracious gifts of God to a sordid soul.

CHAPTER XLI

MY mother's decision that I should have a "talent," and her selection of what she termed "art" which included architecture, sculpture, lamp shades, painting on velvet, painting on china, etc., etc., really moulded my life. Poor dyspeptic Mr. Perelli and that awful ear of David established the tradition in the family that "May is artistic." What then more natural than that our relations should look us over pretty carefully, appraising our respective qualifications for entering upon the long struggle with the wolf whose shadow even then was falling across the threshold?

Yes, I was unquestionably "artistic" and Lucy was "musical." The others were too juvenile and nondescript to be classified. It was my wise Aunt Ida who suggested that somebody take me to the Corcoran Gallery in Washington, to ask about lessons; I had been there once with Father. As no one arose to carry out her suggestion, Aunt Ida took me herself.

If one is already seventeen, and has missed a perfectly good opportunity to get married, one is rather apologetic. If one is poor, and has no earning capacity, and the problem of what to do with one is becoming an anxiety to one's relatives, one is downright abject. Aunt Ida and I went together to Washington, and to my Cousin Rozier's house to lunch and saw that miracle, my Cousin Rozier's little Rozier. But my poor pate was full of conflicting thoughts, and that apologetic feeling just ruining everything—the baby Rozier and all. And then we went to the Art Gallery.

I did not like the nude. Grandma's modesty, I suppose, set me to thinking of all the things I ought not to have thought of, and I was glad my Aunt Ida could not see inside my head. The figleaves made me uncomfortable. My demure little face may have suggested great innocence but I had an evil mind. When we escaped the statuary, we went upstairs among the pictures. I stood before Mr. Corcoran's portrait and conceded that he was a great philanthropist, but I wondered why he wanted an "Odelisk" in his gallery. A very ignorant girl!

We were informed that I must submit a certain specimen of my genius before I could hope to enter Professor Andrews' class. This I perpetrated in Cousin Rebecca's studio, under her instruction. It was rejected. It was rather nice, I thought, and the rejection made me mad. There was no sense in expecting me to be a finished artist—if I were, would I be seeking instruction?

So I went again, alone, to the Art Gallery, to find out about this thing. I demanded Professor Andrews. I thought, as he stood in the statuary hall leaning against the pedestal of the dying gladiator, that he was the handsomest man I had ever seen—and so he was, as he explained so kindly to me the faults in my work. Light broke. I kept my eyes on him as he spoke, understanding precisely what he meant me to understand. Before the words were out of his mouth, I knew. I was afraid to speak. Goose-flesh was all over me, and a cold perspiration. But I kept my eyes fastened on his, and listened, wondered, worshipped, learned. For some days after this event I concentrated my massive intellect upon the business of gleaning some news as to what manner of man this should be. He was from Ohio, went to Europe every summer, sometimes stayed there for years, lived in a fashionable part of Washington, wore a dress-suit to parties and a "dinner coat" every evening. I became inflamed with interest in the society column of the papers to learn where he went to dinner. His studio was in his home, it had tapestries and carvings and armor in it, on the order of a museum.

Yet, he had treated me with great distinction, as though I, too, were a person of consequence. Is anything more soothing? I had told him, of course, why I was going to be an artist, and how it must immediately bring in some money—a good deal, I told him.

The other students told me later, when I was one of them, of how he had come into the class that day, and whistled a long, low whistle; and then given notice to them that they would soon be put through their paces. "There's a little girl coming over from Virginia," he said, "who will show you a thing or two."

CHAPTER XLII

IT was twilight of a raw winter day—January 25, 1888—that found my mother and Lucy and me standing close together by the front window of an upper bedroom, talking in an undertone, wondering what to do next. Our rabble of little ones were playing in the dirty snow outside. The man was lighting the street lamps. Other people did not know the straits we were in: we did not tell. Mother's people did not know, for his sake she kept it from them. We tried to put the best face on the situation. Another baby was coming.

It was dark and cold. Our hearts were like lead, and we knew not why.

Father had wandered about restlessly and forlornly all day, upstairs and down, speaking to no one, had sat with his face buried in his transparent hands, had left the table abruptly without touching food and had climbed to the third floor where odds and ends were stored, things out of use, tumbled together. We did not know there was such a thing in the house, but he must have found it there.

Then he lay himself down on the bed in the back room, next to the one in which we three women were. No one disturbed him. He had been miserably ill, one scheme after another had fallen through. We were glad that he could lie still, and that his poor brain could rest.

Mammy had "Our Baby Girl" on her knees in the little anteroom, undressing her. Suddenly we heard a pistol shot. Mother and my sister hurried to the window and looked down into the darkening street. I stepped into the next room and took it out of his hand.

In a moment the house was in mad confusion. Only he and I were very still. Cousin Bob, the doctor, came and said there was nothing to be done. Dear Aunt Di, good woman and devoted Catholic, dropped on her knees beside the bed and as long as he breathed, recited without cessation the prayers appointed by her church for the dying, helping that poor tortured soul on its way to peace. God bless her for those well-meant orisons!

We took him to Oatlands for burial. The old rusty iron doors of the vault in the bottom of the garden swung to, as my mother's people, who had been his friends in life, received him in death.

I left Mother and her awe-struck little brood with my Aunt Katie, and returned alone to Alexandria, to hunt up some sort of work, to get out of the furnished house we had been renting, and had unintentionally depreciated in value, and to try to puzzle out a new program for the family.

The following editorial notice appeared the day after his death in the Charleston, S. C., "News and Courier," written by his old comrade in arms, Frank Dawson, of Fitz Lee's staff:

> Captain Charles Minnigerode, whose lamentable death was announced yesterday, ran away from school in Richmond to enter the Confederate Service, and served under the Southern flag from the beginning of the war to the very surrender of the Army of Northern Virginia. Indeed, he was the last man wounded in the Army of Northern Virginia at Appomattox. It was while he was riding along the lines giving orders for the Confederate columns to halt, because General Lee had determined to ask for suspension of hostilities, that he was shot across the body and received injuries which left their mark upon him to the very end of his loving and indefatigable life.
>
> When Col. Fitzhugh Lee, the present Governor of Virginia, was appointed Brigadier General he selected Charles Minnigerode as his Aide-de-camp and retained him as a member of his military family until the end of the long struggle. The relations between General Lee and his Aide-de-camp were of the most intimate and affectionate character. The regard in which he held him is both tenderly and worthily expressed in his report of the operations of the Confederate Cavalry of Northern Virginia on their last campaign.
>
> * * * * * * *
>
> Charles Minnigerode was a model of courage and the pink of buoyant courtesy beside. Boyish always, in the freshness of his feelings, he was a man in everything that constitutes true manhood.
>
> Captain Minnigerode was most carefully nursed by the Federal surgeons upon his capture and afterwards; but was partly paralyzed for many months and never recovered altogether from the effects of his wound.
>
> In Memphis, however, he succeeded in establishing himself as a dealer in railway supplies; thence he went

to New Orleans where he was so highly thought of as to be elected President of the Survivors' Association. The failure of a railway company largely in his debt caused his mercantile suspension there. Undaunted, he went to New York and began in the world anew, meeting with successes which promised an early turn to the period of largest anxiety and exertion. It is all ended now.

There were few men in the Army of Northern Virginia who were better known than Charlie Minnigerode was; to few men has it been given to have more devoted friends; to fewer still is it accorded to deserve confidence and trust and affection as entirely as they were deserved by the battle-scarred soldier whose campaigns are ended, and who found, like so many others, that peace had its defeats no less heartbreaking than those of war.

This was mercifully written by one who knew him as he was, and it gave me texts by which to live. "He discharged his duties with an affectionate fidelity," said Fitz Lee in that report. So would I. He "deserved trust and confidence and affection"—so would I. And that "Impetuous spirit which often carried him where the fire was hottest" could surely carry me too, through whatever I might have to face. It has done so. And it goes on in my son.

Cousin Bob and his wife* asked me to stay with them for a while. They opened their pleasant home to the drawing class which I had the assurance to undertake, inadequate as my preparation was. I tried by hard study to keep ahead of my

*Mrs. Mary (Mollie) G. Powell, historian for the D.A.R. and Colonial Dames, and other patriotic organizations. Author of the "Story of Valentine Peyton."

pupils, and was deeply touched by the generosity with which the people of the old town held up my hands. Art broke out like an epidemic, those who had little time or money to spare applied to me for a few lessons. Many of whom it had never been suspected, became wildly enthusiastic over painting. My heart was ready to burst. It did not dawn upon me that this was the purest charity. I thought it a renaissance of art in Alexandria, and threw myself enthusiastically into becoming the guiding star of a new culture.

I was more than ever faithful in my attendance at the Corcoran Art School. Mr. Andrews gave me an order upon his dealer for all my art materials. Mr. W. W. Corcoran sent Mother $500.00 proving himself a philanthropist. Bills long neglected were sent to me receipted without comment. Our grocer, Mr. Ramsay, to whom we owed several hundred dollars, sent Mother the receipt. Beautiful old ex-Confederate soldier! After my Cousin Rozier had collected Father's life insurance, he paid this sum. But Mr. Ramsay's generosity is none the less sweet to remember. The greatest kindness was shown, it was not unmixed with curiosity, and there was much conflicting advice, but poor relations must learn to adapt themselves as best they can to much advice.

It behooves an unprotected girl to walk warily. An old family friend brought me a pair of storm-shoes. Mother and all the children were still at

Oatlands and Father had not been dead two weeks. It was February. I needed exactly those shoes for the walks to and from the railway stations four times a day in all weathers. Exercise was good and it was twenty cents a day saved in carfare. The snow and slush soaked the soles off a pair of shoes very soon, and the storm-shoes were a gift most welcome. I was truly pleased—suddenly he kissed me, a crushing, uncomfortable, horrid kiss, such as I did not know was possible—he held me disgustingly to him, and I had to fight him. This was a revelation of grossness. It was a violation—in the spirit sense—it thrust upon me a sudden sickening realization of sex—my own imagination did the rest, told me plainly what such moods led to. So, thought I, it is not only to find bread, but never to relax one's vigilance against such assaults.

Nevertheless, I hung on to the storm-shoes. I suppose a self-respecting young lady who had been kissed with such enthusiasm should have marked her disapproval by returning them. Not I; I said to myself, "I will watch him and I get the storm-shoes and he gets nothing." Fear vanished.

His next gift to me was a copy of Swinburne's "Laus Veneris." I accepted the book without hesitation. He had had it many years and it opened itself at the most salacious of the poet's rhapsodies. Last night I located the shabby old volume after many years of neglect and scratched his book plate out of it.

POOR RELATION

Picture the little eighteen-year-old, a broken-hearted mother and seven little brothers and sisters on her mind, burning the midnight oil, "In Praise of Venus." When Cousin Mollie and Cousin Bob were asleep (and their guest should have been), behold her sitting propped against her pillows, a lamp at her elbow, saturating her mind with Swinburne's devilish music. But two themes had he—lawless love and hopeless death, hopeless death and lawless love. With the book in her hand and her face flushed with excitement, this young lady jumped as if she had been shot when a mouse ran across the floor—stuck the volume under her pillow guiltily, if the old mahogany furniture cracked or groaned. She felt far more guilty than the poet ever felt during these nocturnal orgies with printer's ink and a disturbed imagination. And yet she could not put the book down. It was too interesting. The word "erotic" she had never heard, and the thing it stands for was hardly understood, but it fascinated while it repelled. She was exploring a new field.

> Wilt thou yet take all, Galilean?
> But these thou shalt not take,
> The laurel, the palm and the pæan,
> The breasts of the nymphs in the brake.

This was blasphemy. And the thought of the complete sacrifice made by Christ that men's minds might be purged, that their souls might be strengthened to resist what was in themselves unworthy, brought tears.

> I am tired of tears and laughter,
> And of men that laugh and weep;
> Of what may come hereafter,
> For men that sow to reap——

That was a slap at Grandma, and at the doctrine of justification by good works.

> I am weary of days and hours,
> Blown buds of barren flowers,
> Desires and hopes and powers,
> And everything but sleep.

He was tired of too much, and it must have been his own fault. All days are not rainy days. This sounded like chronic dyspepsia. He was a "fast" man, the reader feared, and pessimism is contagious.

> To lull you till one stilled you,
> To kiss you till one killed you,
> To feed you till one filled you,
> Sweet lips, if love could fill—
> To hunt sweet Love and lose him
> Between white arms and bosom,
> Between the bud and blossom,
> Between your throat and chin,
> To say of shame—what is it?
> Of virtue—we can miss it—
> Of sin—we can but kiss it,
> And it's no longer sin——

Good gracious! She did not know that such stuff was allowed in print! She did not know how poor it was, as poetry. The nobler work of Swinburne came to her later. This set her cold and hot with intoxication, agitation, imagination, indignation. At last she sickened of it, and childishly replying to the erotic ravings of the poet in a few lines of her own, dismissed him from her mind.

> How great, Oh, Poet, is thine Art,
> Could we but hear thee sing
> Some strain to touch the pure in heart
> Full homage might we bring.
> But thou hast won thy laurel wreath
> By singing, with God-given breath,
> Of lawless love and hopeless death,
> And every tainted thing.
>
> Rather we prize the humbler bard
> Who lacks thy golden speech,
> But pure in thought and clean in word,
> Whose gentle measures teach
> Of self-restraint, the saving power;
> Of love that outlives passion's hour;
> Of God in stream and child and flower;
> And heaven's far heights in reach.

So I digested the songs to Venus. This is the way it is. This is what Mother had hinted, when I lay close beside her in the dark and talked about my Cousin Stanley. It must be wonderful—but can it last? No, Swinburne always said it could not. It was like a storm or a sunset—too intense and tragic to last. It has the quality of music—too evanescent to grow old, to become threadbare and hackneyed, a part of the daily routine. No sense of service or of duty to sanctify it, how can it face the years? The agony of its honest fulfilment makes the ecstasy of its beginnings also noble, this my own mother had proven. So the delicious nasty lines which had sung themselves into my mind sung themselves out again, and only good was done. I had learned something. I knew suddenly more about my mother—more of the mystery that had given me life. That was what she could not tell us, long ago, in New Orleans; that was what she tried to make me know, when we talked in the dark about my Cousin Stanley. And that sacramental, glorifying thing had suddenly been taken away from her! I wept for her in deeper understanding.

Looking back to that old man, dead many years, who gave me those gifts—the sensible storm-shoes, the kiss, and the book,—I feel not the least resentment.

And looking back to my first knowledge of Swinburne, and the influence for a short time of his intemperate imagination, the contaminating degradation of his own magnificent mind (as I came to know it later) I have learned that we must know a man's work as a whole, and not in scraps, to know it truly. None of us could stand the test of judgment upon our unworthiest productions, each of us is entitled to classification according to that which we have most nobly produced. Not by our delinquencies should we be judged. Who knew better than Bobbie Burns?

POOR RELATION

Who made the heart, 'tis He alone
Decidedly can try us;
He knows each chord, its various tone,
Each spring, its various bias:
Then at the balance let's be mute,
We never can adjust it;
What's done, we partly may compute,
But know not what's resisted.

CHAPTER XLIII

THE drawing class at Cousin Bob's house had increased tremendously; the young girls of the town, gay and happy, prosperous and protected, seemed to suddenly awake to the desirability of painting. Busy housewives declared that a little "art" was a real recreation, and a change from the kitchen, nursery, and sewing machine. Business women held the opinion that the routine of office work was unromantic and the love of the beautiful must be cultivated. So it seemed that it would not be too reckless to rent a little house and gather my family together now that I was earning some money. Mother could not remain at Oatlands indefinitely with such a tribe as hers, nor could I permit my generous cousins, Doctor and Mrs. Powell, to turn their pretty home upside-down indefinitely for me. So I rented a wee sma' bit of a house ($200.00 a year) and bought some cheap furniture on the instalment plan, trusting to my wits to make more out of barrels and boxes (as people who have bird's-eye maple and mahogany tell you can be done easily by anybody as clever as you!)—and then I brought them all down from Oatlands to begin a new chapter.

Mother had at once bought a piano with the $500.00 Mr. Corcoran had given her. She said it was an investment. How, she asked, was Lucy to become, as destined, a musician without a piano? And she looked so sweet as she asked this unanswerable question that it would have been too hard to have opposed her. When our cousin heard of it he was very impatient—he said it was a plain question with Mother and her children of bread and meat—not of luxuries and pianos. I was furious. I had eaten his bread for weeks, but that made no difference. Criticism of Mother wiped all gratitude off the slate (I had been very cross myself about it, but did not say so—and why should he say to Mother the thing I would not say?)—I told him it was all very well for him, having a piano, to discourage Mother— and that she had as much right to one, and more use for it, than he had. He looked hard at me and said very kindly that my sister might have used his and welcome. A crop of advisers sprung up over night and Mother was all at sea. She did not want to act contrary to any advice, but opinions were contradictory, and we were glad when interest in our affairs waned a little and other matters engrossed our friends.

It was impossible for us to be put into orphanages, or to be cash girls in the Ten Cent Store, or to be companions to old ladies who did not want us, or do any of the things we were told to try. And the blue blood was such a handicap. It was impossible to quarrel over small matters with petty tradesmen, and it was impossible for Mother to make any kind of a bargain.

She was a defenseless little thing whose sweet eyes filled with tears when her firm and well-disposed friends told her they thought only of her good, which she knew; that she must be grateful, which she knew; that her children must not expect to do or wear or eat or say or be the things they wanted—that not what they would *like*, but what they could get, was the question. She knew all that. When young chaps came to her and asked for board, she felt she should not refuse—her own boys would some day be out in the world, too, and she would be only too thankful to have them mothered by someone. Acknowledging the claim of universal motherhood, she never refused. They paid her what they said they could afford—not what she knew it would cost her to provide for them.

She made them go to church—to Old Christ Church, where our pew, against the wall in the "Amen" corner, was the longest and fullest in the church, except its counterpart opposite, in which the Lawrence Washingtons and their twelve children outnumbered us. Sweet Old Christ Church, with its plain white walls and its associations with Mt. Vernon and Arlington, and the "Simple great ones gone."

Butter became the curse of my life. It is so easily wasted! It is a perishable commodity, is butter,

Old Christ Church, Alexandria, Va.

Pulpit of Old Christ Church, Alexandria, Virginia.

and expensive, and Mother was an honorable soul, despising margarine. Such "boarders" as Mother had, were fond of butter. Butter became in my eyes a gauge of character and gentility, almost of integrity. I watched these ravenous wretches "gaum" their batter-cakes with it, help themselves to more than they really wanted, leaving great golden chunks of it half melted and wholly useless, mixed as it was with gravy or jam, and I called down anathemas upon their greedy heads and arraigned them at the throne of grace as persons whose god was their belly. If the suggestion was made again to substitute cold loaf for batter-cakes and waffles, and thus economize in butter, Mother looked worried, said butter was nourishing, and she still wondered how a Yankee streak had got into one of her children. "No, my dear, we must economize in some other way—we must have hot cakes."

A lady does not notice such things. I did. Therefore, I could not be a lady. Very often I was as far from being a lady of the fine old school as it was possible to be.

We had a slovenly old servant named Emmeline. The nomenclature of the Southern darky would furnish a chapter in itself. Their love of high-sounding names is significant. Some touch of grandeur is the inborn right of each of us. The labial and vowel sounds are sweet to the African ear, and those simple negroes of the older type built up musical combinations in the way of names, which are only amusing to the careless and indifferent. "Magdalina" is very popular, the association being unknown, though often appropriate. "Magdalina Asperine" sounds well. You will admit it, if you repeat the combination regardless of the sense of the words. "Alpha and Omega" had great vogue—and I was brought up on stories of the doings of an order called the "Magdalina Daughters of Cleopatra." They were prone to invent musical names, Cleonora, Letheanna, the psychology of the matter being that such a name compensated the bearer of it for much that was ignominious in that state of life to which we are pleased to say, it "has pleased God" to call him. Emmeline was no exception. She was very exact that no abbreviation became habitual with the children—no "Em" or "Lina"——.

June brought an end to dear Mother's weary waiting for her eleventh child, the sweetest of them all. We could not afford a nurse, but a cousin of Mother's, one of the one hundred and eighty, came to be with her; we had Emmeline, who was fairly faithful, and I walked the floor that night beside the closed door, until I heard the baby cry. Soon I had him in my arms, and have held him in my heart from that day. His badness when he has been naughty has been sweeter than the goodness of some others, and his goodness has been entrancing; for better, for worse, he has been mine.

Our cousin was very charming on this visit. She was more—she was wonderful. Her gaiety, in spite of the discomforts of our cramped little house in mid-June, was wonderful, and she kept the children in transports of joy with the large freezers of ice-cream which she ordered from the confectioner and which the little ones demolished in short order.

The following Christmas she invited our whole tribe to dinner—that first Christmas, so hard for Mother to face without our father. This black-eyed Cousin Annette was witty and quaint, full of tact and of kindness. Her fun and foresight held the tears back and kept the sad thoughts under. Mother was only thirty-eight and very pretty in her mourning. I had to chaperone her—I was not anxious for her to have admirers. I felt that she had been admired sufficiently. I can not recall if my younger sisters were enveloped in crêpe on this occasion, but I know that I was. Our Cousin Annette had taken great trouble, the dinner was served as it might have been for the French Ambassador himself—all the beautiful linen, silver and porcelain that the house possessed was brought out for these nine fatherless children and their mother. The food was served in courses to the great astonishment of the little ones accustomed only to Emmeline's unsophisticated methods. Before the dessert, two immaculate maids appeared with great trays loaded down with gifts for each of us, selected with thoughtful consideration as to individual tastes and needs. Mine was a little travelling bag. The whole thing was so kind—too kind! I was filled with a dull pain, an utterly inexplicable desire to be dead.

CHAPTER XLIV

FREQUENTLY our relatives asked me to drop in to lunch at their homes in Washington, especially this Cousin Annette, and I fear that I became the most faithful dropper-in of history. Hurrying off from breakfast before eight o'clock, walking several miles in the nipping air each day, standing over my own or someone's easel all the morning, talking in criticism, studying the model with as much accuracy as was in me, using all there was of brawn and brain, noon found me ravenously hungry. And I had not done growing. So I frequently—too frequently—but unconsciously, overtaxed this hospitality.

There were places where one could lunch cheap. Only, in such places one is hungry again before he has counted the change. In dairy lunchrooms, griddle cakes—three—with maple syrup, could be had for fifteen cents, but a dirty boy in a dirty jacket with a dirty thumb in your plate, spoiled that. At Trueworthy's oyster-pie was served on Monday, Wednesday and Friday, and chicken-pie on Tuesday, Thursday and Saturday. Pie is filling. The crust helps so, and the gravy. Three or four dejected oysters at least flavored the gravy, and necks and drumsticks of questionable fowls gave the chicken-pie its title clear. The lumps of dumpling were really valuable, and one regretted there were not more of them for twenty cents. The gnawing wolf at one's vitals could be held at bay for exactly one hour, by a plate of ice-cream for twenty-five cents at Demonet's, spotlessly served and therefore appetizing. And when pay-day came, why not be reckless and spend money? A deviled crab and a tomato salad at Fussell's for forty-five cents.

Yet there are days when man cannot live by bread alone, one must have violets. The desire, probably a mere desire of the flesh, a lust of the eye, overpowered one. Every street corner purple with them—and so on spring days there is sometimes no lunch, for an extravagant bread-winner has thrown away fifty cents in flowers. Sayings of the Syrian Christ break upon the mind with new significance as one stands hesitating between a sandwich and a bunch of violets. Nature screaming for both. How much He knew—how deep He saw—"Man cannot live by bread alone."

Soon I secured a position to teach drawing at a girls' school in the country, at a yearly stipend of ninety dollars. Ten dollars a month for two lessons a week. A whole forenoon devoted to it and a long freezing drive.

The music teacher and I drove out together in Uncle Ned's old dayton. The equipage was as venerable as the driver. There were cracks in the floor, the curtains beat and flapped their wretched rags in the wind, the harness was tied up with shoestrings and bits of rope. The horse should have been condemned to a painless death in any Christian city. The roads were deep in mud. The drive was not exhilarating. My little jacket was very thin.

For the first five minutes I was conservative, sitting as far from the fatherly old piano teacher as I could, but as the minutes and the miles dragged on and the bitter wind whistled through my clothing, I became increasingly democratic, and snuggled closer and closer to my companion, who was warm and comforting. When we reached the place our employers thawed us out with tea.

Relatives who were in society (mysterious term) bought dinner-cards from me, and when conversation flagged at their dull and deadly dinners, my dinner-cards and my personal history would serve to stimulate cerebral processes, flagging under over-feeding.

The palm-leaf fan industry of New Orleans also revived but in place of the noble floor-walker Cousin Cary Nicholas was the benevolent angel. The idea originated with his sister, Cousin Lizzie. Cousin Cary spent his life obediently carrying out the orders of his sister, a bustling, excellent little elderly person. Her suggestion also, as regarded Saint Peter, brought me many a dollar, though it cost me many a tear. She said that a great many of her friends had Catholic cooks who were crazy to have portraits of Saint Peter with the keys of heaven. That if I would get a penny print of some old master's portrayal of Saint Peter, enlarge it in full color, and sell the results for $2.00 each, she, Cousin Lizzie, would see that they were sold. "Special offer, portrait of Saint Peter!" This was pot boiling of the most degrading kind, and if my pupils had known that I did it I would have felt my authority and influence at an end— I preached so about ideals, and sacrifice, and ranted against commercialism in art. Yet I could not afford to be squeamish, it was up to me to say one thing and do another—the old, old warfare. There were many devout cooks for whom I ground out the Saint Peters, and Cousin Lizzie raked in the two dollarses for a long, long time until that field was exhausted. Saint Peter did more than pay for the damnable butter that melted so fast! Cousin Lizzie gave me her old clothes too, and they kept me warm. They cannot have greatly enhanced my personal pulchritude.

My sisters were pretty and blessed with the elasticity of youth and after that first period of mourning for Father was over they went as the other girls did to dances and parties, light of feet and light of heart. Mother was often hurt when people told her that we should not feel conscious of our deficiencies of wardrobe, but go and be glad to go where we were invited. Poor mother,

her blue eyes would sometimes fill, and she has been known to protest with some little spunk that we could not enjoy it if we were at a disadvantage and had not the high-heeled slippers and long gloves which were deemed necessary then for evening dress. Whereupon the advisory board would go on record as congratulating us that we were not unattractive, even so. Occasionally another girl would give us a little finery.

One rose-colored bodice was given to me. I presume the giver had use for the skirt, perhaps would make a petticoat of it. This bodice was cut low in the neck, and was quite sleeveless. It laced up the front with a pink cord. I never went to parties; I played with wise old gentlemen and read Carlyle and Schopenhauer. Yet in my own room sometimes, in great secrecy, I donned this rose-colored bodice, this mere fraction of a party dress. It was very becoming, entirely too becoming. The low-neck-ed-ness of it was entrancing and by drawing the cord very tight I could make it as outrageously low as the portraits of the ancestral dames looking down from the walls at Oatlands. Then I struck poses similar to those in the old masters as I knew them from the prints in the shop windows. It was impossible to bring my strong, stout little fingers into the postures of those boneless hands of long ago, but head and shoulders fell in well with the old type. This solitary bit of cast-off finery, this old rose bodice stained under the arms and slightly frayed, afforded me a reaction from the ugliness of Cousin Lizzie's misfits. How would it seem if one curled one's hair? And instead of painting a Saint Peter or two, to pay for some butter, I deliberately sat down before the glass with a rag and a cake of soap, carefully twisting little rings, such as were termed "beau catchers" or "spit curls," plastering them down with soap and tying the band around them until they were dry. Then to run the comb through and loosen the hair, and Lo and Behold! I was pretty! Very pretty—in the spit curls and the rose bodice! But mortal eye never beheld me.

This is a confession that few of my friends will believe for I always openly scorned the vanities that I inwardly coveted. I knew that this secret vanity was sinful as I knew the subterfuges by which I concealed my bleeding pride were sinful. And my ingratitude to Cousin Lizzie—well, perhaps it was not exactly ingratitude, but I could not enjoy her things—whatever it was, it was wrong, and I knew it.

And one can be very sinful and deeply religious at the same time.

CHAPTER XLV

THERE was no doubt but that the religious training of early childhood weighed me down. Only after association with the noblest and best did the tyranny of this self-righteousness relax a little. Habitual courtesy and generosity on the part of those who laid no claim to orthodox religion finally broke it down.

During the adolescent period religion affords a rather decent outlet for emotional fervor. It also scares one to death. Instead of kissing boys a growing girl may pray often and hysterically and enter into confidential relations with the Holy Ghost. I hope this is not flippant. I mean I hope it does not seem so. I know that it is not, and cannot be, for it is God's truth.

Moody and Sankey were holding a religious orgy in Washington in which I felt obliged to participate. Nothing could have restrained me from Convention Hall and that carnival of repentance. Lucy and Powell accompanied me. The audience was at high tension—5000 people swayed by a single impulse—Bishop Penick offered a sensational prayer—Dr. McKim read the lesson with fine effect. Then Mr. Moody tackled the Prodigal Son.

Looked at in cold blood and through the perspective of years, my own life tallies in few respects with the briefly hilarious progress of the prodigal son, yet that immortal story which has fired the imaginations of men for these two thousand years again struck home that night and the sins of omission and commission of all 5000 of us arose to stare us out of countenance.

Then, unaccompanied, Mr. Sankey sang in that sweet untrained voice that tugged at the heartstrings of his hearers:

> There were ninety and nine that safely lay
> In the shelter of the fold,
> But one that was off in the hills away,
> Away from the gates of gold—
> Away on the mountains cold and bare,
> Away from the tender shepherd's care——

Who cares if the poetry is not of the highest quality and the voice an uncultivated one? There is that in the hymn which beggars all art—which stands the test of all time. Something which transcends the things we know and opens to us the things for which we can but hope. That great plea to come and be forgiven—that far-reaching promise of redemption——

When Mr. Moody called for the repentant sinners to come forward to the "Mourners Bench" I instantly arose. Deep repentance and firm determination lifted me to my feet.

My respectable young brother grabbed me, "Please don't—sit down, dear—don't make yourself conspicuous."

POOR RELATION

Conspicuous? Was not Christ conspicuous? I must go.

Then my sister Lucy turned to me, "SIT DOWN YOU FOOL!"

I sat down. Something died. And my garments of repentance I flung away from that day.

Somehow the sense of poor-relationdom falls away from the art student. All are poor together and the aristocracy is one of talent. The currency is one of ideas. Lust of possession is lost in the love of beauty. If I see and admire a rare thing it is mine, to all intents and purposes. Mine, without the responsibility of caring for it. You, who own it, must insure it, or pack it in moth balls, or lock it up in your strong box, or hire detectives to watch it. But I perceive its color and glint, its form and charm, I reap the riches of its suggestiveness, without paying a tax on it or sinking a lot of money in it or glaring ferociously at any fellow creatures because of it.

Your gardens, your jewels, your bric-à-brac, your expensive complexion, your Oriental rugs, are mine as long as my eyes rest on them and my memory holds them for reference. And in return I am willing to open to you the riches of the art student's small world that is so boundless—nature, as I see her, and try to paint her for you. Nature spoke to Shelley and he told it in words. She spoke to Turner, and he repeated the message in paint. She spoke to Beethoven, and he set such soul-searching sounds together that the most ignorant is moved to inexplicable tears. There we feel all of man's poor persistent effort to understand, his loyal purpose to praise. Ancient Hebrew, mystical Hindu, medieval Saint, modern impressionist, all, in every conceivable medium, ringing the changes through the ages as they testify that "the heavens declare the glory of God and the firmament showeth his handiwork."

Nature speaks to us all in her many voices, and we repeat her message in the manner best suited to ourselves. Some express the functions of sense, some of intellect, some spread the poison that is also part of her mysterious makeup. This little art student, with soul sincere, reminded herself continually of the wealth, the grace and beauty that were hers, without money and without price.

The Bible, which I had soaked up like a sponge under Grandma's tutelage, encourages a sort of vanity and mild self-appreciation. There is in its dear philosophy a reassuring suggestion to those whose bread is watered with tears and whose daily experience is of belittlement or indignity. The first shall be last, and the last shall be first; the stone which the builders rejected became the headstone of the corner; the grain of mustard seed outgrew all the great trees around it; the people brought in from the highways and hedges were as acceptable as the invited guests; the humble guest was told to go up higher and was addressed as "friend"; the Publican went home from the Temple justified rather than the other; the servants hired at the eleventh hour; the Prodigal Son; the woman with the precious ointment; the good Samaritan; the dying Thief!

Christ spotted the Poor Relations of his own day, and intimated not infrequently that tables might one day be turned; people and things which the world overlooked and undervalued were precious in His sight!

CHAPTER XLVI

AFTER she secured father's life insurance and my Cousin Rozier had paid some pressing bills, mother put a part of the remainder into the purchase of a plain, substantial brick house in the same street where we had spent a most eventful year. Eventful? Our new baby had been born there, we had learned our first lessons of working together, of making concessions and sacrifices for each other, we had established some precedents—namely, that we were doing our best and angels could do no more, and we would not apologize to the whole world because we happened to have been born. Moreover we had tested our friends and found many of them staunch. It had not been such a bad year.

After the house was paid for there was little money left, and on that mother drew steadily until it was gone. The interest upon so small a sum would have been negligible and the comfort to her of having a little balance in the bank was great, too great to have been denied her. Mother had very innocent ideas of business.

She proposed to Franklin Edwards who had toiled for us too many years and had loved father so faithfully, that he and she should enter into a business partnership—he in New York in the office which still stood in father's name on Broadway, where Frank would contribute to the partnership his work and his time, while she would contribute the prestige of the name, and they would divide the earnings. The prestige of the name—which spelled failure and bankruptcy! God has, does and will bless that man for his conduct to her. He was filling a clerical position, at a small salary, at that time, the "business" having long been as dead as a door-nail—but he never told mother that; he entered into this "partnership" with her without ever a hint at the true status of the case and she never saw the comedy or the poetry of the situation. In fact she doubted now and then if he divided the emoluments of the business fairly with her "Because," she would say, "it was not mentioned in the arrangements that any of the running expense was to be charged to me—New York is a wild place for young fellows—and I hope——"

And all the while he was sharing with mother his hard-earned salary, a piece of knight-errantry, if ever there was such! For shabby and apologetic as this young man must have been, was he not rescuing a lady in distress and sharing his all with the helpless?

Just as in my childhood I had thought myself good because I so sincerely wished to be good, and had bent my energies toward making all of my mother's other children good like me, now as a young—a very young—woman, I concluded that I was more intellectual than the rest of my little world. Instead of joining in the harmless foolishness of the mob of boys and girls who frequented my mother's house, singing comic songs and playing brainless games and laughing and romping and making much merriment out of nothing, I adopted a sweet sad smile, one of infinite superiority and patient forbearance, took Emerson and Ruskin to my bosom and eschewed the noisy life of my own home. I never have known why I acted in this way. It must have been that unfortunate disposition.

Yet work all day and books all night left little time to mope. Nobody's feelings were hurt by my absence. They only laughed at me.

The family rather overdid the thing of ridiculing my faithful swains. They were not dancers and comic song singers. They were men. But I, too, thought them a little queer, and wondered along with the rest of the family what on earth they could see in me.

There was a Spanish artist, Allessandre Casarin, in his long linen duster and the inevitable palm-leaf fan which he always carried in both hands behind him. I was not ashamed of his broken English or his broadbrimmed hat, and I was very proud of his deferential old-world manner and his beautiful Castilian head. And more so, of the way he could paint—with anything—on anything. Studies on the tops of cigar boxes, which are good in size, color and texture for small sketches, and his tiny pictures had in them all the bigness of sea and sky and mountain for he saw and felt in a large way and one never thought of inches in looking at his work. There was no fumbling, no muddy tones—he transcended the means he employed and gave us nature herself— nature, generous, robust, like himself.

He told me to form the habit of studying without any material, to follow the lines of all objects with the thumb upon the forefinger; not to look at it, but feel, feel, feel, form. A painter is not an artist. An artist may not be a painter. The artist must be a poet and a painter. When he said this I felt a burning pleasure for my own bureau drawer was full of attempts at expression in verse. No one ever saw these ravings—the family was not appreciative and when it had to break out, like a strawberry rash, I concealed the results. Then when I was ten minutes late dressing and scratching in the bureau for a pair of clean stockings, nothing came to hand but odes and epics, in among the handkerchiefs and ribbons.

I was tempted to unbosom myself of these effusions upon the sympathetic Spaniard, but was too sensitive about them to show them even to him. My master, William M. Chase, Casarin said, was a painter because of his mastery of material, but was not an artist because the poetic aspects of nature meant little to him. He thought in terms of paint. Corot and Millet were artists, technique being subservient to mood and the imaginative and poetic always there to invite and charm the mind. He told me a great deal of Meissonier with whom he studied many years. He claimed that Meissonier was the king of draughtsmen, among the old masters as among modern painters. Once he said to Meissonier, "I wish to break away from your rigid academic training and draw freely my own way. I see others do so without this careful training." Meissonier replied, "I wish you success and compliment you upon your ambition; but remember that though it seems difficult and irksome to study accurately the forms of nature, it is perhaps more difficult to invent." He also told me how Meissonier would have a costume made for a certain character, hire the model by the day, tell him to put the costume on and wear it every day for a month, and then come back to the studio. Of course, in that time the clothing would have become a part of the man, an expression of personality.

Casarin considered Rubens an inventor of this kind—one whose lust for color so outran his discrimination that he absolved himself from that study, a little of which would have redeemed his brilliant work from the charge of slovenly drawing. He called my attention to Puvis de Chavannes, whose classroom drawings were marvels of academic correctness, and to the fact that, having learned to draw, Chavannes could throw drawing away when it suited his purpose to do so and when the figure served another purpose in his scheme. To know, then to choose. To possess, then to eliminate. And he told me not once, but often, that in spite of the outcry against the literary in art, the mission of art was to uplift and that it should appeal to all classes and elevate all men. That those who shock the world into admiration of their smartness have no enduring hold upon posterity.

CHAPTER XLVII

THE first touch of spring in the air lured us from our skylight into the open. The contrast was delightful, we wondered how we had endured the air of the life class so long, regulated for the nude model and far too hot for us. We realized then that the close application to the black-and-white had been exhausting, the strict academic almost devitalizing. From the stuffy room to the open spaces, from the naked human to outdoor nature, dramatic or gentle as its moods happened to be, above all from that accuracy which in figure and head drawing is absolutely imperative to the freedom of trees and rocks, which allow many liberties. Rock Creek Park was our haunt, more beautiful than any park I know in Europe or America.

Derelicts of society posed for us in the parks. There were many swarthy foreigners and sometimes a Chinaman or Jap in native costume, but our models on those sketching trips were principally the negroes because they were willing to pose for a trifling tip, which is all we could afford to give them. Washington was a provincial town in those old days, with a strong flavor of Southern life, and in spite of the fact that it was the seat of the administration and temporary home of a shifting population, the old residential society was similar to that of Richmond or Baltimore. The immense negro population has always been and probably will always be a characteristic of Washington, and certainly those of us in the old art student days who came in contact with these merry models had many reasons for thinking of them kindly.

There is the army of old colored women who start out every Monday morning pushing empty baby carriages of a prehistoric pattern on their way to collect the laundry, and on Friday these same ancient crones will be seen in the afternoon delivering the freshly laundered clothes. They are typical of Washington. And there are also rusty and battered old clothes boilers, which within the memory of my lifetime have always been used by an army of negro men for putting away coal, even in the most exclusive sections. The coal is dumped at the curbstone opposite the front door and several of these sweating negroes are in attendance to carry it in and put it in the bins. These "coal toters" with their rusty old boilers are typical of Washington.

But of the many subjects which we found for sketching, the most popular was "Mary, the Wild Cat." An ancient negro, with bent back and snowy beard, would be seen slowly trundling a push-cart along the shady walks bordering the parks and calling out in weary voice, "Cheese and Sa'sage," "Cheese and Sa'sage," to the laborers at their hour of noon-tide rest. The cart which served him as a vehicle for these refreshments bore on both sides a crudely painted legend, "Mary, the Wild Cat," and thereby hung a quaint pathetic tale. In the old man's youth he had lived on a plantation and had loved a saucy wench whose nickname was Mary, the Wild Cat. The Civil War came on, followed by the emancipation of the slaves, and Mary, the Wild Cat, vanished from the horizon. Her lover never ceased to seek for her and during many years in many cities pushed his little cart about, hoping that she or some friend of hers would be struck by the title he had given it and that in this way, while earning his daily bread, he might find some clue to his lost love.

We sought out the romantic places all around Washington—there is Bladensburg, in Prince George County, and don't you love our loyal old Royalist names, the King streets and William and Mary College, the Queen Anne and Orange Counties, the capes, Prince Charles and Prince Henry, holding in remembrance the sons of the Stuarts, scamps though they were, in this new world? They trace our history, these names of towns and counties, and the evolution of the Nation, for as influences succeeded each other in our building up, so names changed, until Greek and Latin, German and French, English and

Spanish, make a hodge-podge extraordinary, with the native Indian. And to these we must add the baptism of romance which swept the country with the appearance of Scott's novels, leaving Waverleys and Montroses scattered among the Indianapolises and Annapolises and Minneapolises, the various "villes" and "burgs" of America!

Bladensburg, Maryland, with its low-roofed buildings, the inevitable "Washington's Headquarters," the Police Station, with a sign as big as itself striking terror to the souls of sinners, no evidence of life around except a patriarchal guardian of the law asleep in a dilapidated old wicker rocking-chair on the porch! No wonder Bladensburg was the chosen rendezvous for duellists in the days when we were quick on the trigger, scene of the bloody endings of affairs we can hardly call romances—hardly affairs of honor —vulgar meddlings with other men's wives, and the irrational animal revenge.

Politics or adultery, jealousy in one form or another, stretched many a handsome figure out its length, there where the soft little willows border the brooks; Barron and Decatur, Mason and McCarthy, and others too recent for mention here. All problems solved now as they are gathered like children to rest in the wideness of God's mercy.

When we students could scrape up enough money we would go as far as Fredericktown, with its clustered spires, birthplace of Francis Scott Key and Whittier's "Barbara Frietchie"; who, by the way, did not live on the street through which Stonewall Jackson led his troops, and who, according to her own nephew, was bedridden and ninety years old at the time. In the "Southern Historical Papers," August 27, 1879, appears an open letter by Valerius Ebert, executor of Barbara's will, and at one time Mayor of Fredericktown, in which he refutes the whole story and calls it "fiction, pure fiction." It is harmless fiction and the town is not to be criticised for capitalizing Mr. Whittier's sentimentality and adding one more attraction for the lovers of history and tradition.

If we are to know anything of a locality we must have entré to the homes of the people. This was freely accorded the art students in many places, conspicuously in Frederick. To actually have access to the private homes, which in the South is almost impossible for tourists and sightseers, was a privilege we tremendously appreciated. The town is full of historic associations and these are materialized in rare furniture, spindle-legged old chairs and tables, material for wonderful still-life studies in Wedgewood china, queer brass candlesticks, copper pots and time-stained engravings, with perhaps a Paisley or an Indian shawl as a background. Even the patch-quilts were worthy of study, being unusual in color, design and needlework. We did little

Farmington, Albemarle Co., Virginia; Property of Mrs. Warner Wood; Showing the Part of the House Designed by Thomas Jefferson.

The Box-wood Labyrinth at Farmington and the Covered Corridors, Originally Slave Quarters.

painting on these trips to Frederick but gathered what was of great value—impressions. Impressions of a leisurely, calm life, of delicate, patient faces, of pleasant voices, gentle manners and mellow, honorable backgrounds. Every corner of old Frederick was rich in "Studio Properties," bits of form, texture and color reminiscent of the olden time.

Georgetown afforded us our nearest, most picturesque and least expensive sketching ground. The Pennsylvania Avenue street car took one for five cents to scenes that rival the palisades of the Hudson, the heights of Edinburgh or Genoa, the castle-crowned hills of the Rhine. Of course you do not believe this—but it is true. Old bridges—what is more paintable than an old bridge? A mighty river in its adolescence—useless as far as traffic is concerned, filled with small rocky islands and great gray boulders, on which every wild flower delights to grow—around which endlessly, untiringly, the water eddies with perpetual song.

Where else in addition to all this can you find a canal, loitering lovers along its banks, shabby old house-boats upon it, from which at six o'clock an odor of coffee and hot bread fills the air; the mules resting near the towpath; the boatman's wife and babies on the cramped deck, the comfortable thread of smoke ascending. A glance further, and the rugged bluffs of the Virginia side of the river fill the background of the picture.

The masterful arms of the sycamore trees, with generous gestures, point you to where green little Analostan Island smiles at you—a spot that by all we revere, love and cherish, should be set aside to perpetuity as an asylum for wild birds and wild flowers—our sweet and rapidly disappearing friends whose haunts are sadly few as "progress" rushes onward.

Nowhere did I find in my student days more lovely motifs for the study of Nature than in the Shenandoah Valley and about Charlottesville, Virginia, and in Greenbrier County, West Virginia. In all of these localities I was able to live at small expense for long times or short, because good friends took care of me. That wonderful system of "Southern hospitality" had its amusing side, but was in the main a noble institution by which those who had more shared with those who had less as ungrudgingly as God gives air and rain. So my little talents were often recognized and exploited, and I soon had my head turned by the girls who welcomed me into their own smoothly running homes. There was my cousin Nannie McCormick in Berryville, as sweet a thing as ever grew, who made her beaux take me horseback riding to hunt out the best "views" and made her old uncles take me "buggy riding" with my paint box and easel, when the spirit moved me to paint the charming bits discovered. That winding Shenandoah River with its dear old reddish, rusty, mossy bridges and the great sycamores throwing brave arms across from side to side, a magic roof——

Elmwood was where my old school-mate Hallie Patton lived, a fine old house not far from the White Sulphur Springs, where I often visited. "Deleraine" was Hallie's own saddle horse, but she never had a chance to ride him herself, or in fact any of the best horses, for her numerous guests were always given the best mounts, and I had Deleraine myself. Hallie was self-sacrifice in the flesh, and in fact all the cardinal virtues, and would sing the hymn-book through while she patiently mixed gallons of mayonnaise dressing for the houseful of girls and boys who were out enjoying themselves with her horses and her mother's carriage. When she was not singing hymns and mixing mayonnaise she was cutting sandwiches or darning my stockings. And at night she kept me awake talking about the rascal her mother would not let her marry.

Holkham was the home near Charlottesville, of Dr. John Rodes Woods, whose numerous children were my contemporaries. Dr. Woods was a grand old chap, who gave up his promising profession in order to pay off more quickly a debt of his father, who, like the rest of us, was too courteous to decline to endorse the notes of his friends and bore other people's burdens until he was bankrupt! $30,000.00 does not seem much now, but in the years just prior to the Civil War, when things were all uncertain, it was a big obligation, and this boy assumed it without so much as batting an eye, and set himself to work to earn it out of the land. He did. It took long years and unremitting labor and self-denial, but he did it; and his six sons helped. His daughter Margaret became the wife of Mr. Warner Wood, an English gentleman who had inherited the great estate of Farmington from English relatives who liked Virginia, and had been for many years established in Albemarle. Farmington is a famous landmark of the Piedmont section, part of the house was designed by Thomas Jefferson, and it is a fair rival in stately grace to Monticello itself. I have spent many happy days there, and the old friendship has stood the tests of time. Margaret Wood has five children, who are contemporaries of my own children, and Farmington receives me into its protecting old walls as affectionately as ever. One thousand acres still surround it, and the fine volumes, marble busts and heavy old furniture, all brought from England, are as they were forty years ago.

CHAPTER XLVIII

IN their anxiety to acquire suitable studio properties, art students go to very great lengths. Haunt junk shops, picking up microbious old rags as draperies, and unsavory articles of bric-à-brac. Brass pots and copper kettles from negro cabins, old chairs and tables, sofas with their stuffings falling out, and their joints infested with little fellow creatures which shall be nameless.

A human skull is deemed indispensable. It is a thing not easily acquired. A certain medical student got me one from college—that of some poor subject from the dissecting room. It was a nasty thing. It had enormous amalgam fillings in its back teeth. This treasure was not fit to be taken home—it had to be cured. The janitor of the Art School kindly boiled it for me, but it still made me sick. Then he put it on the roof of the Art School on top of the skylight in a soap box, that wind and weather might accelerate the process. As we worked in the life class, we often heard this thing rolling and rattling on the roof when the wind blew, and—silly creatures—we would giggle! We were such young idiots under that blessed old skylight!

After a year of wind and rain this thing was unobjectionable to me though I did not reckon upon the moral predilections of my mother's servants. With an excellent "rib basket" which I also had secured, I conveyed it to my mother's house—Immediate mutiny! The servants would not stay a minute in the house with my treasures. So I bestowed them with tears upon another girl whose home was not ruled by an Emmeline.

I forgot to mention that with the Life Insurance and the purchase of a larger house, Emmeline had secured a sort of lieutenant in the person of John, who waited on the table, and a Mary came in the forenoon to clean the house. These retainers had been sufficiently scandalized by the drawings from the nude which they pronounced after minute scrutiny, "warn't natu'al." Mother said human bones were out of the question. And I believed her, when I saw Emmeline, John, and Mary assemble in my studio, pointing the finger of reproach at my innovations and the awe-struck tone of Emmeline—"Does you all know what dem dare things is? DEM DARE THINGS IS DEAD MEN'S BONESES!"

You have met Emmeline. I want you to know Mary. Mother loved Mary. She was a sharp-tongued, bright-eyed mulattress, who one night, moved by generosity, had taken into her house a vagrant colored girl out of a blizzard. It happened in this case that Mary was not entertaining an angel unawares. A three-cornered domestic situation ensued, which laid the guest low with a cracked crown, and landed Mary in the Station House. Learning of Mary's incarceration, mother at once tied on her bonnet and went to the Mayor. Mary, she deposed, had not yet made up the beds in *our* house, and it was out of the question to detain her. Would the Mayor please send her at once? She was released.

Mary was pretty sharp but mother was always a match for her, "Miz Minnigrew," Mary would say, "please Ma'am, len' me seventy-five cents to go see a man git hung."

"Of course not, Mary. You will be hanged yourself if you go about knocking people in the head with chairs."

"Miz Minnigrew, all my tooths is achin' somethin' scan'alous. Please, Ma'am, 'dvance me fifteen dollars to get 'em pulled out."

"Of course not, Mary. I will give you a present of fifteen cents to buy a tooth brush—that is all in the world you need."

John was another of mother's faithful retainers. A diminutive imp who filled in odd gaps and for stretches of weeks at a time was in complete control of culinary and other matters—at such times, very grandiloquent. A tradesman at the door (probably with a dun) demanding mother in person, was met by this immovable menial, who insisted that he was mother's representative with plenipotentiary powers; the person enquiring, "Are you Miz Minnigro's servant?" received the magnificent answer, "*One of 'em, Sah.*"

Art School life was stimulating and happy if home life was a little discouraging. Day by day the debit column lengthened. Do what one could, one could not catch up. It was hopeless to try. And still I had a vague sense that some day my turn would come, and busy as I was at night there came visions of someone whose face I could not see, who would come after a while to make all things straight and fill every void full.

My Cousin Annette found for Charlie his first job. It was with a party of railroad engineers in the mountains. He was to report at once, to get thirty dollars a month, and to live in a camp with the other men. He left Alexandria on the Southbound train one night at eleven o'clock. We were not a sentimental family. We did for each other practical services now and then but never put ourselves out at all for mere sentiment. So it happened that no one planned to walk out to the Railway Station with the boy at that late hour. To me it seemed a crisis—(it was dear old Thomas Hovenden's pictures, "Breaking Home Ties," or "Out in the Great World"—It was the doleful ditty, "Oh, where's My Wandering Boy Tonight," etc.)—at least one of us would see the boy off. So I called upon that little friend of everybody, the man who the year before had sold my godmother's watch for me, to act as the squire of dames once more, and he and I escorted the young traveller on his way. Charlie was but fifteen and still in knickerbockers. He had a small nose and a square chin. His expression was determined—what the Germans call "booldoggisch." He was not an affectionate little boy but he was conscientious and faithful, absolutely bound up in and devoted to his mother. He looked so small, so plucky, scrambling up the high rear step of the train. He wore ribbed stockings. His little thin legs in ribbed stockings and the knapsack on his back, moved me to tears. There *is* something about a knapsack!

My old escort consoled me on the homeward walk, telling me not to cry and giving rein to a rather fervid imagination, pictured the brilliant future before this, the oldest brother, and the lovely things that he would do for me in the years to come. He went down the line, child by child, telling me that I was laying up for myself peace and devotion for all my years when these little ones were all old enough to realize how hard I tried. As he talked I clung to his shabby coat-sleeve and lifted up my voice and wept in the midnight streets.

When one stands openly advertised as an applicant for favors, as a wearer of other people's cast-off clothing, as a seeker after small, semi-charitable commissions, pride should die. Why prolong the agony? One suffers the pangs of one knows not what—self-respect is in tatters. One dares refuse nothing, resent nothing. Utter shamelessness is the only way out. Forget the sources from which you are sprung, starve the finer side of your nature —cringe, boot-lick, beg, flatter, be grateful, be cheerful, oh, by all means be cheerful—make yourself acceptable, even if you become an object of contempt in your own eyes.

Take anything and thank all the world that you may breathe the air, and live, and be a spectator of all in which you may not share. Where is the line to be drawn? What is more ludicrous than a snobbish poor relation? What is more exasperating than a sensitive impecunious person? Can you accept a fur coat and feel hurt when a street car ticket is proffered you? "Oh, she jumps at large services, but turns up her nose at small ones. Do not make the mistake of offering her anything short of a brown stone front or a diamond tiara!" This is wit. There is no way, my dears, to control the situation. If you are "by the grace of God" called to that state of life which we are beginning to recognize in these pages as poor relationdom, stand on the street corner with open hands and beg.

One dear friend kept in the back hallway of her second floor, a barrel, which she dubbed "The Minni Barrel." This was wit. A playful allusion to our distinguished name. Into the Minni Barrel were dumped all the odds and ends which her own family did not want, and her outside friends also knew of it, and sent over contributions. It was a sort of sanctified and magnified wastepaper basket—a clever idea—a real clearinghouse. We suddenly sprang into fame because of the Minni Barrel—there were times when I could have followed my father and blown out my useless brains, which were so little resourceful as not to spare my mother this. When the Minni Barrel was full it was boarded up and shipped to mother.

Sick at my stomach, I would watch them unpack it. How could they? To mother—to mother! Yet indeed the things were useful. We would have missed the Minni Barrel. Many of the most serviceable things I had came out of its depths—and I was the only one of us who had a nasty, grudging, ungracious mood regarding it. I hated myself that I could not make such experiences impossible, or at least feel the gratitude I expected of myself. A pair of shoes from the Minni Barrel fell to me. They were handmade, and indestructible; agonizing. It is a wonder they did not lame me for life. You see they were too long in the vamp, and the seam bit into the instep excruciatingly. You know what that is— for a moment, perhaps. This seam must have hurt the person who contributed the shoes to the Minni Barrel. It also hurt me. But poor relations have no business with arching insteps. It was entirely my own fault if they hurt, and I doggedly continued to wear them for months though they took all the buoyancy and joy out of life every minute of every day, until they went into the ash-barrel, which was my Minni Barrel.

Shoes are an item when ten people must have them. The more these infernal things hurt me, the more resentful I felt toward all the nice rich people who threw things away.

I was told to come one day for a package. A friend had been doing her spring cleaning. She sent for me instead of calling the Salvation Army wagon. The package was an enormous bundle, almost more than I could lift, but seeing that she wished to be rid of it at once, I got both arms around it and started down Pennsylvania Avenue with it. It was carelessly tied up and right in front of the War Department the vile little string broke and the heterogeneous contents of the parcel were scattered far and wide over the street. An old, faded bed-comfort, some spraddling old-fashioned kitchen forks, the two-pronged sort that I used to see in the Oakley kitchen, a pair of half-worn corsets, and some shoes of various sizes. If the reader has ever cleared out a closet or two, after several years' accumulation of trash, he may picture the assortment without difficulty.

In later years, as I have stood in company with great and distinguished people, this scene has arisen before my eyes to hold me unspoiled and sincere, to make me grateful, and to maintain always in a mind too easily swayed, a sense of balance. My black velvet and Brussels lace and the great bunch of violets which is apt to finish off my evening dress have all vanished, and I have seen myself a hot, annoyed little girl, lifting a flushed face to thank the big darkey who so kindly gathered up the plunder for me that day. I gave him a tip anyhow. I was that much of a princess.

CHAPTER XLIX

THAT delicious self-confidence which is a psychological accompaniment of proper dress, is never the Poor Relation's. She holds her own by some other means—the triumph of mind over matter, perhaps! From the first fig-leaf, which saved their faces for Adam and Eve upon the fateful day, to the filmy draperies with which the modern descendants of this simple couple reveal their structures, dress has played an important part in the doings and development of men. Clothes are symbolic, emphasizing things mental and moral, proclaiming the tastes, standards and type of the wearer. Clothes are evidential, testifying silently to the condition and rank of their owners. You see an old woman at a ball, painted, massaged, strapped down and built up, overfed and under-dressed, and you read her mind as if you were a gypsy fortune-teller. Royalty is an amazing spectacle in this age of the world's history, a grown man, supposedly intelligent, almost crushed under the panoply of rank, trailing velvet and ermine, weighted down with jewels and decorations which are next to meaningless since they bespeak no personal achievement or effort. Yet the world is not ready to discard these trappings, emblematic as they are of rank, and crowds still gather along life's highways as royalty passes by.

To the nun and the trained nurse renunciation would be made more difficult did not the habit they adopt sustain them in their purpose and command respectful attention from the world at large. They live more or less up to the standard, the ideal, which their garb proclaims. Our clothing publishes to the world our way of life. Upon it rests largely the respect of others for us, and our self-respect as well.

We should make it a rule to be very careful how we distribute old clothes. If we decide that we or our children will not use a garment again we should mend it, send it to the cleaner, and make it as decent and attractive as it can be made before offering it to anyone. Winter clothes one should brush and do up in camphor and put away during the summer, for in the autumn they really will be acceptable whereas in the spring no one would experience a pleasure in receiving them. When the nipping autumn days come on and organdies and muslins have seen their best, press them and fold them up and in April they come out with the violets, to help someone whose outfit is limited, tide over the first warm days. This is very small trouble and it more than doubles the graciousness of the gift.

CHAPTER L

WHEN the little Art class which I had first entered quite outgrew the original plan, the Trustees of the Corcoran Gallery built an annex on Seventeenth Street and opened a real Art School. Mr. Andrews' gratuitous services were also suspended and a salary offered him, which he accepted and devoted to the use of those among his students who were in need of financial help, of whom I was perhaps the neediest. In the opening of the new school I was designated as assistant to Mr. Andrews, to do the clerical work and instruct the classes in drawing from the antique. This appointment was due to his kindness, hardly to my own merit. It was most valuable to me, for my stock instantly rose in every way. My private class boomed; I had more opportunities for commissions and private pupils; indeed, absurd as it seemed, I had to have an assistant myself in my private studio. I stopped painting Saint Peters and paid for the butter in less degrading ways.

I wondered now and then if Mr. Andrews could be in love with me—but he never said a word. He was fond of all the students, girls and boys; so good to us all that I ceased to speculate on that point. We certainly were a great deal together, he took it for granted that we were to lunch together, to drive every afternoon for an hour or so, to go frequently to the theater, but all of this was pure nobility. What else could it be? He never said a word. And I stopped guessing but kept an observant eye upon the maneuvers of certain other maidens.

There was one toward whom he had been especially generous, who in a burst of gratitude one day fell upon him in what should have been a secluded corner and kissed him. Another aspirant beheld this act and spread abroad a highly colored account of the incident. Behold then this paragon among men, in a state of considerable embarrassment, and confiding his predicament to his meek and humble little assistant, "Now, my dear, I'm just an old fellow, you know"; I didn't know—I knew that he was the handsomest man in Washington, delightfully free from relatives and incumbrances—really filling the requirements of my little mother, "beautiful legs and no relations"—and that he was comfortably provided with this world's goods and had a very sweet nature. "You see, you must remember, when I asked you to go out and buy her those—eh—those articles of wearing apparel—those warm things—well, my dear, in a burst of gratitude, most natural, most touching, she—she—er—kissed me—just kissed a friendly old chap, you see—and that damned Blankety-Blank saw her do it and spread it around and the poor girl feels dreadfully compromised. What you do they all do—so be a good girl and befriend her—go to lunch with her—pity her distress—will you?"

Of course I did. I would have poisoned anybody, just as readily, at his request. And I did my utmost to reassure and console the temperamental young lady who in a burst of perfectly natural gratitude had kissed the handsomest man in Washington.

I was having a good deal of fun in my own way—so interested in many things and people. To say one's prayers and read one's Bible, to do one's daily work, to envy no one, to defraud no one, to live in an atmosphere of cordial admiration and generous competition, to visit the poor and earn enough to keep the pot boiling, to be in excellent health, and have always one or two men making love to me, while running around all day with the handsomest man in Washington, was enough for any poor relation.

The burning question now was how to educate our boys. We had five of them—snub-nosed, spindle-legged little rascals, with blue or gray eyes far apart and pale hair standing up erect or falling over their foreheads, according to whether they had cow-licks or not. They were intelligent and, to me, absorbingly interesting. In their mannishness they reminded me of young roosters making laudable but not very successful efforts

Eliphalet Fraser Andrews, Late Director of the Corcoran School of Art, Washington, D. C.

Lieut. Col. Fitzhugh Lee Minnigerode, U.S.A.

to crow. Charlie was at work, engineering in the mountains, such a little fellow to be pitched out with men! Powell, as the grandson of a clergyman, was eligible for a scholarship at a Church School where by the payment of a moderate supplementary fee (which I borrowed from Mr. Andrews and never repaid) we were able to place him—a good school, Southern, Episcopalian, conducted by our own connections—all of which at that time we regarded as advantageous. Later my husband placed him in a clerical position at the Corcoran Art Gallery, a child in knickerbockers—and in thirty years he has never wavered in his devotion there, has declined tempting offers to identify himself with other art institutions, and is at this time the Director of the Gallery. As he was my favorite brother, and the one most scholarly by nature, I was wild to give him a University education. The University of Virginia was out of the question, as too expensive, but in Washington we had our then Columbia University, with night classes.

I planned to work this out by appealing to a member of Congress who was closely affiliated with this University and who I believed would be only too happy to be of service to my brother for my sake—having seriously offended me once and who (as I judged others by myself) would welcome an opportunity to make amends! This man I pursued with my axe ready to grind.

Anyone who has attempted to promote a personal interest through a public man knows how many flunkeys and subordinates stand between the great man and all importunate impecunious unimportant persons who, to the experienced eyes of these buffers, are labeled and classified in some mysterious fashion and firmly but politely held at bay. These wretches would not let me see him but one day I happened to run into him on the street. He was affability itself, surprised and glad to see me. When my object was made clear his change of manner was instantaneous. Portrait painters, even third-rate ones, note these changes, the narrowing of the eyes, the tightening of the lips, the chin seeming to project a little more than usual. Ugly moods. People in society have no idea how surly, how unblushingly brutal, these dear fatherly intellectual old gentlemen can be. "O ho," he said, looking very hard at me," you want something now, do you? A brother educated? And you think I will arrange a matter of that kind for you! You earn money. If you want a thing, pay for it. If you want a thing," he repeated very distinctly and slowly," pay for it."

There was also an Educational Fund for the benefit of orphans in the hands of Mr. Skipwith Wilmer in Baltimore, so to him I telegraphed asking for an appointment, having my next little brother in mind. A wretched little scrap of determination, I went to his office, rigged out as usual in other people's old clothes; faced a group of men in his outer office, waited, and was let in.

Never letting the idea out of my mind with which I had gone to meet him, I stated the case concisely, my eyes fastened on his. He was kindly indefinite; non-committal, after the fashion of his sex and age—he was, I should say, past the years of discretion. Patiently I went over the whole ground again, keeping my eyes on him as though he were the Wedding Guest and I the Ancient Mariner. He parried—the matter would be taken up in turn, and considered—he would write. No, I thought as long as I had come over for this purpose I would just wait while he took it under consideration, which I felt would not take him long, since no one could be more deserving, more intelligent, more Episcopalian, more impecunious, than "Our Third Son"—I would wait. We got this scholarship and by the time it ran out my husband belonged to the family and met the bills!

"Our Fourth Son," George, named for my uncle, George Carter of Oatlands, was but a little boy, a very funny, sensitive, long-headed little boy. Mother's deep-rooted objection to the public schools had weakened and she entered him there. He came home one day very indignant.

"Mother," he said. "They whip boys in that old school!"

"Well, son, behave yourself, and no one will whip you," answered mother.

"Well if they ever whip me," he said, "I shall turn around and walk right straight home."

"Well you will get whipped again at home, my dear, and walk right straight back," said mother.

She supported the teacher and the discipline of the school, just as she had forgiven and shielded our teacher in New Orleans years before. Mother did not feel that a higher education was necessary, nor could we find the money for it; she comforted herself with the hallucination that a distinguished name and aristocratic connections would take the place of it. Of all my mother's nine children, none ever had a day's regular schooling after the age of fifteen. Yet look at Fitz. Little Fitz, with his green eyes and spindling Minnigerode legs! Some soldier! He left school at fifteen; spent twenty odd years in the Army; came up from the ranks.

He came back from the World War merrier, more alert, more upstanding than before, only quite deaf. He had been promoted for gallantry in action, as his father had been in the Army of Northern Virginia, the modern equivalent of that "Belohnung seiner Tapferkeit" bestowed on the old Roman forefather who fought under Charlemagne, or of that "Knighted on the field of battle" of his Peyton ancestor, Sir Robert, in 1487. Fitz, on his homecoming, as Colonel of the 113th Infantry, 29th Division, led the Virginia troops through Richmond, still echoing the footfall of his father's marching feet in 1862, and of his grandfather's moving prayers. His slim figure, his happy face, his breast covered with decorations, stirred the populace tremendously for he was of their own.

Actually, the boy looked like a Christmas tree, with everything but candles! The Distinguished Service Medal, the Distinguished Service Cross, the Croix de Guerre, the Legion of Honor of France, and I know not what other honors.

Because of his deafness, he was retired, and has taken to journalism as a duck to water, lives abroad and wields the pen as well as he did the sword, though Karl, my mother's baby, my own darling always, has remained in the Army since the War.

Look at Lucy. A woman of definite authority, of an honesty so pure and direct as to become the most astute diplomacy. The sort of diplomacy the male mind finds unaccountable. She is the personification of truth with no vacillating policies of expediency. She has many political affiliations in which her directness is more efficacious than adroitness. She is a fearless fighter.

Step by step she has trained her faculties and disciplined her soul. At eighteen she was governess in Charlottesville, Virginia, for girls almost her own age and almost as well informed as herself; she slept in the room with them, rode horseback with them, sat by the roaring open fire with them of winter evenings in the snow-bound hills of Albemarle County, telling stories or reading aloud, and educating herself and them. About the time I was married, she trained at Bellevue Hospital, New York, as a nurse. She has known all ups and downs, seen the inside of many situations, learned life with harsh and tragic certainty. Her activities have circled the globe and experience has strengthened her power and increased her distinction.

When the World War broke out in 1914, she was one of the first American Red Cross nurses to volunteer overseas. She went in charge of her unit, in September, 1914, and spent nearly a year in the Red Cross Hospital at Kief in Russia; the Russian Government giving her the Cross of St. Anne, the Czar receiving her. She did heroic work, and when America entered the War and her physical condition made it impossible for her to be sent over again, the chagrin occasioned her was such that she never spoke of the matter. To the doctors who pronounced her unfit, she said, tossing her wonderful white head—"Suppose I do die? That's nothing. People worth more to the country than I am, are being killed every hour. I want to go."

As chief of the nursing service of the Public Health Department of the United States, she has been an undaunted defender of her profession and a faithful servant of her country. The Red Cross awarded her the International Florence Nightingale Medal, in 1925.

She is widely and justly recognized; her instructions on hygienic matters are translated into many languages and published in many lands. The accompanying portrait of her is by courtesy of the Pan American Bulletin, in which it appeared in 1923, with an article by her, done into Spanish by the Bureau, embodying the most progressive teachings of the nursing profession. Far be it from me to depreciate scholarship. But it is no fetish. Intelligence and perseverance can compensate for the lack of it. It can be acquired outside of schools. One can arrive, despite a meager early education!

Often our sons were rude and naughty but the male of the species is averse to acknowledge a fault. The more one tries to do right the more one hates to apologize. A man should not find it necessary to say he is sorry—and he will try in a hundred ways to atone, to "say it with flowers," or something else, but very seldom come and say it in English, "Forgive me—I was wrong." Once the child, George, apologized to his sister. Whatever the small offense may have been it is long since forgotten, but the fact that he was sorry and said so, is remembered in love. He wrote the apology and slipped it under my pillow, after the family fashion, and vanished before I could catch him.

Ingratitude and discourtesy to one whose only thought was for his welfare oppressed his little soul, and without coercion he made the *amende honorable!* Happy tears filled my eyes, as, having lit the lamp, I read it. How long ago!

CHAPTER LI

How to make money?—For it had to be made almost by fair means or foul. Quick enough one overcame the early, almost constitutional aversion to talking of money, especially talking about it to people who owed it to one.

What was one slaving and slaving for, in God's name, if not for money? Ambition never moved one—the desire to arrive never once crossed the mind. Money for groceries, shoes, coal, books, money for Emmeline and the roof-man, and the ice-man, and the milk-man—a little money for the Church, and a little money for the poor, and a little money to make oneself look less like a rag-bag!

Two evenings in the week I had a drawing pupil at home—a young sign-painter. Once he brought a friend—who "loved art." A frisky little creature, dressed too much like a gentleman to be taken for one. I looked upon this addition to our class of one with some misgivings—and sure enough one evening this budding genius pranced up to me, leering quite frightfully, an awful little cologne-bottle all done up in artificial flowers, extended toward me. "It is for you!" he exclaimed, in a dramatic voice, while the poor young sign-painter looked from behind his easel like a scared rabbit, perfectly and instinctively aware that this was out of order.

"Oh, no!" I said, "not for me."

"Oh, yes!" he smirked, "for you!"

"Oh, no!" I repeated, "I do not accept presents from gentlemen." (Which was of course a lie, for I accepted anything from anybody.)

The next day I wrote this gentleman a little note suggesting that his talents were of an order quite beyond my range, and advising him to discontinue his lessons.

Mother's cousins, as I pointed out long ago, cannot be excluded from this tale—there were many of them and they meant much to her. There was my Cousin Helen, who stayed with us and paid my mother's coal bill, and did many generous things for us all. She was "fond of art" and gave me an order to do a crayon portrait of her pretty daughter. This I endeavored to do before and after my hours of teaching, and I would tear myself from it in the morning when train time came, looking forward to it in the evening only to find that my Cousin Helen herself had invaded my sanctum during my absence and made such alterations as she deemed advisable. These I carefully did away with, but the next day they had reappeared. Added to her activities, anyone of my mother's multitudinous progeny who felt the stirrings of the muse, would also lend a hand—

and thus the lovely Nancy was grossly misrepresented.

My Cousin Helen secured also a photograph of the old Emperor William of Germany, dead, and lying in state, which she said would bring large emoluments to the house of Minnigerode if I industriously reproduced it. She borrowed it from John Bassett Moore. I set to work making full-sized copies of this gruesome but beautiful thing—the dignified bald old head, the long Hanoverian nose exactly the shape of my father's, as also I must say, was the head—tipped down almost into the lilies which lay upon his breast. These I sold for five dollars each, though they were less successful than the Saint Peters; we resurrected several of them in the family attics of late years. One was taken by my good friend Rebecca Ramsay, to Washington, and exhibited with pride and generous admiration to various dealers, who promptly turned it down. I look back upon that bit of bravery on the part of another young girl with surprise and gratitude. It is not pleasant to peddle things, even when successful. It is less pleasant to have them refused. It is quite painful to report to an impecunious friend that your attempts to sell her works of art have failed.

All these small experiences returning to my thoughts after so many years, work out as a mosaic the pattern of a life. Can you see the picture of many well-meaning adults in conference as to what one little girl ought to do and ought not to do, and how hard she tried to be politic, for the sake of little brothers and sisters, and tried to do everything and please everybody? Oh, the luxury of being at last even as they were then—old enough to be arbitrary! Oh, and well off; comfortably well off—thanks to the wholesale grocery business established on the Ohio and Mississippi Rivers, by my husband's pioneer grandfather—that stalwart Martin Andriesen, who started west from Trenton on his twenty-first birthday, arriving at Marietta, Ohio, with his name changed to Martin Andrews, an axe on his shoulder, a half-dollar in his trouser-pocket, but folded in his breast-pocket a baptismal certificate, precious to him as was that family Bible to John Halifax—with the magic word "gentleman" written after his name—! Running his flat-boats up and down the rivers this great broad-shouldered, big-hearted round-headed pioneer grocery-man grew to be as handsome as Mr. Gladstone, whom he greatly resembled, and opened up a trade in sugar and rice and coffee and liquor, establishing a big business, and incidentally founding a family upon one branch of which this egotistical little Virginian was grafted, after more than a hundred years.

CHAPTER LII

NEWSPAPERS took me on. Through Dr. James Nevins Hyde I was brought in touch with the "Chicago Evening Post." It happened this way. A representative from a Bureau of Information in Washington came to the Art Gallery one day to ascertain how a Dr. Hyde of Chicago could obtain a water-color drawing of a continental costume on exhibition in the State, War and Navy Department. I happened to meet the man and told him at once that I would do the drawing myself. He asked me if I had access to these exhibits. I said, "Oh yes,"—though I never had heard of them until that moment. They were for the benefit of the public, and I was of the public, and I was sure it would be quite easy. It was—the drawing was made, and mailed with a bill for $5.00, which was promptly paid, and I forgot the whole transaction.

Several months later another matter took me to the Navy Department and in curiosity I went to take a look at the figure I had sketched for Dr. Hyde. The color of the costume was navy blue—not plum color, as I had painted it—the difference between daylight and artificial light. I at once wrote to Dr. Hyde explaining and apologizing for my error and returned the $5.00. In reply, he wrote most kindly that the mistake had occasioned him no inconvenience at all, and returning the money, inquired if I had ever thought of writing for newspapers. This was a bolt out of a clear sky and I wrote at once that I would be very glad to write for newspapers. Thereupon he advised me that a Mrs. Van Horstman Wakeman, on the "Chicago Evening Post," would look over any material I offered and give me expert advice. This was very remarkable—for that woman did write me several long and most explicit letters, pointing out the difference between journalistic writing and other forms of literary work, suggesting subjects within the range of my knowledge which might be readable and the manner in which such matter should be treated. She wrote by hand and almost affectionately—a warm human touch marked her letters—they were clear and kind and entirely gratuitous. My articles were descriptive, or local, mostly of darkies and queer old-fashioned Southern homefolks—I didn't know much else. They were illustrated; the staff artist always did the drawings over—perhaps my technique was not good for newspaper reproduction—and his name, not mine, was signed to them. I did not care. The six dollars a column came to me, and the honor and glory was the least of my troubles! The money was all I cared about.

Washington papers took my stuff too sometimes but I never wrote under my own name. I had taste enough to realize that my work does not strike a very high note—but I was out for business and that was all. The faculty of observation sharpens under this sort of exercise. I did this work in my goings and comings, on trains and in street cars. I hitched people together who never heard of each other, because somehow they seemed to fit, swapped experiences around and lied like a trooper, made little pencil sketches of types I met and faked the story to match the face, and every day found me ahead of the game, with some little episode or anecdote grabbed up and ready for use. It took no time and was great fun.

I was very diffident about my attempts at writing for I had so little education, and the family always ridiculed my efforts. Verse broke out like a rash—I could not help it! Things I saw sung themselves into my head—started little poems automatically. To voice these moods gave me a pleasure which I would not deny myself though I had not the nerve to show my effusions to anyone. It had been tried on mother with no success and after our marriage I sprang some verses one evening on Mr. Andrews as he and I sat before the studio fire. He held the newspaper in his hands as he looked over his spectacles at me. I tried to read the lines in a way to win his sympathy. It was the first time I had ever dared to read them to anyone. He was very nice about it. Still clinging to his newspaper—"Very pretty,

my dear,—very pretty; but isn't it rather long?"
So, back to the bureau drawer they went, and
many years afterwards, at the request of my
children, were published. Commonplace little
things, only good in intention.

The love for common things grew daily, things
that cost nothing, and life was full of them.
That is what the study of art will do—open blind
eyes. I had no time for actual study, my hours
were too broken up but I stored up impressions
at every turn. Impressions are like capital in the
bank, bearing hourly interest. On the train
twice every day, between Alexandria and Washington, an hour to look out of the window—a
lot of landscape can be photographed upon the
mental retina in an hour every day. Eyes tired
with the black-and-white of charcoal drawings
could rest on expanses of blue and green of swamp
or snowy hill, an endless panorama.

In the winter, the anatomy of the trees, their
naked limbs thrown in silhouette against the sky;
the delicate tracery of last year's weeds, goldenrod and aster whose seeds were long since sown
by friendly winds; the long sweeping lines of
drifted snow, poems in themselves; and across
the wintry landscape how full of meaning, as the
darkness fell and the train sped on, was the yellow lamplight shining from the window of some
poor man's home, taking the loneliness out of
the whole world and the coldness out of the

winter night. And the people's faces and hands! Faces were like a long picture gallery, portraits all painted by masters!

The great book of life was opening of itself, full of romance and tragedy.

Painfully and by the assimilation of varied experience, we come into our own. Develop some sort of character, find some sort of an ideal. And having found it, fight all of our lives to hold on to it!

So there came the realization that everything is a part of everything. Physically and spiritually. "The fountains mingle with the river, the river with the ocean; the winds of heaven mix together with a sweet emotion; nothing in the world is single—all things by a law divine in one another's being mingle"—filling the woods with violets, the nests with birdlings, the cradles with babies.

CHAPTER LIII

FOR a portrait sketch class Mr. Andrews had been able to secure a room free of rent for us in a public building in the city, and there a class of specially ambitious students worked faithfully, under him, hiring their own models and expending excellent effort on portraiture.

As this club worked only in the forenoon he suggested to me to utilize the same room in the afternoons for my private pupils and save studio rent, which for a time I did. Eventually both classes became troublesome and the people in control of the building withdrew the privilege. This necessitated an expense which to me was far from welcome, in hiring a suitable room, but we planned to continue on the original basis, the portrait class using the room in the forenoon, I in the afternoon, thus dividing the cost. Rather an amusing fracas resulted. We took a room at 1700 Pennsylvania Avenue, near the Art Gallery and convenient for all. The rent was $20.00 a month. I hired two colored boys and a push-cart to convey my effects—plaster casts, easels, chairs, etc., and such poor studio furnishings as I possessed—to the new studio, and while they were thus engaged I went out for lunch. On my return I found my own stuff dumped on the sidewalk.

the plaster Venuses without a rag to cover them, creating something of a sensation among the newsboys and loafers, while my darkey boys were busily loading the belongings of my colleagues of the portrait class into the push-cart. My remonstrance was met by my thirteen fellow portrait painters with open contempt, and I saw at once that there were breakers ahead. Permitting them undisturbed control of my boys and cart for the time, I trotted to the Gallery, drew $20.00 in advance on next month's pay, and went over to the studio, asked for the janitor, told him that I was the artist who had leased the room and that I wished to pay the rent in advance. He grabbed at it, for artists are temperamental as regards rent, and gave me the lease in my own name. Returning to the midst of the portrait-painting sisterhood, I said very quietly, "Ladies, I think after all it will be more satisfactory for us not to begin this partnership in one studio—so you may look for a room elsewhere."

"How utterly absurd," they tuned up in chorus, "look for another place yourself——"

"Well, you see," cooed I, "I have the lease in my own name and have paid the rent."

Another disconcerting experience in the taking of a studio is worth remembering. This time I rented in a large studio building, giving the room up always in July and taking it again after the vacation, if it were not already leased. As there was no demand in the summer, I practically held the same room without paying the rent for three summer months, taking, however, the risk each year of not getting it in the fall.

On October first, one season, as I came back for it, the janitor told me that the agent wished to see me on business. "Aha!" said I to myself, "Business! probably a portrait of his wife——" and in great satisfaction I betook myself to his office.

He was a handsome man, socially well-known, and he remained seated as I approached his desk—the sort of discourtesy to which one never becomes quite accustomed. He wished to see me—yes—he wished to bring to my attention the fact that I continued season after season to hold that room, without paying for it three months in the year. I was terrified—he looked so important. "Oh," I answered, "That's all right—I move everything out, and take the chance of not getting it—if it is for rent in October, I have as much right as anyone." "Ah!" he said, looking very pained—disappointed—"from you I had looked for a higher ethical sense—legally, perhaps, you are exempt from financial responsibility, but do you not feel morally bound to consider the matter as a sort of debt of honor?"

He was a vestryman, an honorary pall-bearer, a benign godfather, and relative of several philanthropists; he belonged to that clique in Washington who claim that in order to be in exclusive society, one must be a member of the Metropolitan Club, keep his cash in Riggs Bank, and worship his God (probably everybody's God) in St. John's Church.

His voice was so sad, appealing as it were to my nobler nature, that had I had sixty dollars in my possession, I fancy I would have let him take it. That would have meant my lunch for one hundred and twenty days—I know now he would have taken it. The wolf!

A friend in the country had the agreeable habit of sending Mother a gallon of skimmed milk every day when the wagon went in to market. The children lapped it up eagerly, it helped in the cooking of soups and desserts, and we were thankful. One day, meeting Mother, this lady mentioned quite casually that we would get no more skimmed milk for they needed it all, she said, for their own pigs.

It may be foolish of me to remember such things but they are all parts of the story, and it is with no rancour whatever that I recall them.

My husband has long ago paid back that skimmed milk, drop for drop, in champagne.

And in my heart there is only gratitude to all those who in any way lightened my mother's burdens. In her crowded household, the skimmed milk, the bruised tomatoes, the old shoes, all filled some place in the general economy. Many a substantial service her friends rendered her—my own utmost and uttermost was not enough to meet her necessities.

Back and forth—back and forth—all those summer days. Uncomfortably crowded the street cars, stuffy and dirty the trains; long the walk up Pennsylvania Avenue, when the asphalt pavement yielded in the heat to the pressure of the foot but always—everywhere—compensations. I was one with my kind.

Always the thought that step by step, day by day, inch by inch, I was winning. Doing what I had undertaken to do for my dear father—doing what he had left undone—"discharging his duties with an affectionate fidelity"—holding his house together—fitting his children for the fight. Always buoyed up by my dreams.

And always behind me that best and kindest of friends—Mr. Andrews. I was not anxious, he was there. I cannot enumerate all his kindnesses—they were obvious every hour of every day. But I promised myself a thousand times that if it were in my power to serve him, I would make good at any cost—absolutely and without reservation.

People sometimes teased me about him—said he wanted to marry me—but what would have been more simple than for him to have said so, if that was what he had wished? No, he was good to us all—more so to me, for my need was greater. He never once hinted at love, and I went blindly on, letting other men, scattered through those few years, talk of marriage to me.

I accepted his kindness, as I had to accept everybody's, as part and parcel of the condition of Poor Relationdom. So the debit column lengthened. Obligations, gifts, services from many sources. And always in my mind the honest purpose to render to Cæsar the things that were Cæsar's and to God the things that are God's.

CHAPTER LIV

ON rare occasions during these years Lucy and I went on visits to relatives in the country and tasted the pleasures of life forgetful of the responsibilities of Poor Relationdom. At our Cousin Janie's! At · The Plains! Oh, that good old vine-covered porch—and the delicious agitations of love-making!—some country cousin whose steed is hitched to the fence-post and whinnying with impatience, while his young master plumps down on his knees, exclaiming, "Be mine! Be mine!" Or at Avenel, the Beverley estate, presided over by Aunt Jane, the wife of Col. Robert Beverley, an exquisite saintly creature, whom I see before me as I write, standing at evening in her old garden of roses. Her grandsons, Bev Mason—dear Bev—who died so young—and Billy and Dick and Steenie—were our playmates, and her younger son, Bradshaw, and her nephew Loughborough Turner (to whom descended Kinloch, the estate of my great-grandfather Turner) were the objects of our profoundest interest. These youths were great singers and I assure you that guitars have been thrummed under my window on moonlight nights with all the romance of ancient Spain, and Lucy and I have sprung from our virtuous couches and listened, thrilled and spell-bound, to sentimental ditties which never disturbed Uncle Robert Beverley's heavy slumbers. The fine tenor and baritone voices of our handsome cousins rendered the Serenade from Longfellow's "Spanish Student" with great effect.

> Stars of the summer night
> Far in yon azure deeps,
> Hide, hide your golden light!
>   She sleeps!
> My lady sleeps!
>   Sleeps!

Continual disenchantment met all my efforts to make my mother's children good, but for these disappointments there were unexpected compensations. There seemed to be a good many *men* who really wanted to be helped—who were not very good and needed someone to lead them. Disciples who were willing, even anxious, to sit at my feet and learn wisdom!

At last my moralizing, which was but an echo of Grandma, began to have effect, for old men listened respectfully to my philosophy and young ones held my hand and told me of their spiritual difficulties; but the men began to be sentimental long before their regeneration was under way.

After my Cousin Stanley's exit, the next aspirant for my chubby hand in lawful marriage was an elderly paralytic of excellent family. I know now that it was a case of paresis. I brought this

Lucy Minnigerode, in Uniform as Chief of the Nursing Service of the Public Health Department, U.S.A.

Lucy Minnigerode (Fifth from the Right, Front Row) and Her Red Cross Unit, Sailing for Europe.

humiliation upon myself by going out of my way to read to him and to sit under the trees with him, imagining myself a ministering angel. He was not at all disgusting until he assumed the character of a lover. Mother, still anxious to see some of us settled, and having no indication that I could be more useful unmarried than married, wondered if I had not better think it over!

The next was a fine, hearty old fellow, who frankly told me that he would like to see life a little easier for me and, if I could be patient for a few years with an old chap in a brown wig, he could leave me well provided for. No, I couldn't.

The next was very good. He had short legs and a high forehead, a bad complexion and a good conscience. He loaned me Yankee histories of the Civil War and took me to instructive lectures when he had some money and to church when he had none. He waited for me on Sunday afternoons when I went visiting the poor in Bull-dog alley and other questionable back streets, trying with thick Bibles and thin soup to make them "good." He *was* good, still is good. Was intellectual, and is more so today.

There was a man named Jimmie. Jimmie was young. Very. For a year in copious correspondence he showered his "beautiful thoughts" upon my unworthy head. The fact that Jimmie was clerking in a small country store did not prevent his having many beautiful thoughts. He wrote to me on commercial paper with artistic embellishments, relative to boots, shoes, coal, corsets, agricultural implements, feed, fertilizers, and general merchandise. Was it not a great soul that in the face of such disconcerting suggestions could still write copiously of love? Inscribing the words "Would that I were lying on the greensward at my darling's feet" just as a young colored lady comes to buy a couple of salted herring!

Among them was a square-shouldered handsome creature, named Tom, with a rich baritone voice. He came first to Mother's house to sing duets with Lucy, who, as you may remember, was "musical." While warbling with her, he came to cast an approving eye upon me, and she always declared I took him away from her, just as I was prepared to cheat her out of her share in the two-headed lamb.

With Mother dropping notes about him into my pocketbook and tea-cup, and my sister playing accompaniments to his love-songs, and he so much better looking than anybody else, it is easy to understand that we soon were engaged. Grandma disapproved of him, and so did my Cousin Helen, who always paid Mother's coal bills, and I saw myself up against those coal bills of Mother's for the rest of my life.

Tom died in my mother's house when I was

twenty-one. I have always been glad that he loved me. When Cousin Helen saw in the newspapers that he was dead, she regretted her disparaging remarks and bolted over at once to see me. I knew she was sorry and seemed to sense the coal bills travelling again in their old accustomed track, and so tried not to be resentful or ungrateful.

Genteel poverty is degrading. The habit of expecting other people to share with you what is absolutely theirs, the tendency to criticize their decisions and divisions, grows upon you. The necessity of some ulterior motive, of selling your personal convictions in consideration of anticipated benefit. The compulsory appraising of everything—the butter that goes down the throats of your guests—oh! butter, butter, butter! Mother said I was a monomaniac on the subject of the butter,—the log of wood your admirer puts on the fire—the street car fare you must have, the shoes on your mother's feet, the coffin in which you place your dead—to continually calculate the price of these things, does not broaden and sweeten character.

Life is one long succession of poverty-dodges, compromises and makeshifts. Is it any wonder that pride and often honor go down under the strain? With tradition imposing upon you a standard altogether incompatible with your resources, and that ridiculous blue blood, always getting in the way!

CHAPTER LV

AFTER Tom died I enveloped myself in crêpe and was pointed out as a broken-hearted young lady who could never smile again.

Washington is not even now an Art center, and thirty years ago was downright provincial in all matters of the fine arts. Local artists did their best and scraped and starved along, and the patronage of the wealthy and influential went, as usual, to foreign or out-of-town artists. The local painters got very little. But such as we were our newspapers treated us generously and we young students came in for a liberal share of praise. Our work did not merit praise but we did not know enough to know that, and I have a big fat scrapbook full of my "puffs" and "notices" and "write-ups"!

There was an exhibition of pictures on at the time Tom died, and I, dressed like a little widow and with no idea of the length and beauty of life as it still lay before me, decided that it was useless for me to exhibit my pictures, as I should be living the remainder of my life in complete retirement, and that the wall-space allotted me would serve someone else to better purpose. So I went to Donald MacFarland, then the President of the Art Society, and asked him to withdraw my pictures and give the space assigned me to some "ambitious young artist," rather than to one who would never smile again. He seemed a little amused!

There were many persons in Washington whose names had been familiar to me all my life and many who were indebted in one way or another to my people, though it is not nice of me to mention that. These old friends were sharing in the pleasant features of social life, were entertaining frequently and could quite easily now and then have included me. They didn't. They forgot. Everybody forgets that poor people like a little fun—especially their own Poor Relations. Poor Relations, frankly, are not ornamental—who knows that better than I?

Without suitable clothes, and living ten miles away, it would not have been reasonable to expect dinner invitations—I often wondered what a "formal" dinner was like—but there were other things—the things fashionable people do in Lent, for instance. There's a splendid opportunity to gratify your Poor Relations—let them come to the lectures at your house where they will sit quietly in corners and never be obtrusive—but just look on and learn, and get relaxation, recreation and inspiration. Distinguished travellers and scientists and artists were always giving "chalk talks" and "chamber concerts" at somebody's house, and it would have cost nothing at all to have let me in—nobody ever thought of it!

Much of the beautiful and constructive in life

was flowing, flowing past—but I grabbed at all the strands within my reach. For which reason, and out of many years of gratitude, I here record the beautiful hospitality of Mr. and Mrs. Thomas E. Waggaman, of Georgetown; their art collection was distinguished in that day, and their spacious old-fashioned home at Thirty-second and O Streets looked very handsome and imposing to young artists who lived from hand to mouth as most of us did. The pictures and bronzes were a factor in our education, the opportunities to meet distinguished visitors to Washington were real privileges, and the good suppers furnished at their receptions were also highly appreciated. To participate in any brilliant occasion, even in the most modest capacity, is a pleasure and an education; poise and finish come unconsciously with such opportunity; and in this house there was always a total absence of that subtle distinction between the rich and the poor, the conspicuous and the inconspicuous among their guests.

At the time in my life when I never was invited anywhere, I did enjoy these invitations to the Waggaman receptions and to the lasting credit and honor of the host and hostess be it written, they did what they could to share their own pleasure with many whose pleasures were too few.

The breaking up of the Waggaman collection was a loss to Washington, and Mr. and Mrs. Waggaman deserve to be held in affectionate memory.

CHAPTER LVI

DIRECTLY or indirectly, my pleasures were all traceable to Mr. Andrews. I knew nothing that was of value. Even my education, such as it is today, is directly due to my intercourse with him—his keen observation, his poetic comprehension, his broad democracy, his wit, his knowledge of the world, his mental activity and originality, the extensive travelling I did in his dear companionship.

My Cousin Helen—she who had always paid my mother's coal bill, was planning a trip abroad with her two daughters and included me. The girls were younger than I and owing to exceptional circumstances were comparative strangers to their mother.

I had several hundred dollars (saved for the purpose of buying wedding clothes) and that, with my passage over provided by her, enabled me to go. So one day I told Mr. Andrews.

"Would you like to go?" he asked.

I recall the weary gesture with which I stretched out my hands—"I have never seen anything nor been anywhere," I answered, "and sometimes I think I will die if I cannot get away from everybody and everything I ever have seen."

"Then you must go," he said gravely. He was

sending over another student that year, a girl who had been very ill, and he told me he would reserve a double room for the pair of us, and have us return on the ship with him.

So my good cousins and I sailed in May for the Mediterranean trip, to land at Genoa. Countless crossings since have not dimmed the memory of that first voyage. It is like first love. Like first anything, I suppose. Precisely the same thing, the same way, never comes again.

Every detail was magical. The rattling of trucks and busses along the wharves, the shouts and songs of deck hands and dock hands; the swinging bales and boxes of the cargo, and the luggage dropping into the hold; the hurrying feet of negroes running smaller freight aboard on push-carts, the creaking of chains and rasping of ropes, the passengers hurrying up, up the gangplank, bags and flowers and rugs in hand, friends crowding to say good-bye; the dexterous throwing of cables from deck to dock, the shrill imperious repeated whistles, the thrill of the first shudder of the ship as her moorings loosen; the hustling back and forth of bell boys and deck hands; people locating their state-rooms and the distribution of hand luggage; the unexpected meetings with acquaintances; the great ropes straining as the ship swings round a little, the piles to which they bind her, green and slimy, reflected in strange fantastic wiggling forms in the dirty water, and groaning as if in sympathy; then the call "All ashore" and the tearful good-byes, especially of the steerage passengers, many of whom register unspeakable tragedy and disappointment in their faces; the blur of the many faces of those left watching, the individual lost in the mass, as those thronging the pier fade into the distance. The masterful skyline of New York with its giant buildings like the castles in a dream, honeycombed like a bee-hive with millions of windows, the skyscrapers dwindling to the size of blocks with which children build their towers that fall with a breath or a step, no more enduring than the mists of the morning. The prolonged salutations of other ships. The splotches of sunlight in the dirty water.

And then the sea. That of which we have read and dreamed, but never seen. The self-possessed passengers, not astonished or thrilled at anything. Sunsets unlike anything ever dreamed or painted—impossible to paint—too glorious, too transient—a world without limitations. The sweetness of the buoy-bells, the bright, intermittent friendly signals of lighthouses—the splendid unbroken expanses, the soothing, caressing sound of water lapping against the hull of the ship.

How calmly these other people settled themselves into the scheme of things, how soon they changed from travelling suits to sport; how obsequiously the deck stewards were placing chairs and opening rugs and passing bouillon and tea! Complacently each was studying the passenger list, separating the sheep from the goats, connecting names with faces as those already established in their chairs inspected those who felt impelled to take an immediate constitutional around the decks.

I think I was the first person on board to be classified. Every stitch of raiment I possessed proclaimed my Poor Relationdom. I had no change of outer clothing and wore the one little shabby black serge suit in which I went aboard morning and evening, for breakfast and for dinner, concert or what not. My young cousins were very smart, good-looking and well-groomed; had they realized the contrast between us they would have enjoyed fitting me out properly before we left, but never having been identified so intimately with anyone so poor, they did not know. Generous girls. Generous to this day. Daisy will probably join me at the Louise Home, if we are lucky enough to be admitted, for we both are headed for bankruptcy. The first day or two I spent fighting off a horrid depression. There was a little artist on board to whom my cousin Helen introduced me as a person of promise, asking him to criticize my sketches. I took a dislike to him and did not intend to be his protégée, in fact believed that I could have criticized his stuff just as intelligently as he could mine, and I firmly resolved to repudiate his instructions. My private opinion was that he was about to pull off a deal of some sort with my cousin. He did get a commission from her to paint one of the girls! So the little sketch-book the Art students of our school had given me could only be brought out surreptitiously for fear of this man.

I stuck around the deck rather alone, until from among the passengers a few began to seek me. When conversation opened up in which I was interested, I forgot all about my shabby clothes, and in a short time had made some interesting friends.

Do you know what a vista is opened in a contracted life, by a few new points of contact? And the question comes, "Do these people always see so far and know so much? Do they never slump as we do? What air is it that they breathe and that we know nothing of?" It seemed to me that the bigness of the sea was theirs, and I suddenly became very happy on that ship.

Then I could shake off the depression of being a little second fiddle, for realms opened in which I saw myself no second fiddle whatsoever. The salt air and the wide blue and the multicolored sunsets did their work—then I began to eat as though I had never seen food, and to laugh as though I had never heard of butter and shoes, of duns and bills, and notes and protested checks, and to walk the deck with pleasant people as though the clothes on my back had actually been made for me!

And suddenly I began to contradict the little artist and to bring out my sketch-book unblushingly and accept the admiration of my own friends for the outlines I drew of the coast of Portugal, with the little silhouetted crosses against the sky, which marked the places of violent deaths in the mountains. People sat for me, and we had a merry time making portraits of the Presbyterian preacher from New Brunswick and the Unitarian from Boston—all of my friends autographed their likenesses, and a young fellow from Boston with the beautiful name of Trowbridge, was very agreeable to me.

Glimpses of the Balearic Isles and of the Azores—airy nothings becoming concrete facts—a day full of color and adventure at Gibraltar—the little sketch-book confiscated by a handsome English officer; an old dignified Moor making beseeching gestures to me not to endanger his immortal soul by depicting his mortal body upon paper. The splendid jade green of the Mediterranean, the geraniums that flamed wild over every available plot of ground, the Spanish women on donkey-back, with enormous panniers on either side of their tiny beasts; the smart English women in sport suits or riding habits, such a jumble of picturesque impressions as I took to bed with me when I scrambled up that night, for the last time, to the shelf that was my berth!

We landed by night at Genoa; the heights of the city bejewelled with lights that were reflected in the water—the queer little rambling uphill streets. A big moon, the sort of moon that was indispensable to the picture.

I was in Italy. Going to sleep—in Italy. Italy—I-t-a-l-y——.

CHAPTER LVII

THE next morning we began on the business of life—my cousins were going to buy things. Among the first purchases they made were clothes for me. Then we bought filagree silver—filagree silver is a specialty of Genoa—and we inspected necklaces and tucking-combs and picture-frames and all sorts of things in filagree silver—I sat on a stool in the shop, getting such glimpses as I could of the beggars that swarmed the streets and a sense of the color and mood of the place as we went from shop to shop.

Then we went to Naples. That is where we bought tortoise shell. Necklaces and tucking-combs and picture-frames of tortoise shell. Tortoise shell is a specialty of Naples. But no tortoise shell could hide the bay or Vesuvius or the picturesque peasantry, and there was no escape from the beggars, from the teeming filth and burning sun. I made some small water-color drawings in the Museum, and we went to Pompeii.

My friend, Mr. Dole of Boston, a Unitarian preacher and writer, our fellow passenger, happened to be on the same excursion train and joined us. It was intensely hot. He bought us cherries. We ate a great many of them. When we were going through the ruins of Pompeii later in the day, he was taken violently ill in the baths of Venus. Under these trying circumstances he preserved the same remarkable calmness that impressed me on the ship—he lived above all disturbing things. But on the way back he declined cherries.

The following letter speaks for itself as to the continuance of our friendship, for in the spring of 1922 Dr. Dole visited me on his way back to Boston, after participating in the ceremonies at the dedication at Tuskegee of a memorial to Booker T. Washington, who was his devoted friend. He was a frail old man very pale and thin, but with that indomitable spirit which marks those who persistently, lovingly see the best and think the best, even of the worst. He lingered in Washington hoping to do something toward the release of the one hundred and three political prisoners still held in Fort Leavenworth prison for sedition. The war being over, and nearly all nations having freed their political prisoners, he felt that these men, many of them foreign-born, were less of a liability to the nation free than bound. He visited one great official after the other, dear gentle old friend of humanity, only to be turned down by clerks and secretaries in our circumlocution offices, where every hired servant of the people, the great and sovereign people, has his smiling but adamant subordinate to stand as a buffer between his august person and that public he is supposed to serve.

Dr. Dole came in for luncheon with me day after day, undiscouraged, but a little tired; the President could not be seen; Mr. Daugherty, the Cabinet officer in whose department the matter rested, could not be seen; senators and congressmen made oily promises, but no more—and the time came for the old saint to go, without having accomplished his mission. Yet within a few months the thing he had set his heart upon came to pass—those one hundred and three political prisoners were released.

Jamaica Plain, Mass.
April 19, 1922.

Dear Mrs. Andrews:

All good greetings to you and the friends of your household. I have a very delightful sense of your kindly hospitality. I had good company with your verses on my journey and my daughter Winifred at Richmond and Mrs. Dole here have enjoyed them. I am glad to put the little volume among my poets.

I am happy in believing that, when great and beautiful thoughts come to us, they are the communications and messages of the Eternal Creative Life of the Universe "in which we live."

More and more what people used to call "Prayer," that is, petition, seems to me more truly to be intercourse, or communion of spirit, as between friends, where we, at our best and our consciousness at its height of activity, *listen* and receive, and thus see the better how to act. Whatever, now, of the theory which one adopts concerning your automatic writing, I like in it the fact that you keep your consciousness and are quite alive and aware, are doing it all in the light—not under cover of darkness, or through some alien mediumship.

It is to this wholesome fact that you owe the high value and quality of the thoughts and the counsels. Further than to say this, I do not need or venture to dogmatize. "Ye shall know them by their fruits" is a very wise word.*

I think I shall give myself the pleasure of sending you my last book, though it will be rather to express my respect and affection, than because I see how, with your busy life, you can possibly read it. If you should peep into it so far as to spy certain heresies, I count on your wide sympathies to translate them into what you think I ought to say, or at least to mean.

Yours hastily,
Charles F. Dole.

The color of the world was a revelation to me in these strange places. Such purity of tone—such simplicity and softness. Such perfect harmony. The red poppies and the gray-green of the olive trees at Sorrento. The vapor that pulled all colors together without obscuring anything! No wonder that English literature is full of the blueness of Italian sky and water!

We went on to Rome, where we bought silk stockings. Rome is a great market for silk stockings. We "did" all the things customary there, all the churches and picture-galleries, and even tried to get an audience with the Pope. My cousins were Catholics, and one of them, of whom I am peculiarly fond, was anxious to have a rosary blessed.

*This is a reference to my book, "The Darker Drink," which contains the automatically received instructions of my dear Mary Lord.

So we pinned lace bows on our heads, she and I, every day, and hired cabs to take us to see the Pope, but after a while abandoned the idea as it appeared more difficult than we supposed. I was glad to miss it for he had given my Cousin Stanley a special dispensation to marry me and I had failed to take advantage of it and could not be quite sure that the Pope did not hold a little grudge against me! We went to Florence, where we bought leather goods—card-cases and shaving-cases and hand-bags and portfolios—and "did" Florence too, in a very businesslike way. But anxiety was beginning to prey upon my vitals as I saw my small fortune dwindling day by day, and I was getting so little of what I really had come for.

CHAPTER LVIII

THEN my Uncle Meade Minnigerode invited me to Paris where he, with a wife and one child, were living in the American quarter and I saw my way clear to escape the "specialties" and probably save a little money.

A glimpse of Venice and the Italian lakes, of San Gotthard, and Lucerne and then—Paris.

I arrived, a very shrunken little person in purse and wardrobe, at my uncle's elaborate apartment, and began again to run the gauntlet of Poor Relationdom. I think I was rather ungrateful. Here were people making it possible for me, a little pauper, to do what many people never, never do—see Italy and Paris—and here was I, eternally feeling apologetic, because I did not fit into their scale of life. I hate things that are out of relation to the background and in all these places I was out of relation to the background.

Every morning a French maid came into my room on tiptoe, lowering the window shades, that no ray of early sunshine disturb my august slumbers; prepared my bath, that my noble fingers need not so much as lift a towel for myself; then she went into my bureau to lay out my clothing, which (as I observed her out of the corner of my eye while drawing the cover up and pretending to be still asleep) she inspected with great attention, but never changing her facial expression. She was beautiful, slim, noiseless—I liked her—and felt entirely unabashed that my belongings were not finer.

I liked my uncle's wife—she was just a young girl like myself and named Nellie. My uncle made fun of me all the time and I detested him. He told people that I went to the Louvre and with my head on one side contemplated the masterpieces in silence a while and then announced, "Well, I can say this much for Raphael—he certainly could draw." Or, "I think Mr. Andrews would have told Murillo that his shadows are too black" which things never happened, were mere inventions, and made me feel like a fool. He made fun of my religion, of my clothes, of my wretched little beginnings in art, of my Southern accent—which infuriated me. And then I understood why Grandma used to say, at Oakley, that she would not like to live in the house with Meade Minnigerode.

I stayed in his house a month and learned a good many things and left there full of liking for his wife, affection for his baby son, disgust for Paris, and fear of him. He frightened me—and Paris frightened me—I was too green to understand or to enjoy either. My uncle's beauty was in itself terrifying—he was so tall, so unearthly, his profile the purest Greek, his hair intensely black and waving and rippling back, like Lord Byron's. Those same monstrous gray eyes wide apart, that my father had, long transparent hands, and intense pallor added to these features. His contempt for mediocrity, for labor, for everything the average man must accept, the clever and cynical comments upon religion and conventionality with which he puzzled, embarrassed and fascinated me, all combined to make me a most ungracious and ungrateful guest, so far as my host was concerned. However he made so much fun of me that I believe my visit was a real pleasure to him. And looking back I see that I lost, through sheer ignorance, self-righteousness, and the survival of my grandmother's teachings in me, much merriment in association with this relative.

When this invitation was at an end, I had still three weeks on my hands before the date of sailing for home, and so decided to go to Dresden. Some old New Orleans friends were there studying music—so I betook myself one fine morning away from Paris—travelled all day, spent a night in Cologne, and never even looking out of the hotel window to see what the city was like, went on early the next day to Dresden.

This itinerary proves the traveller's inexperience—but it was long ago, the money spent, the small miscalculations forgotten, the many inspirations remembered. In Dresden, I was a perfect fit. We all were Southerners, all Art students, all "broken down" aristocrats, all as poor as Job's blue turkey!

My friends had a big, cold, half-furnished apartment in an unfashionable quarter and were as happy as larks and as independent as jay-birds all the time. A noble mother, four girls and a boy. The boy was young—the girls just grown. One had a voice to train, one was a violinist, one a pianist, and I cannot recall now what study the fourth girl followed. There was a big piano in the living room which knew no rest—when the family were not hammering on it, American students from outside were—and it banged all day.

The violinist practiced seven hours a day—practiced until she almost fainted. The singer (soprano) practiced at brief intervals all day—and there was the pianist too.

Then at meal times there tumbled in boys and girls from schools and pensions and all of them stayed for dinner or supper. The members of the family, hard-working and still growing, would exhibit the sweetest spirit of fellowship and hospitality I ever witnessed, making downright sacrifices, for they needed food themselves, and it was none too plentiful.

At the head of the table the handsome mother presided with all the grace of dear old New Orleans days, and around the board sat these big greedy American boys far from their own mothers. The younger members of the family, concealing the fact that the jam or the beef or the beans were conspicuously absent from their own plates, ate potatoes and bread with perfect good humor, swearing by all their gods that it was entirely from preference.

These girls had one brown skirt and a long coat which they wore by turns, and when any one of them was due for a lesson there was a scurrying to locate the skirt. If the last wearer had lingered overtime somewhere and the best skirt was not available, some second-best garment served the purpose, but the brown skirt was the first choice of all. "Where's the brown skirt?" was the query with which one became soon familiar. It was a dear garment, with something of the association of the mittens Grandma made for me from Cousin Rozier's old pants—for to it clung the warmth and kindness of those generous souls.

The violinist came in one day and reported that her master had struck her with the bow and called her an "Esel"—which I was told meant "ass." I was scandalized, but she seemed quite pleased. Once, as a great treat she took me to gaze upon him—she said I must not leave Europe without having seen him. I saw a disreputable-looking old Jew, with a dirty, bushy beard, and he received us in his undershirt—a greasy gray flannel garment, only half buttoned down the front, most disgusting. I saw the whiskers all over his breast through the gaps in it. And this beautiful girl, stately as a lily, crowned with a glory of pale gold hair, her dimples coming and going, as she talked, idolized him. That is art. Idolized something in his heart and brain, oblivious of his greasy shirt and disgraceful finger-nails.

Here I had my own background and was happy along with the rest. It was an echo of home— of that glorious "sans souci de lendemain ' that is born in New Orleans. They were so high in their aims, tnis household, so simple in their needs, so aristocratic in the grand old sense of Tennyson, with "manners that are not idle, but the fruit of loyal nature and of a noble mind." There was a delicious human freedom about them—an amazing generosity.

From my grandmother at Oatlands I had a letter prior to my departure on this first momentous journey for which, for its love and anxiety, I beg a little patience.

Oatlands, May 20, 1892

My beloved child:

I have been trying to write to you ever since my disappointment at not seeing you last Saturday. But my dear child, much as I long to look upon the face that for near twenty-two years I have loved so well, I would not have you over-fatigue yourself on the eve of your departure. I would not you should have your strength broken by over-exertion and anxiety. I want you to have a mind at least at ease, that you may profit by the rest and the sea air, and my dear child, may Almighty God in his infinite love and mercy watch over you and restore you to us in health and safety. My prayers shall continually ascend to Him that He will watch over my child and restore her in peace and safety to your home. You must not be surprised that it is a trial to your dear mother to have you separated by so many miles of water and land. I wish I could be with her during your absence. You could not be going with a more desirable party, and my dear child, be guided by your cousin in all things. I hope you will return with Mr. Andrews and his friend—I do not like your coming alone.

Give my best love to your mother and tell her I received her package. And now my dearly loved child, may our Father and our God watch over and keep you and should it not be permitted us to meet again in this life may we reunite in that life where there will be no separations. When or if you meet Mrs. W. make yourself pleasant to her for my sake. I am very fond of her.

And now again farewell if we do not meet and may the everlasting arms be around you shall be the constant and earnest prayer of,

Your devoted Grandmother.

Tell your mother this letter is for you both.

CHAPTER LIX

SHINNECOCK HILLS, Long Island, was the scene for several seasons, of a unique series of performances in connection with the so-called "Summer Art School" which a group of girls attended from the Corcoran School. The existence of the school there was primarily due to the fact that some rich people owned some poor land. To the east is Southampton-on-the-sea, a fashionable and delightful resort. To the west are the Hills, elevations hardly to be called hills, but in a flat country we will allow the term to pass unchallenged; between these lies a hollow, hot and unattractive, a stretch of bad lands for which no use had been discovered until some brilliant mind evolved the idea of an art village. I have noticed that what is not fit for any other purpose is often found available for artists—and this is due firstly to their good nature and superiority to mere inconvenience, and secondly to their talent and vision, which really discover charm where to the Philistine no charm is.

Here in this hot hole there were erected a string of flimsy cottages and a big studio. And the great William M. Chase was urged to open an Art School. He did. And from all over the country girls and boys gathered together all shekels available, and came humbly to his feet in search of knowledge.

The landowners entitled themselves "patrons," which sounded quite nifty, and they gave afternoon teas at which overfed old ladies bristling in silks and satins, and feeble, pale old gentlemen with very good clothes on, and certain evidences of having had too gay a time in the dear dead days beyond recall, would stand graciously in line and "receive" the poverty-stricken and ambitious youth which assembled there for study. They not only patted our hands—I was there with the rest of the mob—and gently reminded us that we must take full advantage of this great opportunity for improving ourselves, but they fed us—which made their axioms and advices a little less unpalatable. In view of the fact that we really were poor and hard-working, the price paid in cash for everything we got precluded all idea of philanthropy. It was worth the money as an experience but it was absolutely no charity—and I who have been "fed up" on charity will not admit that there was a single element of the eleemosynary in the undertaking. So much for the philanthropic aspect of the case.

Long Island is delightful. We did not prostrate ourselves in astonishment because the villas were large upon the hilltops and the vill-i-ans gorgeous with chariots and flunkeys. We had lived in big houses and seen servants—inherited servants, generations of them—so a liveried butler did not leave us gasping for breath! Personally, I was impatient of the old ladies with their pin-cushiony hands, dimpled deep like tufted mattresses, and sparkling with rings; and of the wheezy octogenarians whose trembling hands made me think of oysters, gray and moist and limp—with purplish-greenish-bluish coloration from the upstanding veins, poor old gentlemen with only money and memories! Our own strong little paws with traces of Prussian blue which neither toil nor prayer could remove from the cuticle, lay unwillingly in these lukewarm palms and submitted to the pawing, purring and patting of the "patrons" with some reluctance. Nevertheless, Long Island is delightful. There is a free air that sets the blood to singing. There are skies big and colorful and windswept. Under them the earth and the creatures crawling upon it are properly insignificant. The horizon is low-toned and warm, deepening in blue and growing colder as it rolls towards the zenith. The cumuli are magnificent, billowing and floating and changing so that paint and brush have a merry race to catch up with their manifold variations of form. Way, way up, the baby clouds are playing hide and seek, leap frog, and every game of childhood. Beneath, strong winds—the same that drive the clouds along—are swaying the green-gray grass of the sand-dunes till it looks like a grain field of some other sphere, where

grain ripens to silver instead of gold. And for
drawing and accent, for something out of which
to make a foreground, there are the clumps of
bay-berry bushes—squat and hardy, dark and aromatic, for the same wind sets free a perfume as it
speeds the cloud and sways the sage and grasses.

There are poor scraggy trees, trees which have
varied from the original design because subjected
to a too great stress and pressure in their youth.
Meant to climb straight and certain, they have
been warped and twisted by gales until their very
bodies tell the tale of their struggle for integrity.
To a certain height the trunks are grotesque and
crooked, full of old pain—the pain of youth's
helplessness. But toward the last, they win.
Having taken on girth and strength slowly and
in the face of discouragement, they have reached,
as we do, a point where their own strength is a
match for the force of circumstance, and then
they develop as they should; the original design
is expressed in their maturity, built though it
may be upon a foundation of tragic resistance to
the inevitable. Much comfort and many lessons
have come to me from intercourse with trees.
These little heroes are found straggling along the
coast—breaking the horizontal line of the sea
with their dark and fantastic silhouettes.

The salt meadows are full of bloom, the swamps
offer another variety of landscape, while queer
little farm-houses with gray out-buildings lend
themselves to pleasant study; there are types of

natives too, kindly folk who sitting for a sketch will offer a glass of milk to the artist or a slice of blueberry pie.

And out to sea there are rocks and surf—the endless music of the shore, and the accompaniment of nets and boats and huts and bronzed faces under Sou'westers—a suggestion—only that—of a real fishing village.

CHAPTER LX

IN the Shinnecock summer Art School, on Monday, we had a field day, and Chase criticized for us as we painted out of doors. There was the greatest scrambling to get ready. We looked like a lot of young tramps as we departed from the village with our traps to the appointed rendezvous. The poorer girls tried to walk and were too exhausted with bodily fatigue to paint when they reached their destination. Arriving at the place there was a search for a motif, and such squinting through little card-board frames or "Cherchmotifs"—until each had selected a subject! Then up went the big umbrellas, to dot the world like giant toad-stools as far as eye could see. Sometimes the wind swept easel and artist off the face of the earth; sometimes the sun went under and a gray day settled after your masterpiece was well under way as a broad sunlight effect. And then a smart little trap appeared on the horizon, hearts sank, faces flushed, pulses went up and temperatures went down; all sorts of mental, moral and physical changes took place, as Chase himself loomed up. A very dapper little man to create so much commotion. Your heart almost stopped beating when his chariot wheels ground into the sand alongside of your easel. What would he say? Would he get out? Would he become so interested in you as to forget the thirty-five others waiting breathless for a word—a glance? No—he did not even get out—he waited just one second—leaning a little out of his buggy. "Good morning, I think your sky a little dark." Dark? The whole universe was plunged in gloom. You thought you had better go home and seek a painless death. Five dollars gone the way of all flesh. Your sky was dark. It was indeed.

On Tuesday he criticized in the studio. This was as good as a bull-fight to the cottagers and the loungers from the hotels—the patrons were out in full force to patronize and gave parties at little expense and with great gusto to their friends, inviting all they cared to invite to attend the morning criticisms. Carriages and even motors were at the door, the "nobility" with their lorgnettes ready, the students all sitting on little camp-stools before a large revolving easel. While Chase criticized the studies on one side, a servant filled the other side with more—thus it went round and round, until hundreds of daubs had met their fate.

The audience all assembled, waiting just long enough for the great man to render his entrance dramatic. H—s—s—sh—He is here! Neat—immaculate—the sharpest of creases in his trousers, the reddest of geraniums in the buttonhole of his gray morning coat, his brown Van Dyke beard trimmed to perfection! He holds a mahlstick in his hand as a pointer, steps to the big easel, bows, makes a threat at the first group of sketches on view, and asks: "Whose work is this?"

Almost fainting, you answer in a wretched squeak——

"Mine, Mr. Chase."

"I do not see you——"

And so you wriggle out of ambush, while the patrons and their august guests look you over until you think your vaccination marks must be visible to the naked eye—and Mr. Chase surveys you.

"I should judge that you were in the habit of copying cheap chromos," he says, while the patrons titter.

Sometimes he gave a "talk" in the studio and sometimes an "at home" in his own house. These occasions were of distinct value. The opportunity to see his pictures, his unfinished sketches, his suggestions of compositions, were great eye-openers. And his wife—a mere woman like ourselves—the unsupportable bliss that must be hers—hearing his talk—seeing him eat—breathing the same air with him—how wonderful her ivory skin is—how glossy her black hair—how altogether adorable her children.

Words of William Chase

"I will set you right for all time on one point—it is not only the light picture that succeeds.

Impressionism with the high-keyed picture gave us some things that have come to stay, light, air, space—of which the old painters knew less. But the high-keyed picture is not the only one. You are to avoid recipes. There are no recipes. Not objecting to light pictures, I tell you that the dark, the black picture, in quiet tone, is just as satisfactory. . . .

"Take the thing you care for to your heart of hearts, if it is only a chromo. Love that and the rest will come. Development is gradual. I insist upon this—do not trouble about mediocre people, their doings or opinions. Avoid all but the best. Do not look at cheap pictures. You might catch it. The day is done when pictures will be done indoors. Millet lived out of doors. His soul did not know that he was in a studio. He lived an open-air life, saw, felt, breathed nature as it is. (See Exhibitions.) If you are not in reach of a city get magazines, all you can. Do not read the matter, study the reproductions. Get catalogues of exhibitions. Eat them up. Don't deplore your situation. Be happy—do your best." . . .

On Portraits

"It should be your ambition to produce something that will interest others besides the family. It is never the aim of the master to please the sitter. Rather to produce a work of art. Velazquez, Titian, Hals. Of course, it should resemble the sitter. Get the pleasure of doing something frankly. We have the same material as the masters had. Men and women. Don't degrade your art by doing portraits to be housed. Some day they will see the light and expose you. Insist upon as many sittings as are necessary. Make them short. Don't fatigue your sitter, draw him into conversation on what interests him. Don't do too much at first sitting. Place it on the canvas, well up—head near the top of canvas gives height and dignity. If the subject approaches the left, place head a little to the right. It is awkward if it appears to be trying to get out of the frame. Do not conceal your work. Show it and welcome criticism. Do your work as well as you can and insist on what you believe. You will get more respect for it. Your work should be done so directly and honestly that the painter should know instantly the last touch. It is well to have a frame, it gets rid of the edge."

On Technique and Style

"Technique is the manipulation of the material. The best use of your material means good painting. Pity those who have no cleverness. Turner never did what Mr. Ruskin claims for him. He was very individual, but much influenced by other men. By Claude. Claude, a man of moods. Moods expressed with great distinctness. He succeeded in what he aimed at. He was a great painter. He did great painting. All the old English masters were great, enthused painters. No new movement will detract from their value. There is nothing so rare as style. It is fine manner. Fine treatment. Fine conception. It comes from a general idea of all the phases that go to make a work great. The advantage of European study—art influence in the air—great inspiration—galleries, architecture, color, romance, tradition, history, we will have more of it and more sympathy. Away from extremes and fads. The art which has stood the tests."

On Commercialism

"There is one matter of the utmost importance. I feel bound to speak of it. I see work on this board which has been done with a commercial view. Let me tell you frankly that that spirit is the damnation of art. (Oh, Saint Peter! Saint Peter! I almost groaned aloud.) If you as Art students or as artists, paint with the idea of truckling to possible buyers (I spent my life doing that thing) you degrade the art and yourself. If you paint with the desire of pleasing the vulgar taste, of tickling the fancy of the ignorant, if your aim is to produce what will sell, I beg of you to put up your canvas and brushes and leave them forever. I really do. I cannot speak too warmly on this subject. Art is too sacred to degrade in this way. You will make the mistake of your life if you sell it for a mess of pottage. Paint honestly, paint reverently, paint truthfully. I entreat you to cast out from among you this passion of trade. I have seen many of the best ruined by its influence. I have never seen one succeed. I wish to say a few words to those among my pupils who are compelled to support themselves by their art. One of the most common expedients for such is "pot-boiling." By "pot-boiling" I mean painting the sweet, pretty sort of thing which sells readily. Of all things, this is the most unfortunate. It is death to art. It is hard to lie in the morning and be true in the afternoon. I would urge those of you who can, to lay aside this practice. Teaching is another means frequently resorted to, and that I heartily endorse. It is a means of earning a living and yet keeping yourself in touch with true art. It affords you an opportunity of being true to your ideals, and you should insist that your pupils do each study as you yourself would do it. You are apt also to have one talented pupil who will be to you a real pleasure and satisfaction. If your teaching is sincere and honest you are giving the equivalent of what you receive. Illustrating is a third resource, to be regretted for two reasons. First there is something to relate—a story to be told—an expression to be represented. The literary in art is unfortunate and this is a disadvantage to frank, courageous study of nature. Moreover, the constant use of black and white is disastrous to one's sense of color. Yes (this in answer to a question from myself), I have seen work in black and white so true in value, so atmospheric, that it appeared full of color. Abbey is an instance of how dangerous the constant use of black and white is to the color sense. He is doing better now, but he had a struggle to get good color into his work."

"Use the very best materials. New canvas, good brushes, best colors. Students try to paint with materials a master could not handle.

"Stop when you wonder what to do next.

"It is only safe to consider three tones of color at a time.

"Avoid finish. That will take care of itself.

"Make an edge without having an edge. That is the best kind of an edge.

"If you get home with three absolute facts found in a day, you have accomplished something.

"When we begin a study we would do well if we forgot that we had ever heard a theory, seen a picture or done a study before. Look at it as if for the first time. Lay aside all preconceived ideas. Let me beg of you, never attempt to make a thing stick out. Keep it back.

"Self-entertainment is what I most hope to bring about. Play with your paint, be happy, over it, sing at your work.

"A stained surface is unfortunate.

POOR RELATION

"Your aim is to make it look right, not what you know it to be. Don't start out in one way and finish in another. Experiment as much as you like, but let your study be one impression throughout. Invert your head. Don't squint.

"It is never well to keep your work too much inside the frame. Carry it well out to the edge.

"It is always in the hereafter that criticism is useful. It applies not so much to this study as to what will follow."

The Chase Song, for the authorship of which no one would plead guilty, was high in favor, and used as a serenade on the occasion of circuses, Della Milhau's parties, and all festivities, sung to the classic tune of "Dat Watermelon Hanging on de Vine."

> Oh, to my summer school the students all they come,
>   Seeking the knowledge I impart;
> For we needs must love the highest, oh, I really think we should—
>   And we teach but the highest of high art!
>
> Now, whose sketch is this? It is yours, Ma'am, I believe·
>   Also the two that are below;
> That one there on the floor, the big one by the door,
>   And the three little ones here in a row.
>
> Now, charge well your brush, then note it down,
>   In a way to make the thing exist;
> Play with your paint, oh, I really wish you would,
>   And from niggle-ing and puttering desist.
>
> Now, look well to space and make your skies talk,
>   Even though they noisy, noisy be;

Look well to sizes, oh, I really wish you would,
  Preserving thus my equanimity.

For your shadows use mauve, let your trees be light blue,
  And your grass just as yellow as can be,
Pile on the purple, oh, I really wish you would,
  In a manner that is very loose and free.

If the sky should seem blue, the grass and trees green,
  And the road just an ordinary brown,
Hasten, oh hasten, I really think you should,
  And consult with an oculist in town.

For I am William Chase, for William Chase am I,
  Yes, I am William—William—William Chase.
Believe it, oh, believe it, how I really wish you would,
  I am William—William—William Chase.

CHAPTER LXI

THERE were some clever boys there. They took no notice of girls, so far as I knew—at least not of me. Howard Chandler Christie—a big blond fellow with an acre of canvas strapped on his broad back, swinging out early in the morning and singing—or roaring—until the welkin rang. He painted in a vigorous and manly fashion and gave promise of a great career. As a boy he was a great landscape painter. I ran into him in Washington last winter, after exactly thirty-three years. He was painting portraits of the President and Mrs. Coolidge.

Both of the Beales were at Shinnecock, Reynold and Clifford. Fine boys. They paint just as one would have expected them to paint and just as they would have delivered the goods in any other field of labor. Cadwallader Washburn—a deafmute, also did brilliant work, and is doing it still.

And of the girls—Adelaide Alsop was with me a good deal, and off and on through these years we have kept in touch. She was the best ever, utterly indifferent to dress and men and other vanities. Chase never gave her a good criticism, and neither did Mrs. Nicholls in the water-color class. The girls all liked her and called on her to nurse them when they were sick but thought, poorly of her talent and of her attractiveness. She is the most distinguished of us all today. To see her in her fascinating "Four Winds Cottage" at Syracuse, New York, where she has a big studio—to see the Art publication for which we have to thank also her husband, Samuel Robineau; to know that the Art Institutes of the country pay several thousand dollars for one tiny example of her pottery, a method known only to herself—and that she is a Doctor—with a University degree as Doctor of Arts——! And she has beautiful children, each hitting the high spots in his chosen artistic line.

There was Gertrude Weil. A beautiful Jewish girl—full of fire and kindness, of charm and sympathy. She had a mane of glorious tawny hair, and wore a sweater of the same color. Her uncovered head, deep chest, strong arms, as she rowed in her own boat, far, far out to sea, all golden, sparkled against the blue background of summer sea and sky. A beautiful young thing. At night she would come into my room while I was propped up in my cot reading the Bible, and sit on the foot of the bed, her hair loosened around her, hugging her knees and listening to the Epistle to the Hebrews—her splendid lines all clear to my eyes through the thin nightgown, till I would get tongue-tied over Saint Paul and the Hebrews, trying to look at two things at once. She went to Paris to continue her studies. One bitter day the Seine gave up her corpse.

POOR RELATION

There was Della Milhau. She did not paint, but came to Shinnecock to be with friends, and to make life merry for others in her own absurd and lovable way. She made a practice of giving orgies—innocent orgies—to which she invited the whole settlement by the primitive means of ringing a large bell. The sound of this bell meant food at Milhau's expense. Out we tumbled from every corner, as when the call of "fire" rings through the streets—and pell-mell into Milhau's boxes without ceremony. She kept a horse or two and was a great hunter.

When Miss Alice Tinkham, from Boston, arrived for a few weeks' stay and surveyed the outfit with stern disapprobation, it was Milhau who decided that we must break her in or be ruined. We would have forgiven her almost everything but the Robert Browning which she slapped down on the table, so very Bostonese. Then we began to plot—for had she been permitted to practice her propaganda we should have become ladylike in twenty-four hours. Elizabeth Van Renssalaer thought we might curb Tinkie's flow of erudition by starting an endless narrative which evening after evening should balk Miss Tinkham in her fiendish purpose. This girl was to begin after tea with the tale of her illness in Rome, where she had had an attack of fever; the others were to escape one by one, until the dear and courteous Tinkie was left alone with the narrator, hour after hour, night after night. Miss

Van Renssalaer did her part thoroughly, and as soon as one of us would mention illness, would launch forth—fastening her eye upon the victim, who, after several evenings, was glad to take her Browning to her own room. When Miss Tinkham's sister joined her we agreed that rather than go through this discipline a second time we would conquer the refinement of the second sister all at once. The night of her first appearance in the dining room, pandemonium broke loose. We came in every possible disguise. Some pretended they were drunk, and hiccoughed in the most perfect way. Then came Milhau, in her riding togs, coat-tails over her arm, hat on one side, spurs, whip, everything one could think of, and the brush of a fox she had killed the day before, in her hand. This she extended suddenly before the Tinkham sisters—"Don't it stink?" We danced around then like young Hottentots; some were in evening dress and painted up like Jezebels—others were in painting aprons, most disreputable. Some had used paint brushes instead of hairpins, some were smeared with emerald green across the forehead; and the two sweet little ladies from Boston were filled with consternation of the sincerest sort. Within three days their ruin had been accomplished, the Browning was a volume of forgotten lore, and they were volunteering to jump through burning hoops at the circus we were planning.

Catherine Carter Critcher and I had been

schoolmates at Cousin Rebecca Powell's school in Alexandria, comrades in the Corcoran Art School, fellow-travellers on the old ferryboats on the Potomac River, and were at Shinnecock together. She has forged gallantly ahead, made many sacrifices to hold sincerely to her ideals of art, and today she has "arrived." She spends her summers at Taos, near Santa Fé, and the Corcoran Gallery has bought one of her Indian pictures for its permanent collection. She has a dear face and a buoyant heart, and will never grow jaded or tired or old.

PART V

AN ART STUDENT IN WASHINGTON, 1895

CHAPTER LXII

MY first big order—it seemed big—five hundred dollars—came from Mr. and Mrs. Byam Kirby Stevens, of New York, who commissioned me to paint for them a copy of the painting in the Rotunda of the Capitol, The Surrender of Burgoyne. How important I felt as I mounted daily to the platform built for me by my dear old friend, Mr. Edward Clark, and his young assistant, later his successor, Elliot Woods, then the curators of the Capitol Building. Young women making copies of pictures in public buildings abroad attract little notice but I attracted considerable attention in the Rotunda of the Capitol. Senators and members of Congress took great notice of me, some making themselves a nuisance. And the dearly beloved Public could not go on with its sightseeing without wasting many of my precious minutes.

Mr. Stevens' ancestor—one of his many distinguished ancestors—occupies a conspicuous position in this picture, and he bequeathed my copy to the Massachusetts Historical Society. By means of this piece of work I made some influential friends, besides the Stevens themselves whose kindness was unremitting during many years.

During the work upon this picture for them,

mother found frequent need for money and long before they had even seen it, I began writing for remittances. Mr. Stevens sent me $200 at once without knowing at all how the work had progressed. When I wrote again for money he replied that he hoped I could wait awhile before drawing it all, that I might need it for a rainy day. I wrote him immediately that I had earned the money and that it was mine, and that as my mother wanted it he would oblige me by sending it at once, all days with me being rainy days so far as money was concerned, that his solicitude on that score was kind but superfluous. Instead of thinking me an outrageous little scrap of bad manners, he sent the check promptly with a very affectionate note, and years afterward when I visited them at their summer home at Lenox, Massachusetts, he showed me my letters. "Your Southern blood was up, was it not?" he remarked.

One interesting duty that fell to my share was the employment of models for our various life-classes. The question of study from the nude was greatly agitated in our family, and my mother consulted all the bishops, priests and deacons that came along as to its effect upon my character; they looked wise and virtuous holding heart to heart talks with mother and me, and my argument would be that an engagement was open to any lady or gentleman who thought the wages were the easily won wages of sin, to try posing for a week.

There is not only no seductiveness, there is the reverse of it in the life-class. The lines of the body are much as the lines of trees and of mountains. Flesh covers the frame-work, as foliage drapes the trees, as soil covers the granite.

Our poor models! One by one they arise out of their graves to stand before me at this typewriter. I see their knotty joints, their hairy legs, their moles and blemishes and varicose veins. Their flabby breasts, protruding abdomens, loose flesh, corns and bunions. They had vaccination scars, they showed the unmistakable strains of childbirth. They were always wonderful, and the hideous ones were just as wonderful as the beautiful ones, and far more interesting. Blood glowed through coarse skin as through fine, light played upon the scrawny old men of the Ribera type as upon the rosy nymphs of Bouguereau.

It was I who found them, booked them, paid them and loved them. They were my children. There was old Perryman—we could see every beat of his poor heart, a heart that had hammered out so many wretched years. There was Ed Olden, negro masseur, a giant bronze figure, worthy any classic title. There was one who was hopeless as a model, but became a painter of repute. He only posed because he was hard up. There was red-headed Joe Grant, afterwards a professional boxer. There were now and then the sons of people well known in society who came as models to extricate themselves from some ugly scrape. And there were all my girls who kept the wolf from the door doing this tedious work. One of them fainted on the stand. We sent for a doctor who said she was only hungry. That was true too; Mr. Andrews sent me out with her for food, after this demonstration. There was Nellie Reyburn—a very pretty thing—young, with hardly sense enough to come in out of the rain. She posed for us often, and for the "Living Pictures." One morning the newspapers had big headlines—"ARTISTS' MODEL COMMITS SUICIDE"—and here was Nellie up to mischief—had been taken nearly dead from asphyxiation, to the nearest hospital, which happened to be the colored hospital. There I rushed to see her and if Grandma's peach-switch had been handy I surely would have used it. The little fool had already stuck under her pillow the clippings from the newspapers describing her escapade. Fourteen men wrote by the next mail, some telegraphed, offering to marry her. I believe she began marrying them, one at a time. Most of them were from the rural districts near by, some from the West, breezy, big-hearted fellows, I suppose.

And the poet. The poet was everything a poet should be. During the rests he would become so absorbed in the epic he was inditing that I would almost have to knock the screen over to get him out. We never knew the real names of these people. No doubt the hard times passed by, and many of them have become prosperous. I hope so.

One of our stalwart models, a red-headed fellow, passed me recently on the street, after these thirty years. He was driving a Ford. I was walking. "Like to have a ride, Mrs. Andrews?" was his friendly greeting. "Thank you," I said, and in our three-minutes' drive to my door he told me of his children.

CHAPTER LXIII

IT was impossible to remember that one was a Poor Relation in the midst of these interesting days. It was only on going home that it came over me fresh each night. At the Art School there were a few fashionable girls with whom art was a fad and never lasted. I meet some of them now and wonder if they ever regretted the discourtesies they showed in those old days to the little assistant instructor. One beautiful princess we had—Mary Cantacuzene—daughter of the Russian Ambassador. Her Governess always attended her and sat quietly knitting in a corner of the life-class while Mary studied Perryman's construction or Nellie Reyburn's contour. This noble Russian girl was a genuine inspiration to us and one of the persons from whom I have learned democracy. It does take the conceit out of you to find that you are being outdone on every hand by those you fancied to be your inferiors. Mary was our superior. Not in rank, for that does not count, but in education, in courtesy, in character. But not a student in the school ever had cause to regret the association, not one but recognized the pace she set. When she was present we all were princesses, for she treated us as such.

P O O R   R E L A T I O N ·

This Princess Mary married in her own country some years before I married and when I came again in contact with her she was the mother of six sons and the aftermath of the World War had brought about the downfall of the old regime in Russia.

Thirty or more years and half the world lay between us, but when I heard that she and her family were refugees from Bolshevist rule and among the sufferers in Constantinople, and that she had in such extremity turned to the art she studied with us here in Washington, as a means of providing for herself and her children, I wrote to her. The correspondence which ensued was most significant, picturing as it does the courage and the helplessness of the ancient nobility of Russia.

From the Island of Antigone these letters came to me, and I used them in many ways for the relief of that sorely tried community. One of her boys made me a visit in Washington of a year's duration, and in the summer of 1925 she and I met again in Paris, after thirty-five years. A happy reunion!

The Connoisseur made a practice of coming often into our Gallery and he did know and buy pictures. Knowing which I encouraged him to take cognizance of my masterpieces. My masterpieces impressed him it appeared, wherefore he, in proportion, impressed me. I scented a commission and managed always to be around when this patron of art came in. We talked art and nothing but art. We talked art earnestly and frequently. We suddenly stopped talking anything, for one day, after having declined many invitations to go and see his collection, I went with him.

I did not know whether he was a married man or single and did not care, for the check with which a married man pays for a picture is precisely the same as the check of the bachelor. His apartment was in a hotel. There was, as I later recalled, something sinister in the manner of the elevator man. We went into these rooms and the Connoisseur closed the doors. There was no other person in the rooms and the place showed every evidence of wealth. He pointed out what he regarded as the gems of his collection but with an indifference to art which surprised me. When he took me into his bedroom—a horrid place with clumsy Mid-Victorian furniture—chairs upholstered in yellow brocade, a four-poster bed with a lace spread over yellow satin—I swung around squarely to him and asked him to take me at once to the elevator. I was very much annoyed.

That man, old enough to have been my father, had frittered away a lot of his time and mine. I had no one to blame for this affront but myself, because in the hope of extorting some of his money from him I had shown a decided preference for his society and must have given him a false impression. He died a few years ago leaving his "collection" to a notable institution of art.

Old men buying girls, playing upon their necessities, appealing to their greed, or to some more noble instinct, their self-sacrifice and love of their own people! Counting upon helplessness and poverty to satisfy themselves at a trifling cost. A pleasant thought—pleasant to know that it still goes on, from the Capital of this nation to the darkest back-alley, laying up judgment against judgment and wrath against the day of wrath. In these cases there is little subtlety. The attention is a mere preliminary to a matter of business, of clear traffic. So obvious as to be unmistakable, so crude that it is funny. It happened that this particular young person had no great yearning for fur coats or orchids or the usual bait of these pathetic old pirates.

Her real temptations came from within. Sometimes amounting to actual torture. When, when would this sort of thing come to an end, and she be given her part in the unseen forces that were shaping nations? There had to be a man. All the potentiality, all the fervor, all the creative power packed away in herself awaited the touch of a man. She could not set it free alone. She bumped her round little head against that quite often. She took stock of her opportunities. No. Nothing that had been offered to her satisfied her. The material did not invite her to supreme effort and sacrifice. It was not worthwhile—none of it.

Love alone would never satisfy her and she knew it. Only in maternity would she be content—and in that great business no dull, commonplace material for her.

She must have been very passionate. But for no self-indulgence, no Swinburne stuff, physical and fruitless. Her sex function should count as brain and hand counted, for some constructive work, for ideals expressed and goods delivered. She was destined to be no plaything. She would dry up and blow away, as the maple seed did by the million—but inviolate and aloof she could be, and would be.

You think it is not nice for a young woman to think of such things? How is it to be avoided? Unintelligent indeed the girl must be, or unfamiliar with the most apparent conditions of society and the most ordinary aspects of nature, who does not reason a little upon this sovereign factor.

The dignity of physical love never struck her, its inseparableness from spiritual love, for she did not know it. The dearness of the caress, as such, and its culmination as a thing in itself holy and sacramental, she never calculated upon; but she reckoned on suffering as an intrinsic part of love, and she wrote down maternity as well worth while. Sometimes she was terribly afraid that she would have to go to her grave without ever having had a baby.

By way of parenthesis, I may say that the effort to boil down these Memoirs of a Poor Relation into some less ponderous form seemed a labor suited to the quiet of the country and the lovely September and October days on the wooded hilltops of Vaucluse. Here was my studio, adjoining my bedroom and bath, as I planned it for my dear husband when the new Vaucluse was built, a room, when its own atmosphere is preserved, which lends itself delightfully to study and labor. Here he sat long and tranquil afternoons at his easel, whistling like a boy and painting things that he loved, whether the world took heed or not; and here since he has gone, our son has created in other mediums some worthy works of art. One example of his work is the new gate to the North entrance of the old Episcopal Theological Seminary, the landmark in this part of Virginia. It is a memorial we have given in the name of Dr. Minnigerode, who was officially connected with the Seminary for many years. The wrought-iron arch which Eliphalet Andrews, his great-grandson, designed and executed, is made without bolt or rivet, a solid piece of welding, and it stands outlined against the sky like a bit of old black lace. The symbolism reads "Through Nature to God," the peacock feathers and roses expressions of physical nature, the Cross surmounting them, speaking for the Divine. The seven sprays of roses, the mystic number of perfection. The three crosses, one on each lantern as well as one that finishes the arch, the Three Crosses of Calvary and symbolic of Repentance, Atonement, and Absolution.

So while the young people are abroad I reserved the correction of my story for this beloved spot, while having an eye on their babies, and, said I to myself: My duties will be only nominal; the servants are efficient, the house runs like a clock, and there is Fräulein; the darling babies will be my recreation, my joy and delight, and all responsibility will be hers. I shall walk among these infants as some lovely lady in a garden of roses, the guiding hand, the seeing eye, the generous protector!

The interruptions have been sweet—the walks with a wee one on each hand, in the orchard to pick up apples, in the chapel field to watch the sheep, or down in the woods where the first leaves are already turning; or the excursions with Carter Randolph alone, I pushing the baby carriage; she in a language understood by the angels, apostrophizing the heavens above and staring into them with eyes that must have dropped from there to here. Bathing the children has been so dear; the perfect little dimpled bodies, flawless, rosy, fragrant. Grandmotherhood is a pleasant phase of this mortal life. The things you have always loved taking new forms and going on, on, on; a sort of immortality of mind and body, if not of estate. The question of estate is ever uncertain, and it may be that with the next generation we

NORTH GATE TO THE THEOLOGICAL SEMINARY OF VIRGINIA.

Eliphalet Fraser Andrews II, Veteran of the World War.

POOR   RELATION

take a turn at Poor Relationdom again, wherefore not? Surely life has dealt kindly enough with me and in the perspective that today is mine, every hardship, every apparent self-denial, has served a constructive purpose and added to the value of experience and the breadth of horizon. I would not wipe out a day of it. I would not change a feature of it. God is my witness, here near the end of the day's work, had I another chance, I would travel again the same way, select the same parents, live with the same man, go through the same disappointments and triumphs, the same reactions and the same agonies. Could these things be, and a better judgment be vouchsafed me along the way, I might do some things differently, more wisely, more kindly; but it is as it is, I am content.

The Memoirs might easily have been thrashed into shape to be more readable, in spite of the interruptions, had not the unexpected illness of Mary Lord Andrews the Third come upon us. An unaccountable illness. Fräulein ascribes it to my lack of caution in taking her for a long drive on a lovely day and recklessly exposing her to fresh air—to that deadly foe of the human race, a *Durchzug*. Certainly her stomach is much disturbed. The doctor orders Milk of Magnesia; Fräulein orders boiled milk, but the patient positively declines to touch either referring mysteriously to some other milk, not milk of magnesia, not boiled milk, not milk squeezed out of the old white cow, but a secret known only to herself. With not unusual adult dumbness, her grandmother has passed these hints by, unmindful of the wisdom that proceeds from the mouths of babes and sucklings.

But today a silver goblet was found under the bath tub in my dressing-room. The plebeian broom first discovered it, a more aristocratic parasol coaxed it into the light. It was found to be lined with a pasty whitish substance, of agreeable and familiar odor. Putting Mary Lord Andrews the Third through the third degree, as she sat propped up against the pillows in my four-poster, I elicited the information that she had put the goblet under the tub the same day that she made the milk. Not milk of magnesia, which she hates, nor boiled milk which she does not like, nor plain milk squeezed from the old white cow, which she accepts as a thing *selbstverständlich*, as saying her prayers or cleaning her teeth, but the milk she made for herself that "tasted good and smelled good," and was made out of Grandma's French face powder and a glass of ice water!

This then accounts for the indisposition which has baffled diagnosis, delayed the reorganization of this literary effort, and compelled me, through the inexplicable disappearance of a box of powder, to attend the Garden Party at Twin Oaks in honor of the Interparliamentary Congress, without the merciful embellishment that softens the ravages of time. There is one compensation. I cannot refrain from calling Fräulein's attention to the fact that it was not the deadly *Durchzug!* "But you have gave her ice water, Madame, dat widout wich she cannot mix powder. Ice water is also for the *Magen* no good. So erklärte mir der Herr aus Berlin."

Lengthy and philosophical are the conferences between Fräulein and myself, in which I find myself invariably the vanquished. As a *vernünftige Person* Fräulein firmly contradicts every word that falls from my trembling lips and advises me that had she the absolute control of Mary Lord the Third which her experience entitles her to have, the child would be the *Muster* of all *Fähigkeit* (Pattern of all efficiency). She allows for the *Oppositionsgeist des Kindes* (the contrariness of the child) also for the *unregelmässige Erziehungsart* of a grandmother (the irregular system of bringing up characteristic of a grandmother) and I must admit that often when I could screech with annoyance *she* preserves a perfect calmness which fills me with rage and admiration. During these weeks together I have snapped at Fräulein quite often, but she has never answered me but in the most respectful fashion. A brave soul, the girl is, far from home, and iron bound in her conviction that she is always right. Those who faithfully strive to do right must be forgiven if they believe that they always succeed in doing right. Ja, ja, Fräulein hat immer Recht!

The patience and self-control of domestic servants might be a lesson to those of us who live more indulgently. Recently our precious old colored cook who is not old—the adjective is used as a pet name—kept to herself for more than a week a heart-breaking sorrow that suddenly overtook her family. There are ten children, and one of the older girls left home. No trace could be found as to her whereabouts. When the rumor of the matter reached me I went right to her. "Yas, Ma'am, I knowed you would he'p us but I ain't said nuthin' 'cause youse got yo' own troubles an' ain't no 'casion fer we all to mek you tote ourn too." If any lady could feel or express greater consideration or delicacy of feeling than this, I would like to meet her!

PART VI
At Twenty-Five

CHAPTER LXIV

AT twenty-five one felt very old, for seven years of responsibility had piled the burden up; all one could earn was insufficient to do all one longed to do; the children were no longer children, but strong-willed young things coming into or passing out of the difficult period of adolescence. "Our Oldest Son" came home from Chicago quite a man, and resplendent in a Prince Albert coat and silk hat. Mother was bursting with pride because he was so grand. There was no flavor of Poor Relationdom about that apparel!

Youth would slip away, and one would never for a single day have looked pretty or felt free from care. Girls of twenty-five are fresh and charming in their flowered organdies, under the brims of becoming hats, or tinged with rose or violet from a friendly parasol. But trudging along in a shabby cloth frock which was not made for her, with a portfolio under one arm and a bag of tomatoes under the other, a girl of twenty-five seemed middle-aged and felt it.

Something was going to snap!

Mother became, as do most parents, a spectator of what her children would do. Which was preferable to putting her own stamp too forcefully upon them. Children are themselves, not imitations of parents. Individuality does not develop under a parental trade-mark. The world is not calling for copies of the older generations but for men and women equal to the needs of their own day, abreast of the ever-changing standards and conditions. Each child represents a fusion of many elements and growth and the adjustment of those elements is from within outward. Development cannot be superimposed upon anything.

As my mother's children grew many conflicting impulses were tearing at our hearts. All sorts of theories were wrangling in our heads. Wild desires were torturing our untried souls. Dear mother! One woman long ago "wasted" a box of precious ointment in a moment of supreme self-abnegation. It was all that she had. And down the ages have rung the words which silenced her critics and justified her extravagance: "She hath done what she could." Where judgment errs, when courage fails, where love falters, may these words be heard—"She hath done what she could!"

All the world over women are repeating her action. Giving their best and their all, though that be but the gift of themselves in the apotheosis of suffering nature. Then may the same commendation be for them all, "She hath done what she could."

Not to be a faddist. Not to act upon impulse,

however noble; not to overjump the mark; not to overestimate one's own powers; not to undertake in enthusiasm what can only be accomplished in long years of patience—all this negative wisdom preached itself into my soul, as I jumped and plunged and never knew when I was beaten. Something bigger seemed to drive me on. Was I building a house upon the sand?

What is worth while? Duty, art, society, religion? Is knowledge the real thing? Are children of flesh and blood, warm hands that one can clasp, the real things? Are brick and mortar real? Banks, universities, cathedrals? Or are the dream things real? The pictures never painted, the songs unsung, the poems never written, the thoughts that were turned back upon the soul, the forces that were never needed, the children that were never born?

How weary one grew, struggling with one's self. Contending to muzzle the tiger and silence the ape that are fellow inhabitants with one's immortal soul, in this clay tenement. Seven years. Mystic number. At least some of the things battled for had been attained. Some fraction of the purpose was accomplished. The soul maintains its equilibrium in spite of some upheavals.

I envied my mother her religion. It was of a gentle character, different from Grandma's. There was none of the gall of bitterness in it, little of severe judgment, and no hell-fire.

Mother loved justice and followed after mercy and shut her eyes to many offenses against herself. She visited the fatherless and widows in their affliction and gave liberally of the little that was hers. She used hospitality without grudging, and followed the rules and instructions of her church without argument. The blessing that was on her lips at every meal is the best I know, inherited from old Robert Randolph of Eastern View, beginning as it does with the petition for others—

> Oh, Lord, relieve the wants of others, and make us thankful, for Christ's sake.

She observed family worship every morning before breakfast, gathering her children and her servants around her as long as we would come. As we grew older and more self-assertive, we failed her. Some rushed off to work, others to school, others expressed a democratic independence by lying in bed until too late to join her; and so it befell that only the babies who were in the room with her and dressed by her, little Anne and Karl, attended. Mother and these little children often had family prayers alone, she reading and they kneeling by her side, until they too were "big," and she gave up the dear old custom.

Her voice was so sweet as on Sunday morning she used the special invocation—

> Direct us in all our ways, and let thy holy spirit accompany us to the place of thy public worship;

making us serious and attentive, and raising our minds from the thoughts of this world to the consideration of the next, that we may fervently join in the prayers and praises of Thy Church and listen to our duty with honest hearts in order to practice it.

Gradually the doors of life swung open to this ignorant and self-approving little girl, who was myself, as she studied nature and as she mixed with men.

She was taking her own measure. She was weighing herself in the balance, and finding herself wanting. The self-righteousness was being kicked out of her. Her art work was undistinguished. Interruptions and conflicting interests left her little time for persistent and concentrated study. She measured her talent with that of others and came out second-best. The vanity was being worked out of her system.

Her work brought her in touch with people, who, making her feel small, enlarged her. Gave her vision and a sense of proportion which drawing from the antique was also developing. Do you think there is no ethical side to the study of the antique? Try it. Those noble lines, the perfect repose of the Greek, the idealized representation of what man's body might and should be. The genius in those old masters who were largely self-taught and knew no anatomy or science as we have it dished out to us in every school. Michelangelo in his whole life did not have the anatomical knowledge which any student of a year can have today. We have too much teaching and too little imagination. Yet a small share is better than none and, as this sense of values grows, there comes a glorious new joy in the accomplishment of others—an utterly unselfish and catholic appreciation of the achievement of those who out-do ourselves. That is a big thing to get.

Daily intercourse with highly trained people showed her her own intellectual poverty. She bought many second-hand books at Lowdermilk's. She took time that was worth money, and went to the Capitol to listen to the Solons. She did not know what trivial matters came before Congress, nor that Congressmen lolled and loafed, chewed and spit and quarrelled! And she was living, moving and having her being in the constant companionship of Mr. Andrews, that courtly gentleman and finished scholar.

At last one beats one's music out. Not only the visible and tangible have counted, not only the work of head and hand. Those inarticulate cries for a purer life—those vague impulses toward the beautiful and fine—those moments of shame for the coarseness of one's own nature! The will to do for others more than one ever expected for one's self, the hunger and thirst for righteousness, all have counted. The immortal part pleads always for its share, silencing at last the tiger that growls and the ape that chatters.

"Perplexed in faith but pure in deeds," at last one beats one's music out.

So she slumped and recovered, slumped and recovered many times.

But what is to be done with the power that is not called for? God! How women suffer! The virtue of them is too terrible. Doing perfunctorily the things one finds to do, thoughts crowd the brain like torrents of water in narrow places. Strength of body, strength of mind, not used today. Perhaps not wasted. Stored up, perhaps, like the lost sunshine of long ago, in one of Nature's storehouses for the warmth and brightness of the days to come.

Strange creatures, we, to whom such heights and depths are known. Magnificently selfless or criminally selfish, according as it is our duty or our desire that commands us. Demonstrating too often, in acts that involve the happiness of others and our own honor, the victory of a profuse imagination over an undisciplined will.

CHAPTER LXV

MY Aunt Ida's life had undergone some changes with the death of her husband and the marriage of all three of her children. Grandma was the only tie that bound her to Oakley for the year around. And Oakley, with the absence of those dear ones, and the responsibility all upon her, without the sweet compensations of earlier years, became a great care, an unnecessary care. She was at the threshold of that remarkable period of a woman's life when, her physical functions having been triumphantly fulfilled, her intellectual powers are redoubled. The mental and spiritual, long and rightly dividing her attention with the duties of maternity and home, come into full possession of all her time and energies, as she sees the original home and family disintegrate and become the many homes and families of another generation. Then come the long, sweet, uninterrupted hours for reflection and study, for travel and social intercourse. Then all the training and discipline of the past, which seemed to be but broken and scrappy, model something symmetrical and complete. Oh, those are very precious years, in which we feel our pulses slowing down as our vision widens. In which we are gently weaned one by one from the things by which a short time ago we set such store. We look over all that we have accumulated of experience and of knowledge, practical and ethical; all that we have acquired by labor or inheritance, houses, silver, pictures, books, the things that people buy in unconscious betrayal of their own secret souls—and we try to place all this. We take our grandchildren on our knees and weave for them the stories of our own childhood, with its funny little blunders and punishments; we reach out to our girls and boys a steadying, but not a directing hand; we give the pictures and silver and books to those who will most enjoy them, and we separate the goods which will have meaning for those who follow us, from the things which have served their purpose and only cumber the earth. We see ourselves as a spark of eternal energy, of that force which moves all things, and disdains not so simple a tool as ourselves. This is a woman's right. She has rounded out the life of the man she loved, she has borne and trained her offspring, she has conserved such material things as were entrusted to her hands, and now she looks beyond the personal, and grasps the scheme of things entire, as a preparation for the next chapter in her history. That great chapter to be lived in the house not built with hands.

With Grandma on her hands, my Aunt Ida could not budge from Oakley, and the place was rather lonely, and in case of illness, hardly safe for them. A competent overseer could take care of the farm, if only Grandma would be happy elsewhere. She came to us. To mother, who was her baby, and to our full, noisy home. It was good for her and for us. It was only fair to Aunt Ida.

We fitted up our best room and got hold of an old colored woman, Mammy Lizzie, to act as maid for her, and established the two old ladies together for better, for worse. It was often for worse. Grandma was the wreck of her stately and distinguished self, but even more arrogant than formerly.

My room adjoined hers, and every morning I went in to read the Bible to her before I went off to my work.

The poor old dears were at dagger's draw all the time. Wakening early as old people do, and faint for their breakfast, they could not hold their tongues or tempers a minute, and often I jumped out of bed and rushed in to settle some pathetic dispute in which they both forgot the relative position of mistress and maid, and were wrangling like spoilt children. Mammy Lizzie had very little work to engage her time and Grandma, bedridden, could do nothing but watch Mammy Lizzie in her uprisings and her downsittings and find perpetual fault. The one was ghastly and emaciated, her ancient pride unabated, helplessly dictatorial; the other, equally old, but active, alert, keen as a briar, black as coal, quick as a cat. At four o'clock in the morning they were chirping like sparrows, by one minute past four war had begun. I would hustle to them. Grandma, fuming on the pillow. Mammy Lizzie staring out of the window and talking to herself. Grandma would say:

"I cannot hear you, Aunt Eliza." (She would have scorned the familiarity of "Mammy Lizzie.")

Mammy Lizzie would grunt,

"Tain't no cause fer you to hear me———"

"I wish to know what you are saying."

"Tain't no 'casion fer you to know what's I sayin'."

"Come away from that window, Aunt Eliza. I pay no colored person two dollars and a half a week to do nothing in this world but stare out of a window."

"Ain't goin' to do nothin' o' the kind. I don't see what fer you don't never want me to see nuthin'."

"Aunt Eliza, you are the most impertinent servant I ever knew in my life, and I shall discharge you."

"You don't look like dischargin' nobody. Whar you gwine find nuther pusson in this worl' to put up wid yo' discombobulations? You is exasperatin' an' cantankerous, an' all yo' religion ain't goin' to keep you out o' hell, neither, ef you don't be easy on other folks, I *know*."

"My dear!" Grandma would wail to me as I

leaned over her. "Aunt Eliza has told me that I am going to hell. *Me—Me——*" and a poor little squeal would wind up the altercation; I would suggest to Mammy Lizzie that her prognostications were unduly pessimistic; peace would be restored after the two old dears whose sands were so nearly run had glared and snapped at each other, Mammy Lizzie's eyes reminding me of the eyes of an angry rat, while she hopped up and down in her rage as though the floor were red-hot.

When Mr. Andrews rode over on Sundays, as was his habit, so straight and handsome on his handsome horse, he always paid his respects to Grandma. We had a special counterpane we spread over her bed, and the shades were drawn, by her imperative order. His deference pleased her, though she observed after each visit that she was at a loss to understand his frequent attentions; that so much gallivanting and junketing seemed strange to her, and why in the world did he insist so on seeing her? After all, she was only a poor old lady lying in the bed; her daughter or granddaughter of course, was present during these visits; but the privacy of a lady's bedroom was a sacred thing. From all she had heard, or could observe, Mr. Andrews was a perfect gentleman, but why, could anybody tell her, did he want to see her so often?

Mammy Lizzie would then offer what seemed to her logical explanation, to the effect that seeing her was a mere detail of the day, of which the all-important purpose was, to "he'p Miss May make de ice-cream."

For, be it known, when mother filed her tribe into the Amen corner of Old Christ Church every Sunday morning, it fell to the lot of one of her daughters to stay at home with Grandma and to freeze the ice-cream for the "boarders'" Sunday dinner. Knowing that my distinguished visitor enjoyed that exercise, he being as you have already perceived, a true philanthropist, I often volunteered to stay, even out of turn, and let my sisters go to church and stare at the descendants of Thomas Jefferson. Then Mr. Andrews, after his call upon Grandma, sat on the back kitchen stair, and turned the freezer for me.

Recalling this to him in after years, I asked if he remembered. We were sitting by the studio fire in the Scott Circle house. He was reading, I was scribbling, for it has taken years to collect these simple notes on Poor Relationdom. (By the way, he did not like the term, nor want to think of the fact.)

"Remember?" he looked up in the quick way he had. "Remember that? Do I? Well—it was then that I could see your strong, beautiful arms with the sleeves rolled up."

CHAPTER LXVI

BY long living and honest thinking, Grandma had acquired much valuable knowledge, and this boiled-down wisdom she was determined not to take hence when the hour of her departure should draw nigh. She was going to leave ideas, as well as a mahogany work-table and a pair of silver mugs, to me. Thus the echo of her philosophy comes to me in many an hour of need, and the convictions which she bought so dearly, have become long ago part and parcel of the characters of all her descendants, in whom she lives again. Nothing can dim her memory. It was that commanding personality that laid its impress indelibly upon us all.

The manner in which she awaited death was very striking. God was always with her, and on her side in every question, had always been her friend and ally. It would be more correct to say that having always herself been on God's side of every question, and having been His ally here, and faithfully striven to know and then to do His will, she felt only a great longing to be with Him. She had no resistance to death. That is dramatic in a quiet way, dignified and impressive.

We buried Grandma in Middleburg, with the

POOR RELATION

windows of her bridal chamber looking down upon her grave. A lovely spot, which she herself had made over to the locality for a cemetery, reserving only a rectangular tract for her own connection, in which her two sons and her husband had long been buried. Her own long life enabled her to see this tract gradually fill with those she loved, the children and grandchildren, among whom she divided it.

A country funeral was a dreary thing to me, in the old days, before I understood. A long drive over bad roads, the creeping pace of the horses; the joining all along the way of every conceivable type of ancient vehicle as friends and neighbors fall in line; until, worn out and hungry, we reach the little church. The village darkies throng the streets. At the windows, a few curious faces.

The country parson reads the service and all walk to the little neglected cemetery. We group around the open grave. The red mud is piled high beside it, and the dirty old negro who dug it up leans on his spade, looking on. The burden is clumsily lowered, goes groaning and creaking forever out of sight. The thud of that first handful of dust to dust. The dirty old negro stolidly shovels the earth back whence it came.

And then—the wiping of eyes and the blowing of noses. The furtive glances from behind damp handkerchiefs to see who's who; then the lifting of veils and the rising inflections of voices, as old friends recognize each other—the pleasant intonation as we say, "Poor Cousin Marietta—but my dear,—how well you look!"

Then the walk back to the village, arm in arm with some nice person never met except at a funeral; through the green graveyard, past the old well-known but little noticed names, along the quaint streets, under the arched maple trees; and then the reaction—the excellent dinner at the home of some other cousin, prepared not without care and cost; the noble old square-shouldered gentlemanly black bottles, for which no one apologized, the mint julep or the brandy smash— "Do take it, dear. This has been such an ordeal for you—it will do you good." And dear does take it, for this has been an ordeal and "it" does do one good.

Then a general jollification, and all rattle home over the darkening road as fast as wheels and hoofs can carry them.

CHAPTER LXVII

WITH an ingratiating smile and (I fear) a hypocritical kiss, Mary Lord Andrews the Third assures me that she is not in any "mishtuff, Grandma." Her face has a trace of anxiety as she tries this alibi, for her pretty hands are deep in the mazes of some colored silks which I use for embroidering the collars and cuffs of her dresses, these gay skeins all tangled up and looking now like a drunken rainbow. "I like to fix my Grandma's things for her nice," she continues, diplomatically, if not grammatically. Perhaps some grandmother, made of sterner stuff, could resist her, but not I; for we really are playmates. When no one is looking I do the silliest things to make her laugh during this convalescence, and we hug and kiss each other in a fashion very ridiculous in one of my age. I starved along through my first ten or fifteen years, un-hugged and un-kissed, and imagination cannot picture my grandmother and me indulging in any such superfluous and undignified demonstration.

Fräulein detecting us in the midst of these osculations, states it as *meine Ansicht* that this is not sanitary; though this time she does not quote der Herr von Berlin as her authority. She does not know what Carter Randolph has done with her safety-pin; perhaps Madame have it? "No," I declare, "I have not. And I hope the baby has not swallowed it." "And indeed not, I hope, Madame, for that also is for the *Magen* no good."

My utter lack of intelligence is really mortifying, if it seems to me that the sun is shining, I find that that may be so, but it is a wind also blowing; if I suggest that a wind is blowing and Helen Tucker Andrews the Second had best put on a coat, I ascertain that it may be blow a wind but the sun shine very nice also and a sweater is to the weather more agreeable than a coat, and also for the holding of the body bones excellently *zusammen*. If beef soup presents itself to my mind as suitable refreshment for a sick child on a cold day, I discover that it is milk-toast already for now, beef soup may be for the day after tomorrow; yet when I yearn to spoon milk-toast into Mary Lord's sweet mouth, I find the beef broth Madame is for the *Magen* more good.

The October days are passing. The hickories' and poplars' vivid chromes and cadmiums, the green trees and the oaks sparkling in scarlet and crimson—heavy mists in the morning, sudden cold evenings. The young people are due, are even now on the ocean—and Grandma's reign is drawing to its close. Mary Lord the Third and I have gathered up the photographs, the books, the sweet girlish treasures of my dear Mary Lord; we have handled the things her dear hands touched and to my baby granddaughter I have passed on some little messages from the sweet daughter now seven years dead.

"Be not ashamed, women. Your privilege enclosed the rest and is the exit of the rest. You are the gates of the body. You are the gates of the soul."

"Unfolded out of the folds of the woman's brain come all the folds of the man's brain, duly obedient."

"Unfolded out of the justice of the woman all justice is unfolded."

"Unfolded out of the sympathy of the woman is all sympathy."

"A man is a great thing upon the earth and through eternity, but every jot of the greatness of man is unfolded out of the woman."

Grandma's death crystallized in me the decision to become a mother. I would be what she had been, a breeder and maker of men. All there was of me to the uttermost limit, I would give—investing my small capital of power in what would yield the best and most far-reaching results. This was suddenly and clearly defined. I would be the thing God planned me to be, complete and well rounded I would gather to myself elements finer than I, and send on down the stream of life the sweetness, the intelligence, the kindness, of—whom?

Time would tell.

For I myself was a gate of the soul.

CHAPTER LXVIII

Epilogue

TWENTY, thirty, years have passed and I have seldom found the time to visit the graves of my mother or my grandmother, my Aunt Ida or my Aunt Katie, good as they were to me, richly as they deserved my reverence. But my feet have worn a path to the grave of my child. The love of the old for the young is the law of life. We cannot love our parents as we love our children. Let us remember this, and never expect the younger generation to regard us with the same devotion we gave to it for that must be reserved for those who are yet to come. We will not even wish to turn those great currents backward, their flow is forward, downward, through the years, as the streams flow down to the rivers and the rivers out to the sea.

I have learned my lesson. I have found my spiritual adjustment. Those were dark days, after I buried my Mary Lord beside my mother, my father, and my grandmother, in the same quaint green old cemetery that was once a portion of the estate on which my grandmother's children were born. But I would not change it now. The Service flag with its three stars, one for her young brother, two for my young brothers, all soldiers and in France, went into the grave with her—symbol of love and patriotism.

Oh, the listlessness, the helplessness of those long months, before the light broke. Only that open grave, blood-red as is the soil of Loudoun, only that pouring rain, turning the earth into streams such as flooded the fields of France. Only the friendly faces of people whose own children would gather that evening round the home table, and talk of my daughter in her grave and my boy far away "at the Front." Only the birthday letter he had written to her, for this day was her twenty-second birthday, a greeting from the firing lines, a scrap of crumpled paper in my coat-pocket, clutched in my hand. Rozier Dulany brought it with him when he came to the funeral. Rozier, my lifelong friend and from my baby days adored. Only the dear ones standing around, my sisters and brothers, Archie Randolph and Loughborough Turner; Gay Fleming burdened with delicious blossoms from the garden of Gordonsdale—white and blue—the blues were giant larkspur—the Fairfax Harrisons, the Dulanys, the Carters, the Beverleys, the Randolphs, Virginia Corse, the Turners, the Masons, all our own people, rain dripping from their hats as they stood by me with heavy hearts.

The rain was very sweet; and I beat it in upon my weary brain as though it were the burden of a song "The whole world looks to America for food. The rain is a gift of God. The rain makes the corn and wheat to grow. The rain is a gift of God, and the child is a gift of God."

I could not get beyond that. And they lowered the little gray casket into the wet red ground, covered as it was with lilies—how the frail petals out of sight were bruised and reddened as the clods were tumbled in—little Lyman McCrary singing, "Abide with Me." And I who could never sing, must sing, and in some strange sounds God understood, brought out discordantly the cry.

"Oh, Thou who changest not, abide with me." An answered prayer.

For now I know that love permeates all spaces as light does, struggling, filtering even into those closed corners that would bar it out. Unifying, simplifying, all things; reflected back and forth, as a grim countenance reflects the smile of a child, as bare brick wall or scowling bluff reflect the flush of dawn. Shadows are never permanent, but even as you watch them, shift and change.

From the low level of one little grave my thoughts have reached the skies. From the poor fragments of our human loves there have been built new worlds. And hands left empty of what was most precious overflow with gifts more precious still. For the lost loveliness of one young face a holier grace is given, and in high Heaven the love cut short on earth finds scope and place. For God is good. Error is ours, not His. Ungracious is our egotism, thankless, short-sighted, crude, we merit not the tenderness bestowed. If we look up, not down, we meet His gaze, and in it find our own, our lost, again; all grace, all life, all faith, all hope of youth, and every loveliness we fancied gone!

INDEX

Alexandria, Va., 91, 244–245, 249–255, 256–259, 260–266, 267, 280, 283, 284, 326, 351

Alsop, Adelaide, 401

Andrews, Carter Randolph, 167, 168, 169–170, 171, 420

Andrews, Eliphalet Fraser, 87, 163, 276, 277, 278, 283, 334–336, 337, 350, 353, 356, 357–358, 367, 368, 412, 438, 439

Andrews, Helen Tucker, II, 167–171

Andrews, Mary Lord, 56, 167, 446

Andrews, Mary Lord, III, 56, 106–109, 167–171, 421, 423, 433–444

Arlington, Va., 82, 84, 85, 89, 91, 92

Auger, Gen., 34

Aunt Di (*see* Diana Kearny Powell)

Aunt Ida (*see* Mrs. Henry Grafton Dulany)

Aunt Imogene, 211–212

Aunt Katie (*see* Mrs. George Carter)

Avenel, 92, 359

Baltimore, Md., 35, 90, 338–339

Beale, Clifford, 401

Beale, Reynold, 401

Beauregard, Gen., 190

Beverley, Elizabeth, 61

Beverley, Mrs. Hill Carter ("Becca" Dulany), 6, 34, 67, 74, 77, 137, 160

Beverley, Col. Robert, 359–360

Beverley, Mrs. Robert (Aunt Jane), 359

Bladensburg, Md., 316–319

Bolling, Edith (Mrs. Woodrow Wilson), 165–166

Bolling, Lucy, 165

Bolling, Robert, of Bollingbroke, 165

Bolling, Tabb, 86

Bollingbroke, 165

Bonaparte, Jerome, 90

Buchner, George, 15

Butler, Ben, 35

Cameron, 161

Cantacuzene, Princess Mary, 414–415

Carlyle House, Alexandria, 251

Carter, "Councillor," 202

Carter, Dr., 196

Carter, Mrs. Edward, 359

Carter, George, 198–199, 203–204

Carter, Mrs. George, of Oatlands (Aunt Katie), 44, 75, 198–203, 204–206, 232, 280, 446

Carter, Grace, 189, 203–204, 207, 214, 216, 232–233

Carter, Robert, 199

Carter, Robert, "King" Carter of Corotoman, 96, 101, 165

Casarin, Allessandre, 310–313

Chambers, Mr. 89, 91

Charlemagne, 11, 101

INDEX

Charlottesville, W.Va., 320–321, 341
Chase, William M., 311, 386, 391–400, 401
Christ Church, Alexandria, 91, 268, 272, 292, 439
Christian, Mr., 184, 240
Christie, Howard Chandler, 401
Clark, Edward, 409
Conyers, Sally, 164
Cooper, Jennie (Mrs. Dawson), 22–23
Corcoran, W. W., 276, 283
Corcoran Gallery and Art School, Washington, D.C., 275–278, 283, 334, 337
Cornell, Mr., 80, 98, 129–130, 151
Corotoman, 96, 101, 165
Corregia, Don Heidenrich, 11
Corregia, Don Otto, 11
Corse, Mrs. Montgomery, 46
Cousin Alice (*see* Mrs. Arthur Herbert)
Cousin Annette, 294–296, 297, 326
Cousin Arthur (*see* Col. Arthur Herbert)
Cousin Charles, 263
Cousin Helen, 345–346, 362, 367, 370
Cousin Janie (*see* Mrs. Edward Carter)
Cousin Stanley, 231–232, 256–257, 263, 267–268, 287–288, 360
Critcher, Catherine Carter, 404–405
Custis, George Washington Parke, 82, 85, 92
Custis, Mrs., 82, 85, 92

Davis, Jefferson, 17–20
Dole, Dr. Charles F., 374–377

Dulany, Capt. Henry Grafton, 6, 32, 62, 74, 78, 92, 94, 95, 100, 102, 104–106, 115–116, 125, 138, 141
Dulany, Mrs. (Aunt Ida), 6, 33, 34, 62–64, 66, 72–73, 79, 81, 98–99, 102, 123, 125, 134, 137, 160, 275–276, 435–436
Dulany, May, 6, 47, 67, 77, 79
Dulany, Rozier, 62, 72, 73, 77, 78, 106, 125, 135, 210, 276, 283, 308, 447
Dulany, Mrs. Rozier, 123

Early, Gen. Jubal, 190
Eastern View, 61, 82–84, 92, 165
Edwards, Franklin, 228–229, 237–238, 241, 244, 258, 308–309
Emmeline, 293–296, 324

Farmington, 322
Fauntleroy, Jane, 61
Fauntleroy, Kinloch, 195–196
Fithian, Philip, 96
Fitzhugh, William, 85, 86, 202
Fleming, Gay, 447
Fortress Monroe, 17
Fort Worth, 161

Georgetown, 86, 319–320
Gibbon, Lieut., 163
Gibbon, Major James, 164
Good Intent, 56, 57
Gunston Hall, 22, 84

Haxall, Lou, 22
Hearst, Mrs. Phœbe A., 202, 205
Herbert, Arthur, 161–162, 251
Herbert, Mrs. Arthur, 162
Herbert, Mittie, 251
Hill, The, Middleburg, 32

INDEX

Hyde, Dr. James Nevins, 348

Jefferson, Thomas, 14, 83, 85, 199, 202
Johns, the Rev. Arthur, 97
Johnston, Col. William Preston, 240
Jones, Mr., 190

Keith, the Rev. Ruel, 91
Kennon, Beverly, 86
Kennon, Britania (Peter), 86, 90
Kinloch, 61, 82, 84, 86, 91, 92, 166
Kitchener, Gen., 193–194

Lafayette, Gen., 83
Lasteyrie, Count Louis de, 84
Lee, General Fitz, 22, 24, 26, 27, 28, 190, 196
Lee, Mary, 192–195, 229
Lee, Mary (Custis), 86, 89, 92, 93
Lee, Robert, 92
Lee, Robert C., 255
Lee, Robert E., 17, 83, 85, 86, 89, 92
Lee, General William Henry Fitzhugh ("Rooney"), 22, 85, 86
Lee, Smith, 22
Little Theater in the Hills, The, 56, 57
Louisville, Ky., 27

Mammy, 219–220, 221, 224–227, 280
Mammy Lizzie, 436, 439
Mansion House, Alexandria, 251
Martha, 70, 75, 80, 149, 199, 210
Mary, 324, 325
"Mary, the Wild Cat," 315–316
Mason, Beverley, 359
Mason, Billy, 359

Mason, Dick, 359
Mason, George, of Gunston Hall, 22, 87, 202
Mason, Nannie, 22
Mason, Steenie, 359
McCormick, Cousin Nannie, 320
McCrary, Lyman, 448
McKim, Dr., 303
Menokin, 161
Miles, General Nelson A., 20, 21
Milhau, Della, 399, 403
Minnigerode, Anne Gibbon, 164, 430
Minnigerode, Benjamin, 12, 13
Minnigerode, Charles, 26, 28, 31, 38, 44, 47, 103, 125, 175, 177, 183, 196, 237–241, 244, 264, 267, 269, 270, 271, 273, 274, 275, 279, 280
Minnigerode, Charles, Jr., 184, 326, 327, 336, 427
Minnigerode, Charles Frederick Ernest, 15, 16, 17, 18, 19, 20, 38, 48, 70, 164, 419
Minnigerode, Fitzhugh Lee, 199, 340–341
Minnigerode, George, 339, 340, 343
Minnigerode, James Gibbon, 27
Minnigerode, Johann Ludwig von, 12
Minnigerode, Karl, 341, 430
Minnigerode, Lucy, 94–97, 100, 179, 183, 185, 199, 211, 231, 255, 272, 275, 279, 303, 305, 341–343, 359, 362
Minnigerode, Ludwig, 14
Minnigerode, Meade, 379, 380, 381
Minnigerode, Mrs. Nellie, 380
Minnigerode, Powell, 303, 336, 337
Minnigerode, Virginia, 272

INDEX

Minnigerode, Virginia Cuthbert (Powell), 29, 32, 37–39, 40, 47–49, 50, 52, 61, 99, 101, 102, 162, 163, 176, 177, 178, 179, 182, 183, 184, 185, 186, 188, 208, 214–216, 241, 244, 256, 258, 259, 260, 261, 262, 267, 275, 279, 287, 290–293, 300, 308, 309, 361, 363, 427, 428, 429, 430

Molinari, Mr., 211

Monticello, 83, 84, 85, 199

Monumental Church, 164

Moody, Mr., 303, 304

Mount Vernon, 82, 84

Muckross, 161

New Orleans, 35, 177, 180–182, 183, 185, 190, 192, 194, 195, 207, 211, 221, 228, 232, 235, 240

New York, 258

Nicholas, Cousin Carey, 152, 299

Nicholls, Gov., 190

Nicholls, Mrs., 401

Oak Hill, 84

Oakley, Fauquier Co., 32–39, 40, 47, 49, 50, 62–69, 84, 89, 94, 96, 98, 100, 101, 110, 114, 116, 120, 124, 175, 186, 209, 210, 211, 330, 380, 434, 435

Oatlands, Loudoun Co., 44, 198, 199, 201, 203, 204, 228, 231, 232, 280, 290, 384

Old, Mattie, 22

Old St. Paul's Church, Richmond, 17, 164

Patterson, Margaret, 90

Patton, Hallie, 321

Penick, Bishop, 303

Perelli, Mr., 211, 275

Peter, Thomas, 86

Petersburg, Va., 86

Peyton, Eleanor, 61

Peyton, Col. Francis, 87

Peyton, Valentine, 87

Philadelphia, 17, 90

Philips, Mrs., 35

Plains, The, 359

Powell, Betty, 165

Powell, Carrie, 165

Powell, Diana Kearny, 280, 290

Powell, John, 165

Powell, John Henry, 163, 164

Powell, Mrs. John Henry, 165

Powell, Mary Fauntleroy(Turner), 3–8, 33–37, 61, 66, 70–75, 77, 79, 82, 83, 89, 90, 95, 96, 98, 99, 101, 103, 106, 108, 110, 112, 113, 114, 115, 126, 127, 131, 132, 133, 134, 135–136, 138–142, 149, 151, 154–156, 175, 177, 207, 231, 233, 362, 380, 384, 435, 439, 440–441

Powell, Mrs. Mary G. (Cousin Molly), 282, 285, 290

Powell, Cousin Rebecca, 165, 262–264, 405

Powell, Dr. Robert (Cousin Bob), 280, 282, 285

Powell, Sarah, 165

Princeton, The, 86

Ramsay, Mr., 283

Ramsay, Rebecca, 346

Randolph, Archie, 447

Randolph, Eliza Hill (Carter), 61, 165

Randolph, Peter, of Chatsworth, 165

Randolph, Co. Robert, 83, 84, 165

Ravensworth, 85, 86

INDEX

Richmond, 17, 22, 24, 26, 28, 32, 48, 163, 164, 184, 340
Robineau, Samuel, 402

Sankey, Mr., 303, 304
Seminary Hill, 23
Shinnecock Hills, L.I., 386–390, 391, 401–405
Shirley, 61
Smith, Ellen, 134
Smith, Sallie W., 52, 53, 54, 55
Stevens, Byam Kirby, 409, 410

Thornton, Dr. William, 86
Tilghman, Dick, 89, 91
Tinkham, Alice, 403, 404
Triplett, Mary, 22
Tucker, Jim, 190
Tucker, Laura (Powell), 192
Tucker, Randolph, 190–192
Tudor Place, Georgetown, 86
Turner, Charles, 90
Turner, Edward, 92
Turner, Elisa (Randolph), 165
Turner, Horatio Whitridge, 229
Turner, Loughborough, 447
Turner, Thomas, of Kinloch, 82, 86, 90, 165

Uncle George, 102

"Uncle Robert," 38, 39, 40, 63, 72, 73, 81, 138, 158
Uncle Willie, 211
Upperville, 3, 68, 84

Vaucluse, Fairfax Co., 56, 87, 107, 161, 166, 167, 419
Venable, Col., 240

Waggaman, Thomas E., 366
Waggaman, Mrs. Thomas E., 366
Wakeman, Mrs. Van Horstman, 349
Wallace, General Lew, 35
Warrenton, 68, 82, 84
Washburn, Cadwallader, 401
Washington, D.C., 23, 28, 85, 86, 275, 277, 297, 303, 314, 315, 316, 351, 365
Washington, George, 202, 249
Washington, Martha, 85
Waters, Henry Harcourt, 236–237
Weil, Gertrude, 402
Wilmer, Skipwith, 338–339
Wilson, Mrs. Woodrow, 166
Wise, John S., 22, 24
Wood, Margaret (Woods), 322
Wood, Warner, 322
Woods, Elliot, 409
Woods, Dr. John Rodes, 321–322

www.ingramcontent.com/pod-product-compliance
Lightning Source LLC
Chambersburg PA
CBHW072322170426
43195CB00048B/2194